Abuse of Process and Fairness in Criminal Proceedings

To my wife, Louise

David Corker

To my parents, Maureen and David Young

David Young

Abuse of Process and Fairness in Criminal Proceedings

David Corker, MA
Oriel College, Oxford
and the University of Sheffield
Solicitor, Peters & Peters, London

David Young, BA (Hons), LLM (Lond)
4 Brick Court
of the Middle Temple, Barrister

Butterworths
London Edinburgh Dublin
2000

United Kingdom Butterworths, a Division of Reed Elsevier (UK) Ltd, Halsbury House, 35 Chancery Lane, LONDON WC2A 1EL and 4 Hill Street, EDINBURGH EH2 3JZ

Australia	Butterworths, a Division of Reed International Books Australia Pty Ltd, CHATSWOOD, New South Wales
Canada	Butterworths Canada Ltd, MARKHAM, Ontario
Hong Kong	Butterworths Asia (Hong Kong), HONG KONG
India	Butterworths India, NEW DELHI
Ireland	Butterworth (Ireland) Ltd, DUBLIN
Malaysia	Malayan Law Journal Sdn Bhd, KUALA LUMPUR
New Zealand	Butterworths of New Zealand Ltd, WELLINGTON
Singapore	Butterworths Asia, SINGAPORE
South Africa	Butterworths Publishers (Pty) Ltd, DURBAN
USA	Lexis Law Publishing, CHARLOTTESVILLE, Virginia

A CIP Catalogue record for this book is available from the British Library.

ISBN 0 406 90258 5

Typeset by Connell Publishing Services. Thame, Oxfordshire
Printed by Butler & Tanner, Frome and London

Foreword

By Edmund Lawson QC

A few years ago, I wrote that abuse of process in criminal proceedings was effectively 'dead' (Journal of Criminal Law, Vol. 57, p 96). I was so wrong. As a criminal practitioner, I have since been asked to appear in or to advise on many cases where abuse has arisen as a potential preliminary point.

As the authors of this study point out, 'abuse of process' is a somewhat unnecessarily pejorative misnomer for a simple jurisdiction, as recognised by Garland J in his courageous 1993 decision in *Reade*, when he stayed the prosecution of the policemen alleged to have conspired unlawfully to procure the convictions of those who became known as 'the Birmingham Six'. Essentially, this 'doctrine' is about fairness: can a defendant have a fair trial? Is it fair to try him, even if he can have a 'fair trial', having regard to the prosecutor's or the State's conduct?

In 1991 (in *A-G's Reference No 1 of 1990)* Lord Lane CJ made a spirited attempt to kill off the invocation of the abuse doctrine in criminal law, at least in respect of delay cases. His discouragement to judges, exhorting them to stay for delay only most exceptionally and to trust in 'the trial process', has by and large been followed by first instance judges; it has become increasingly difficult to persuade judges to stay for delay, in particular in sex cases involving huge delays of up to 30 years. Lord Lane suggested that to stay where no fault is established on the prosecutor's part should be even more exceptional: if a man cannot have a fair trial, it is surely irrelevant whether that outcome derives from 'fault' by the prosecutor, Further, his approach appears to overlook the presumption of innocence: a guilty man may well have a reasonable recollection of old events; but the innocent defendant will not. If or when it gets the opportunity, it will be interesting to see whether Strasbourg endorses the Courts' negative approach after our imminent adoption of the Human Rights

Convention: Strasbourg has addressed delay, under Article 6, in the context of delays between notification of charge and the completion of the trial process. Perhaps, that Court will be persuadable that it is 'unfair' to try a man 30 years after the event, where the delay is not his fault.

If the Courts have been reluctant to stay for delay, they have nonetheless been active in the further development of the doctrine in other respects: the 'new' *ex p Bennett* jurisdiction has combined with other innovative steps (for example in respect of enforcement of promises not to prosecute, other alleged prosecutorial malpractices and the effect of prejudicial publicity) to produce a new and productive area for practical application of the doctrine. There is, it appears, a much greater willingness now to entertain submissions, whether to stay proceedings or to exclude evidence, on fairness grounds: a sea change has occurred, compared with the relatively recent approach whereby the courts had no concern as to *how* a defendant or evidence came to be before the court. Whether the 'new' approach derives from greater liberalism among the judiciary or from an anticipation that European standards of fairness are soon to be imposed upon us is speculative.

Some suggest that the 'new' approach to abuse has gone too far and that a retrenchment (such as happened to delay-abuse in 1991) is overdue; but, it is to be hoped that a reasonable fear of condemnation in Strasbourg may inhibit that occurring.

In the meantime, it is vital to the practitioner to know the extent to which the courts have recently been prepared to apply considerations of fairness when considering staying proceedings or quashing convictions. A particular value of this book is that it provides that information. Fairness is an elastic concept; but precedent provides at least a guide to how far the courts have been willing to stretch it.

No criminal lawyer can properly operate without considering the potential for abuse: defenders obviously must consider its application, but so must prosecutors if they are even to pay lip-service to their 'Ministers of Justice' role.

There have been many developments over the last decade. Unfortunately, many cases remain unreported, some of which are important. This book is invaluable to the practitioner: many of those unreported cases and all the important ones are referred to; the commentaries on cases, reported or otherwise, is considered, sensible and practical.

In this book, the practitioner will be brought up to date – and will be both informed and entertained by the critical commentaries. I will use it and I commend it to others.

Edmund Lawson QC
9-12 Bell Yard WC2

October 1999

Preface

In a free society trust is placed in the judiciary to ensure that the state does not use its dominant position to deny fairness to the accused. Where, as in the United Kingdom, there is no written constitution, no constitutional court and where, until recently, the Human Rights Convention was seen as peripheral to our jurisprudence, it has been left to the judges to develop a framework for testing the fairness of the prosecution and trial process. In so doing, they have pressed into service, in a peculiarly Anglo-Saxon way, a jurisprudence with a different and altogether narrower purpose.

Abuse of process is an area of the criminal law that is relatively new. In civil law the concept is well established and for a long time there has been a power of a civil court to stay proceedings, where to permit them to proceed would amount to an abuse of the process. Prior to the Woolf reforms, this power was contained in Ord 18, r 19 of the Rules of the Supreme Court. The 1996 White Book in its commentary in relation to this rule (n 33 at p 344) stated that abuse of process conferred on a court,

> '... powers which the court has hitherto exercised under its inherent jurisdiction where there appeared to be an abuse of the process of the court. This term connoted that the process of the court must be used bona fide and properly and must not be abused. The court will prevent the improper use of its machinery and will, in a proper case, summarily prevent its machinery for being used as a means of vexation and oppression in the process of litigation. The categories of conduct render the claim frivolous, vexatious or an abuse, are not closed but depend on all the relevant circumstances and for this purpose considerations of public policy and the interests of justice maybe very material.'

Since the decision of the House of Lords in *Connolly* the boundaries of abuse of process have gradually been widened. This process is not unique to England and Wales; a similar development of the law in abuse of process has occurred in other commonwealth jurisdictions. In *R v Conway*[1] the Canadian Supreme Court expressed its view of abuse of process in the following terms:

> 'Central to our judicial system is the belief that the integrity of the court must be maintained. If the court is unable to preserve its own dignity by upholding the values that our society views as essential, we will not long have a legal system which can pride itself on its commitment to justice and truth and which commands the respect of the community it serves.'

The court continued:

> 'The prosecution must be set aside not on merits, but because it is tainted to such a degree that to allow it to proceed would tarnish the integrity of the court. The doctrine is one of the safeguards designed to ensure that the repression of crime through the conviction of the guilty is done in a way which reflects our fundamental values as a society. I acknowledge that courts must have the respect and support of the community in order that the administration of criminal justice may properly fulfil its function ... where the affront to fair play and decency is disproportionate to the societal interest in the effective prosecution of criminal cases, then the administration of justice is best served by staying the proceedings' (page 67).

The Commonwealth authorities have generally emphasised that the court must take a broad view, not simply weighing up the potential prejudice to the defendant. For example, in a New Zealand case, *Moevao v Department of Labour,*[2] the court held:

> 'The yardstick is not simply a fairness to a particular accused. It is not whether the initiation and continuation of the particular process seems in circumstances to be unfair to him. That maybe an important consideration. But the focus is on the misuse of the court's process by those responsible for law enforcement. It is whether the continuation of the prosecution is in inconsistent with the recognised purposes of the administration of criminal justice and so constitutes an abuse of process of the court' (page 482).

1 [1989] 1 SCR 1659.
2 [1981] NZLR 464.

In an Australian case, *Ridgeway v R*,[3] the High Court of Australia held:

> 'The question is not one of fairness or unfairness to the appellant, but rather that the ramifications for the process of the court in allowing the proceedings to continue.'

Finally, in the New Zealand case of *R v Ellis*[4] it was held:

> 'Fairness is a broad concept but any consideration of it demands attention to any relevant factor, and to a balancing of all those factors in order to arrive at some overall conclusion. Fairness demands a multi-faceted analysis of particular circumstances.'

No-one concerned to ensure fairness in trials should overlook the judgment of Bingham CJ in the appeal of Derek Bentley, which occurred in 1998, 45 years after Bentley's execution.[5] The trial in November 1952, presided over by Lord Goddard CJ, was a travesty of justice. The scathing judgment of Bingham CJ on the conduct of Lord Goddard concluded:

> 'The summing up here was such to deny Bentley the fair trial which is the birthright of every British citizen ... it had to be a matter of profound and continuing regret that the mistrial occurred and that the defects found here were not recognised at the time.'

In this book we have sought to identify and distinguish the separate heads of abuse of process as they have developed in our criminal law. The chapter headings therefore are an attempt to delineate the application of the concept of abuse to groups of factual situations.

No contemporary book on criminal law, least of all this, could afford to ignore the potential impact of European Court of Human Rights jurisprudence, which will be of direct effect from October 2000 when the relevant provisions of the Human Rights Act 1998 are finally implemented. Fairness, however, is not a concept invented in Strasbourg. The English common law, via the concept of abuse of process, has long sought to bring into effect the provisions of Art 6, the right to a fair trial. Nonetheless, fairness as interpreted by the European Court in particular factual situations will come to play an increasingly important role in our criminal law. It is perhaps likely

3 [1995] ALJR 484.
4 [1993] 3 NZLR 317.
5 [1998] TLR, 31 July.

that in the years ahead the label of abuse of process will wither and be supplanted by a label of either 'fairness' or 'human rights law'. In that sense we stand on the threshold of the ending of one era and the beginning of another.

Whatever the future brings for the law on abuse of process, English common law can be proud of its record. In common with the development of the law on prosecution disclosure in criminal cases, the common law did not lie supine in the face of apparent unfairness and came by a process of, albeit cautious incrementalism, to grapple with some of the clearest instances of unfairness and prejudice. That this should have happened is an enormous tribute to our judiciary.

Errors and omissions remain our responsibility. The law is stated as at 1 January 2000.

David Corker
David Young

14 January 2000

Acknowledgments

We gratefully acknowledge the assistance (witting and unwitting) of the following in helping us to write this book. At the Bar, Michael Hill QC, James Hines, Campaspe Lloyd-Jacob, Alun Jones QC, Ken Macdonald QC, Charles Miskin QC, Colin Nicholls QC, Nicholas Purnell QC, Peter Rook QC, Roger Smart and Stephen Solley QC. At Cambridge University, we are grateful to Professor John Spencer. At Customs and Excise, to the legal advisor Christopher Burke. At Peters and Peters we are grateful to Monty Raphael and colleagues for their encouragement.

We are indebted to Edmund Lawson QC for agreeing to write the Foreword and for his helpful comments on the draft chapters.

Our thanks go to Anne Hutchinson (David Corker's assistant) for her efforts and patience in the many months over which she typed and marshalled the manuscripts.

David Young would like to thank Anne Rafferty QC, and the members of Chambers and Clerks at 4 Brick Court for their encouragement. Other colleagues and friends in the profession, particularly Rock Tansey QC, Steven Kay QC, Jeremy Dein, Martin Lee and Gary Summers.

Contents

Table of statutes

References in the right-hand column are to paragraph number. Where a paragraph number is set in **bold** this indicates that the Statute is set out in part or in full.

Table of cases

PARA

B

1. Delay

TYPES OF DELAY

1.1 This chapter is concerned with delay in the criminal justice process: specifically how the courts recognise that it may prejudice a defendant's right to a fair trial. Delay can occur either because the prosecution has been lethargic in bringing an accused to justice after it has sufficient evidence to merit proceedings or because a complainant delayed coming forward to the authorities with an allegation of crime. Those authorities would only then be in a position to commence proceedings. Prosecutorial delay, broadly speaking, can be divided into two types: first, delay in the investigation of a suspected offence by the police or another investigative agency and second, delay by those responsible for prosecution in deciding to institute proceedings, for example the Crown Prosecution Service.

1.2 In some foreign jurisdictions, establishing which type of prosecutorial delay occurred is an important step in deciding whether it is appropriate that the particular criminal proceedings should be allowed to continue. In the United States for example, the Sixth Amendment to the US Constitution states: 'In all criminal prosecutions, the accused shall enjoy the right to a speedy ... trial.' Violation of this right will result in dismissal of the indictment. However, the US Supreme Court has interpreted the meaning of this Amendment to hold that the right to a speedy trial arises only after a formal charge is instituted and a criminal prosecution has begun. The right is deemed not to apply in relation to complaints about a protracted investigation which results in the charging or summonsing of defendants being delayed provided that once the criminal proceedings were commenced, they were conducted without undue delay. A similar restrictive approach is applied by the courts in Canada.

1.3 In this jurisdiction, the principles which the courts have devised to deal with a complaint of prosecutorial delay are irrespective of how or why it happened. The common law has not devised different rules or standards depending on what type of prosecutorial delay occurred. These same principles also apply when the delay was the result of the complainant coming forward a long time after the alleged offence. There are no special rules which differentiate outcomes depending on who is to blame for the delay.

DEVELOPMENT OF THE LAW ON DELAY

1.4 The impetus for the development of the law in this field was the courts' increasing concern over delay by the prosecution (ie not by a complainant) in the bringing of cases to trial. While complaint by an accused about prosecution delay was not unprecedented before the mid-1980s, it was not until then that the principles of law expounding how the courts should use their abuse of process jurisdiction specifically in the context of delay were adumbrated. In his now landmark judgment in *R v Derby Magistrates' Court, ex p Brooks*,[1] Sir Roger Ormrod sought to provide a definitive statement as to the extent of the court's abuse jurisdiction in this context. He declared:

> 'The power to stop a prosecution arises only when it is an abuse of the process of the court. It may be an abuse of process if either (a) the prosecution have manipulated or misused the process of the court so as to deprive the defendant of a protection provided by the law or to take unfair advantage of a technicality, or (b) on the balance of probability the defendant has been or will be prejudiced in the preparation or conduct of his defence by delay on the part of the prosecution which is unjustifiable: for example, not due to the complexity of the inquiry and preparation of the prosecution case, or to the action of the defendant or his co-accused or to genuine difficulty in effecting service ... The ultimate objective of this discretionary power is to ensure that there should be a fair trial ... '

As this excerpt from Sir Roger Ormrod's judgment demonstrates, he sought to delineate a distinct abuse jurisdiction in relation to prosecutorial delay which he held as a pre-condition, must be judged to be unjustifiable.

1 (1984) 80 Cr App Rep 164.

1.5 This judgment, it is submitted, expressed the emerging view that the courts should possess a power enabling them, if it was appropriate, to respond to claims by defendants as to prejudice caused to them by a prosecutorial delay especially if it was unjustifiable. The other view was that common law should not be powerless to provide a remedy in the face of unreasonable delay. The genesis of this view can perhaps be found in what Lord Devlin said in *Connelly*:[1]

> 'The judges of the High Court have in their inherent jurisdiction, both in civil and in criminal matters, power (subject of course to any statutory rules) to make and enforce rules of practice in order to ensure that the court's process is used fairly and conveniently by both sides ... First, a general power, taking various specific forms, to prevent unfairness to the accused has always been a part of the English criminal law ... nearly the whole of the English criminal law of procedure and evidence has been made by the exercise of the judges of their power to see that what was fair and just was done between prosecution and accused.'

1 [1964] AC 1254.

1.6 The judgment of Sir Roger Ormrod in *ex p Brooks* was echoed and reinforced by Lord Templeman giving the leading judgment in the Privy Council case of *Bell v DPP.*[1] In *Bell* the Privy Council was called on to interpret the meaning of the relevant article of the Constitution of Jamaica which guaranteed an accused's right to a fair hearing in a reasonable time. The applicant alleged this article had been violated by a prosecutorial delay amounting to 32 months. This was the lapse of time between the conclusion of the applicant's first trial and the commencement of his second. In construing the Jamaican constitutional provision, Lord Templeman agreed with the applicant's submissions and held that this delay was unconstitutional. The second trial of the applicant was thus an abuse of process and the applicant's conviction should be quashed. While the judgment of the Board in *Bell* was only a persuasive authority in English law, Lord Templeman suggested that in a domestic situation the abuse jurisdiction could also be used in the context of delay. Lord Templeman said: 'Whenever any person is charged with a criminal offence he shall, unless the charge is withdrawn, be afforded a fair hearing within a reasonable time by an independent and impartial court established by law ...'

1 [1985] AC 937.

1.7 Both *ex p Brooks* and *Bell*, were quickly followed by a large number of first instance decisions in both the Divisional Court and by trial judges in the Crown Court. The rapid growth in this corner of the law continued until the judgment of the Court of Appeal in *A-G's*

Reference (No 1 of 1990)[1] which brought this development of the law largely to an end.

1 [1992] QB 630.

ALTERNATIVE REMEDIES TO THE ABUSE JURISDICTION

1.8 Before considering how delay in the criminal process has been located within the courts' abuse jurisdiction it is important to consider other remedies English criminal law has developed to prevent delay from arising or, if having arisen, to ameliorate its effects in a subsequent criminal trial.

The constitutional position

1.9 In contrast to other jurisdictions, neither Parliament nor the common law has sought to confer on an accused any constitutional or absolute right to a speedy trial or to judgment within a reasonable time. In other words, no over-arching limitation period restricting the right of a prosecutor to bring charges against an accused has been imposed. Possibly the closest English law has come to granting such a right is chapter 29 of Magna Carta which states: 'No freeman shall be taken, or imprisoned, or be disseised of his freehold or liberties, or free customs, or be outlawed or exiled, or any otherwise destroyed; not will we not pass upon him, nor condemn him, but by lawful judgment of his peers, or by the law of the land. We will sell to no man, we will not deny [or defer] to any man, either justice or right.' However, these words were given a very restrictive meaning by Lord Lane CJ in *A-G's Reference*. He construed the word 'defer' as meaning a wrongful rather than a mere deferment. He held that the delay or deferment complained of must be both wrongful and unjustified. In this sense therefore Lord Lane dismissed the relevance of Magna Carta. It merely questioned whether the delay was justifiable or not, an issue which only the courts could seek to resolve.

1.10 A clear illustration of the fact that English criminal law has not imposed any limitation period is the enactment of the War Crimes Act 1991. This legislation was passed in order principally to make it possible to bring to justice in the 1990s persons who were suspected of committing war crimes during the 1939-45 war. In *Serafinowitz*[1] and *Sanouik*[2] the defendants were indicted for war crimes committed during the early 1940s. Both their submissions for abuse based on delay in 1997 and 1999 respectively failed, the trial judges holding that the trial process could overcome any prejudice thereby caused. Moreover, by passing this Act there was a clear parliamentary intention that trials for such crimes should occur despite massive delay.

1 CCC (17 January 1997, unreported).
2 CCC (March 1999, unreported). This defendant was convicted and sentenced to life imprisonment.

Limitation period for summary-only offences

1.11 While there is no over-arching principle in English law imposing a limitation period on the bringing of criminal charges, Parliament has nonetheless imposed a limitation period for a specific category of alleged offences. Section 127 of the Magistrates' Courts Act 1980 which provides: 'Limitations of time (a)–(1) Except as otherwise expressly provided by enactment and subject to subsection (2) below, a magistrates' court shall not try an information or hear a complaint unless the information was laid, or the complaint made, within six months from the time when the offence was committed, or the matter of complaint arose.' Via the discipline of this six-month rule Parliament has sought to ensure that summary offences are both charged and tried as soon as reasonably possible after their alleged commission.

Prosecution delay – s 127

1.12 In the exercise of its supervisory jurisdiction over the magistrates' court where all summary offences are tried, the Divisional Court has sought to ensure that this intention behind s 127 is respected both in its letter and spirit. This determination can be illustrated by the authority of *R v Brentford Justices, ex p Wong.*[1] In that case, the prosecutor decided to lay an information against an accused for the summary only offence of careless driving. However, this information was laid only one day within the six-month period permitted by s 127 and it transpired that the decision by the prosecutor to lay this information had been taken before any decision had been made as to whether proceedings should be continued or not. In other words, the prosecutor had sought to circumvent the six-month limitation period by issuing the information as a holding manoeuvre in order to decide whether to proceed with a prosecution later. The Divisional Court held that such prosecutorial manoeuvring constituted an abuse. Donaldson LJ held that the six-month time limit required prosecuting authorities to act with expedition and to decide within that time limit finally whether to bring proceedings or not. Donaldson LJ said:

> 'The process of laying an information is, I think, assumed by Parliament to be the first stage in a continuous process of bringing a prosecution. (Section 127 of the MCA 1980) is designed to ensure that prosecutions shall be brought within a reasonable time. That purpose is wholly frustrated if it is possible for a prosecutor to obtain summonses and then, in his own good time and at his convenience, serve them ... Here there was a deliberate attempt to gain further time in which to reach a decision. It is perhaps hard on the prosecutor to characterise that as an abuse of the process of the court because I am sure that there was no intention by the prosecutor to abuse the process of the court. He thought he could legitimately do this ... I do not think that he can ... it is a matter which has to be investigated by the justices.'

1 [1981] 1 All ER 884.

1.13 *Wong* is therefore authority that deliberate prosecutorial delay in context of summary offences will not be tolerated by the courts. The prosecution must decide on the institution of criminal proceedings in good time and also decide on which factual basis to proceed.

1.14 The principle in *Wong* has also been held to apply where the prosecution lay an information (and so have decided to bring a prosecution) but are undecided between two factual bases on which the case might proceed. This was the situation in *R v Newcastle-upon-Tyne Justices, ex p Hindle*,[1] the defendant was charged with obstructing a police officer in the execution of his duty but the information did not specify the nature of the obstruction alleged and, in the circumstances of the case, the prosecution might have been alleging two different senses of objectionable behaviour. When the prosecution refused to resolve this ambiguity, the Divisional Court held that the obstruction summons ought not to proceed. Goff LJ said that the situation was '... at least as objectionable a course as the laying of an information where no decision has been taken to prosecute, for, if permitted, it would allow a prosecution to postpone until after the expiry of the six-month period, their decision whether to prosecute for a particular offence' (page 718). Prejudice had also been caused to the defence because, without knowing how the prosecution intended to put its case, it was unable to properly deal with the question of whether the obstruction charge should be tried before or after other charges against the defendant which arise out of the same incident.

1 [1984] 1 All ER 770.

Implicit limitation periods

1.15 While it is submitted that s 127 is the only statutory example of an explicit limitation period being created on the bringing of criminal proceedings, there are however, implicit limitation periods which exist by virtue of the obligation being created by the relevant legislation. For example, regs 5 and 12 of the Money Laundering Regulations 1993[1] makes it an offence for a person who conducts 'relevant financial business' not to preserve records of relevant transactions for a period of five years after those transactions have been completed. If, therefore, a prosecution were to be mounted against a person for an offence under regs 5 and 12 more than five years after the relevant transactions occurred, the accused would have an absolute defence in that he was entitled to destroy the records once the statutory period had elapsed. Another statutory example which also contains such implicit limitation periods on the bringing of proceedings is, for example, s 221 of the Companies Act 1985 which requires the keeping of accounting records for a defined period.

1 The Regulations are a piece of delegated legislation deriving their validity from s 2(2) of the European Community Act 1972.

Practice directions

1.16 In recent years, efforts have been made to streamline and spread the passage of cases in the Crown Court. As part of this process practice directions have been promulgated which set down time limits within which cases should be progressed to a specified point. The best example of this is Practice Direction (Crown Court: Plea and Directions Hearings) which dictates that a plea and directions hearing should take place at the Crown Court of trial within 28 days of the accused being committed for trial by the magistrates. While plea and directions hearings are non-statutory the policy underlying the practice direction referred to above has been reinforced by Part IV of the Criminal Procedure and Investigations Act 1996 (ss 39 to 43) which give judges power to hold pre-trial hearings in the hope that such hearings will clarify the issues in dispute and lead to shorter and more efficient trials.

Custody time limits

1.17 Section 22 of the Prosecution of Offences Act 1985 grants power to the Home Secretary to set time limits in relation to the preliminary stages of criminal proceedings. Subsection (1) provides that:

> '22.-(1) The Secretary of State may by regulations make provision, with respect to any specified preliminary stage of proceedings for an offence, as to the maximum period–

(a) to be allowed to the prosecution to complete that stage;
(b) during which the accused may, while awaiting completion of that stage, be–
(i) in the custody of a magistrates court; or
(ii) in the custody of the Crown Court;
in relation to that offence.'

Significantly, no overall time limits have been promulgated pursuant to subsection (1)(a). However, subsection (1)(b) has been applied for the purpose of introducing the scheme of custody time limits, a scheme primarily intended to ensure that the prosecution act with due expedition once an accused has been charged and remanded in custody awaiting trial.

1.18 The issue concerning extension of time limits has spawned a developing body of jurisprudence which in *R v Manchester Crown Court, ex p McDonald*[1] Bingham CJ referred to as a 'proliferation' of cases. *Ex p McDonald* seeks to provide a comprehensive review of the most important points arising from extension of custody time limits. Bingham CJ places great emphasis on the underlying purpose of the regulations and also the significance of the European Convention on Human Rights, especially Art 5. Detailed consideration of custody time limits is outside the scheme of this book.

1 [1999] 1 All ER 805.

CPS code of practice

1.19 The DPP is enjoined by s 10 of the Prosecution of Offences Act 1985 to issue a code for Crown Prosecutors giving guidance on general principles, inter alia, in determining whether proceedings for an offence should be instituted. In the absence of any limitation period, para 6.5 of the code is headed 'Some common public interest factors against prosecution'. The relevant part of para 6.5 reads as follows:

> 'A prosecution is less likely to be needed if:
> (a) ...
> (b) There has been a long delay between the offence taking place and the date of the trial, unless:
> - The offence is serious;
> - The delay has been caused in part by the defendant;
> - The offence has only recently come to light; or
> - The complexity of the offence has meant that there has been a long investigation.'

1.20 In relation to serious crime, para 6.5 states that the more serious the offence, the greater the public interest in favour of prosecution. There is therefore, despite a long delay, a general presumption in favour of prosecution where the offence is serious. The prosecutor must apply para 6.5 and decide whether to commence a prosecution or not where there has been a long and, perhaps unjustifiable delay. There is no provision within our legal system for a prosecutor to seek a preliminary opinion or declaration from a court as to whether proceeding after a long delay would amount to an abuse of process.

Police and Criminal Evidence Act code of practice

1.21 Code C of the Code of Practice is entitled 'Code of Practice for the Detention, Treatment and Questioning of Persons by Police Officers'. Paragraph 11.4 provides:

> 'As soon as a police officer who is making enquiries of any person about an offence believes that a prosecution should be brought against him and that there is sufficient evidence for it to succeed, he shall ask that person if he has anything further to say. If the person indicates that he has nothing more to say the officer shall [without delay] cease to question him about that offence ...'

1.22 This provision is designed to ensure that once the substance of a prosecution case is apparent to a police officer/investigator he should not continue questioning the suspect for the purpose of trying to turn the case into a stronger and better one. While the avoidance of delay is not the primary aim of this provision it is designed to ensure that once a case is apparent the suspect should be charged and the proceedings should begin at the soonest opportunity. The decision to charge in this context, should not be delayed. This point is made even clearer by para 16.1 which reads: 'When an officer considers that there is sufficient evidence to prosecute a detained person, and that there is sufficient evidence for a prosecution to succeed, and that that person has said all he wishes to say about the offence, he shall [without delay] bring him before the custody officer who shall then be responsible for considering whether or not he should be charged ...'

1.23 It is submitted that several qualifications need to be made to the prescriptions contained in the quoted passages from the PACE code in paras 1.21 and 1.22. First, the custody officer has to know what charge is appropriate, bearing in mind the circumstances of the case. There is in our system no provision for a holding charge to enable a suspect to be charged with an offence merely for the purpose of firstly complying with the code and second for enabling the prosecution to be given a breathing-space for the purpose of formulating more specific and appropriate charges. It may therefore be entirely understandable for the police to delay charging in order for their understanding of the case to improve, leading to the decision to charge an appropriate offence. Second, it is understandable to defer charging for the purpose of carrying out certain investigations which may have been instigated by the suspect himself in answers he gave during his interview.

1.24 It is submitted that while the wording of the relevant paragraphs of the code encourage charges to be levelled as soon as the police believe there is sufficient evidence to merit such charges, the courts have been reluctant to adopt this strict approach. Instead, they have preferred a flexible approach allowing investigators not to charge until all relevant evidence is gathered so long as this is achieved within a reasonable period. A recent example of such judicial tolerance is the judgment of the Lord Chief Justice in *R v Cardiff Magistrates' Court, ex p Hole.*[1] In answer to a specific defence submission that there had been a breach of paras 11.4 and 16.1 Lord Bingham CJ observed that the decision of the police officer to defer charging was reasonable, bearing in mind the complexity of the case and the need to conduct additional enquiries based on what the defendants had said during their respective interviews.

1 [1997] COD 84.

1.25 Other than the discrete provisions referred in paras 1.21 to 1.24, the common law via the abuse jurisdiction has been left to confront and resolve the issue of delay in the criminal process causing unfairness to an accused. Unsurprisingly, it is an established tenet of this jurisdiction that delay is inimical to a fair trial and the efficient working of our criminal justice system. However, despite their adherence to this tenet the courts have, it is submitted, been reluctant to embrace a further principle flowing from the first: that failure to ensure a trial within a reasonable time constitutes infringement of the accused's right to a fair trial.

Why 'abuse of process'?

1.26 It is perhaps especially unfortunate that the perjorative phrase of 'abuse of process' in the context of delay has become so entrenched. 'abuse of process' connotes impropriety, perhaps even misconduct, by the prosecution whereas the test for abuse in this context is not necessarily connected to any finding of fault by the prosecution. Blameless delay can warrant the staying of criminal proceedings if the accused can demonstrate sufficient consequential prejudice. As Garland J said in *R v Reade*,[1] 'Although this jurisdiction is usually referred to as "abuse of process of the court" this phrase is something of a misnomer and that the jurisdiction would be better described as exerciseable in "circumstances in which a fair trial is no longer possible"' (page 1). However, thus far this label of abuse has successfully resisted any attempt at being dislodged in favour of a different and more accurate phrase. Accordingly it will be used henceforth in this chapter.

1 (1993) Independent, 19 October.

THE GENERAL LAW ON DELAY

1.27 By the early 1990s the law in this field was developing rapidly with trial judges increasingly holding that prosecutorial delay could justify a stay. Such rapid developments inevitably threw up anomalies and inconsistencies, thus causing uncertainty as to the general principles to be applied. For example, the law was unclear whether, in order to justify a stay, evidence of actual prejudice arising from delay had to be established by the defence or alternatively, whether prejudice could be inferred from prosecutorial delay simpliciter. Furthermore, in *R v Telford Justice, ex p Badhan*[1] Mann LJ suggested that a distinction should be drawn between two types of delay case: that where the prosecution had been responsible or culpable for the delay and that where the delay was not its fault. Mann LJ opined that in the former a stay might be ordered if the accused could show that he had been prejudiced in the conduct of his defence, whereas in the latter, an elapse of time case, the accused had to show that he could not have a fair trial. However, shortly thereafter in *R v Bow Street Stipendiary Magistrates, ex p Judd*[2] a different constitution on the Divisional Court rejected this dichotomy holding that there was only one test to be applied irrespective of any justification for the delay: the fair trial test.

1 [1991] 2 All ER 854/862.
2 (23 November 1992, unreported).

1.28 In early January 1992 in *Bow Street Stipendiary Magistrates, ex p DPP*[1] (The Guildford Four case) Neill LJ summarised the law in relation to delay:

'The authorities establish that an abuse of process may exist in the following circumstances:

(a) if the prosecution have manipulated or misused the process of the court so as to deprive the defendant of a protection provided by the law or to take advantage of a technicality;

(b) if on the balance of probability the defendant has been, or will be, prejudiced in the preparation or conduct of his defence by delay on the part of the prosecution which is unjustifiable; or

(c) if, even though the prosecution are in no way responsible for the delay, the delay has produced genuine prejudice and unfairness for the defendant;

(d) in a case involving delay, the court will consider the reasons for the delay and the responsibility, if any, of either the prosecution or the defence for the delay. The court will also consider the issues which are likely to arise at the hearing and the nature of the evidence which is likely to be relevant. Thus a case which depends largely on documentary evidence may be regarded very differently from one where witnesses will have to try to recollect some swiftly moving event which passed before their eyes years ago.

(e) the purpose and existence of this discretionary power is to ensure that there should be a fair trial according to law' (page 16).

In seeking to apply these general principles Neill LJ upheld the prosecution's submissions that the respondent magistrate had been wrong to hold that the proceedings against the defendants should be stayed on the ground of delay. Neill LJ held that the magistrate had fallen into error because he had agreed with the defence submission that the delay had been sufficiently extreme so as to raise a general inference of prejudice. This was the wrong approach to adopt and what Neill LJ held the magistrate ought to have done was to focus his attention on what he held was the critical issue, which was what specific prejudice would be suffered by the defence as a result of delay at the eventual trial? Neill LJ held in answer to this question that, while inevitably the defence would suffer some prejudice, a fair trial was still nonetheless possible. He rejected the view first, that the accused's right to a fair trial meant that he should not suffer any prejudice at all and second, that prejudice could simply be inferred from mere delay even when, as in this case, the delay was enormous.

1 [1992] Crim LR 790.

Attorney General's Reference

1.29 *R v Bow Street Stipendiary Magistrates, ex p DPP* was shortly followed by what has become the leading case on delay and abuse of process, *A-G's Reference (No 1 of 1990)* ('*A-G's Reference*').[1] In *ex p Hole*[2] Lord Bingham CJ in October 1996 observed that as regards delay (page 7) and the court's abuse jurisdiction, '... there can be no doubt that the leading authority is Attorney General's Reference'.

1 See para 1.7.
2 See para 1.23.

1.30 The decision by the Attorney General to seek the authoritative guidance of the Court of Appeal regarding delay demonstrated the degree of official concern regarding the then willingness of courts to stay prosecutions. In allowing the Criminal Division of the Court of Appeal a full opportunity to consider delay in the context of abuse it was obviously hoped, by those responsible for criminal prosecutions, that the Court would issue clear guidance which would dramatically restrict the extent of trial courts' jurisdiction to stay cases on the ground of delay. In this respect, prosecutors were not to be disappointed. As Lord Lane CJ commented at the end of his judgment: 'This judgment will, we hope, result in a significant reduction the number of applications to stay proceedings on the ground of delay' (page 177).

1.31 The facts which gave rise to *A-G's Reference* concerned a police officer who attended an incident in August 1987 giving rise to subsequent complaint. He was summonsed for an offence in March 1989. At the commencement of his Crown Court trial in December 1989 the trial judge accepted a submission that, because of the August 1987 to March 1989 delay in prosecuting him, this alone constituted an abuse and his trial should accordingly be stayed. The Attorney General felt this approach was flawed and pursuant to s 36 of the Criminal Justice Act 1972, the Attorney sought a ruling from the Court in relation to the following two questions:

> (1) Whether proceedings on indictment may be stayed on the grounds of prejudice resulting from delay in the institution of those proceedings even though the delay had not be occasioned by any fault of the prosecution.
>
> (2) If the answer to (1) is in the affirmative, what is the degree of:

(a) likelihood, and
(b) the seriousness of any prejudice which is required to justify a stay of such proceedings.

1.32 During the hearing of *A-G's Reference* the Attorney argued that the trial judge had been wrong to hold that the period of delay in the case before him could properly be said to amount to an abuse. Two arguments in support of this were canvassed. First, the delay which did occur was reasonable and justifiable in the circumstances. Second, there was no evidence of any specific prejudice to the accused in the preparation of his defence caused by the delay. In reply, the defence submitted that the delay amounted to a breach of chapter 29 of Magna Carta (see para 1.9): the word 'defer' meaning any period which was longer than that required for proper preparation for the trial.

1.33 Lord Lane unhesitatingly rejected this defence submission holding that the deferment meant wrongful deferment or delay which Chapter 29 of Magna Carta could not even begin to offer any guidance about.

1.34 Lord Lane CJ in giving the judgment of the Court answered the first question as follows:

> 'On the basis of the decision in *R v Telford Justices, ex p Badhan*, Mr Hooper, appearing before us on behalf of the Attorney General, constrained to concede that the answer to the Attorney-General's first question is a qualified "yes". As it is not possible to anticipate in advance all the infinitely variable circumstances which may arise in the future, we feel ourselves, albeit reluctantly, forced to agree to a limited extent with that concession'.
>
> However, we remind ourselves of the principles outlined earlier in this judgment and the observation of Lord Morris in *Connolly*, 48 Cr App Rep 183, [1964] AC 1254 at page 211 and page 1304 that:
>
> '... Generally speaking a prosecutor has as much right as a defendant to demand a-verdict of a jury on an outstanding indictment, and where either demands a verdict a judge has no jurisdiction to stand in the way of it.'
>
> 'Stays granted on the grounds of delay or for any other reason should only be employed in exceptional circumstances ... In principle ... even where the delay can be said to have been unjustifiable, the imposition of a permanent stay should be the exception rather than the rule. Still more rare would be cases where a stay can properly be imposed in the

> absence of any fault on the part of the complainant or prosecution. Delay due merely to the complexity of the case or contributed to by the action of the defendant himself should never be the foundation for a stay.'

In answer to the second question Lord Lane said:

> '... no stay should be imposed unless the defendant shows on the balance of probabilities that owing to the delay he will suffer serious prejudice to the extent that no fair trial can be held...In asserting whether there is likely to be prejudice and if so whether it can properly be described as serious, the following matters should be borne in mind: first, the power of the judge at common law and under (PACE) to regulate the admissibility of evidence; secondly, the trial process itself should ensure that all relevant factual issues arising from delay will be placed before the jury as part of the evidence for their consideration, together with the powers of the judge to give appropriate directions to the jury before they consider their verdict.'

1.35 Turning to the facts of the case as set out above, Lord Lane held that the trial judge had been in error in agreeing to stay the proceedings: 'The delay, such as it was, was not unjustifiable; the chances of prejudice were remote; the degree of potential prejudice was small; the powers of the judge and the trial process itself would have provided ample protection for the respondent; there was no danger of the trial being unfair; in any event the case was in no sense exceptional so as to justify the ruling.'

1.36 It is notable that this is all Lord Lane said by way of judgment on the facts of the case before him and the erroneous ruling of the trial judge. He did not, for instance, provide any guidance on exactly what material facts in the case led him to his conclusions; why for example the degree of prejudice was small and what the trial judge should have done during the trial to have prevented it from being unfair. It is perhaps regrettable that Lord Lane apparently shied away from providing this sort of practical analysis of the factual issues before him. This perhaps would have rendered his judgment of much greater direct practical assistance to subsequent proceedings.

1.37 In *Ex p Hole* Lord Bingham CJ summarised the judgment of Lord Lane thus:

> 'The clear upshot of that decision therefore is that there must be exceptional circumstances before a stay should be granted; and even where there is unjustified delay a stay should be the exception of the

> rule; that a stay should be more exceptional in the absence of fault; and that complexity itself should not be the ground for a stay. Furthermore, the decision indicates that there should be no stay unless the defendant can show on a balance of probabilities that, owing to the delay, he has suffered serious prejudice to the extent that no fair trial can be held so as to render the prosecution a misuse of process' (page 8).

1.38 The judgment of Lord Lane was approved by the House of Lords in the Privy Council case of *Tan v Cameron*[1] who quoted with approval the above quoted passages from his judgment. Furthermore, in his speech Lord Mustill sought to remove the confusion which had arisen in relation to burdens of proof to be satisfied when a submission of delay causing prejudice and unfairness was made. There were some authorities to the effect that burdens of proof differed depending on whether the delay was excusable or inexcusable. Lord Mustill sought to eliminate this dichotomy in favour of a more simple and unified approach:

> 'Naturally, the longer the delay the more likely it will be that the prosecution is at fault, and that the delay has caused prejudice to the defendant; and the less that the prosecution has to offer by explanation, the more easily can fault be inferred. But the establishment of these facts is only one step on the way to a consideration of whether, in all the circumstances, the situation created by the delay is such as to make it an unfair employment of the powers of the court any longer to hold the defendant to account. [This is a question to be considered in the round,] and nothing is gained by the introduction of shifting burdens of proof, which serves only to break down into formal steps what is in reality [a single appreciation of what is or is not unfair]'.

1 [1993] 2 All ER 493.

1.39 Lord Mustill was therefore exhorting judges not to over-complicate the application of principles on delay to their abuse jurisdiction. Little was to be gained in his view by having separate rules and standards depending on whether the delay was characterised by adjectives such as inadvertent, inordinate or inexcusable. Furthermore, by focusing attention on the question of what prejudice was really suffered by the accused occasioned by delay and the real importance of it to issues of dispute in a particular case, Lord Mustill was, in common with Lord Lane, seeking to diminish the importance of issues like the actual length of the delay complained of and whether the prosecution could satisfactorily explain or justify their delay.

1.40 A similar approach is to be found in the House of Lords case of *R v Horseferry Road Magistrates' Court, ex p Bennett*[1] which unlike *Tan v Cameron* (a Privy Council case) is of binding authority. In his speech Lord Lowry said:

> '... I consider that a court has the discretion to stay any criminal proceedings on the ground that to try those proceedings will amount to an abuse of its own process either (1) because it will be impossible (usually by reason of delay) to give the accused a fair trial or (2) because it offends the court's sense of justice and propriety to be asked to try the accused the those circumstances of a particular case. I agree that prima facie it is the duty of a court to try a person who is charged before it with an offence which the court has power to try and therefore that the jurisdiction to stay must be exercised carefully and sparingly and only for very compelling reasons. The discretion to stay is not a disciplinary jurisdiction and ought not to be exercised in order to express the court's disapproval of official conduct. Accordingly, if the prosecuting authorities have been guilty of culpable delay but the prospect of a fair trial has not been prejudiced the court ought not to stay the proceedings merely for "pour encourager les autres"' (page 135).

1 [1993] 3 All ER 138.

Analysis of Lord Lane's judgment

1.41 Bearing in mind that Lord Lane's judgment has remained the cornerstone of the law on delay, it is necessary to consider in some detail. It is submitted that the following points are pertinent:

(1) *Some prejudice must be tolerated by the defence* – The hurdle to be surmounted by defendants seeking a stay is a high one. The prejudice must be serious to the extent that no fair trial can be held. A defendant must therefore tolerate some prejudice or unfairness to his case caused by delay even if this is no fault of his own. This unfortunate predicament, Lord Lane contended, can however be largely eliminated, as faith can be placed in the flexibility of the trial process to eliminate residual unfairness caused by delay.

(2) *The remedial effects of the trial process* – Lord Lane, as his answer to the second point above demonstrates, urged trial judges to recognise the existence of their other powers to ensure a fair trial as alternatives to the exercise of a stay, ie excluding evidence and ensuring that the jury are made aware of the facts concerning

delay. In Lord Lane's view, the exercise of such powers would in most cases where there had been significant delay be a sufficient remedy and so would ensure that the proceedings were fair.

However, against this it is difficult to see how the use of such powers and protections will be effective in delay cases. How, for example, is a jury to deal, when it retires to consider its verdict, with the issue presumably raised by the defence and echoed by the judge as to what the evidence might have been but for the delay? It would appear that this is an open-ended issue which can only be resolved by speculation rather than by fact. How, in a concrete case, can a tribunal of fact seek to resolve this issue based only on the evidence presented to it?

(3) *The culpability of the prosecution* – In his answer to the first question Lord Lane suggests that judges should be more reluctant to stay proceedings on account of delay if there has been no fault on the part of the prosecution than if there has been such fault. It is submitted, however, that this distinction creates an immediate uncertainty because in answer to the second question, Lord Lane held that the criterion to be followed is always to be the same, that of serious prejudice to the accused. What then is the relevance of considering the extent of the prosecution's culpability for the delay? Unless Lord Lane meant to suggest that if the prosecution has been culpable then the threshold for imposing a stay should be lower than if it has not, this consideration has no legitimate role. But as Lord Lane did not suggest this, it is submitted that there is an inconsistency between his answers to the two questions vis-à-vis the relevance of prosecution fault. Despite Lord Lane's insistence that there is only one criterion, he appears to concede that the issue of any fault on the part of the prosecution for delay is to be included in the equation, although unfortunately does not explain how. It would appear that almost sotto voce, Lord Lane accepts that the courts have a role in disciplining the prosecution in this regard.

(4) *Causes of delay to be excluded from consideration*: In his answer to the first question Lord Lane makes plain that two factors should never militate in favour of the exercise of a stay:

(i) *Complexity*: where delay is due to the complexity of the prosecution's allegations or genuine difficulty in investigating the alleged crime. Delay may be inevitable in complicated cases especially in those involving allegations of fraud.

Lord Lane's view here was reflected earlier in *Holyoake*[1] where the defendant was tried in 1990 for offences alleged to have occurred between 1983 and 1986. It was submitted on appeal that this prolonged delay was prejudicial to the defendant. The defence submitted that a material witness had died and an important part of the prosecution case related to a conversation between defendant and victim which had occurred four years previously and where there was a conflict of recollection. Farquharson LJ, however, did not agree either that the delay had caused an unfair trial or that the prosecution delay had been unjustifiable: 'These are matters which might give rise to some degree of prejudice it is true ... It must be perfectly obviously to everybody concerned that it was a case which required consideration and investigation in depth. Everybody is aware that these company fraud cases (a) take a long time to prepare, (b) generally arrive at the Crown Court at a late date because of the commitments of the people concerned in the case.'

(ii) *The culpability of the defendant*: unsurprisingly Lord Lane held that when the accused is responsible for the delay he cannot then complain about possible prejudice arising therefrom. Accordingly, a defendant who flees the jurisdiction in order to avoid criminal proceedings against him is in effect estopped from arguing that he cannot receive a fair trial on the grounds of delay.

This principle, easy to explain and apply in straightforward situations, although has called for qualification when in the light of a defence complaint about delay the prosecution riposte that the delay was caused by the defendant's conduct, which itself is to be an issue of dispute in the trial. For example, where the defence complain about delay and deny guilt and the prosecution contend that the accused committed subsequent offences to conceal his principal offence and such attempted concealment caused delay in discovery of the principal offence. In *A-G of Hong Kong v Wai-bun*[2] the question arose as to the accused's responsibility for the delay. The prosecution argued that the defendant was primarily responsible for the delay because he had sought to hinder and delay the investigation by falsifying accounts, the subject of the charge against him. On behalf of the Privy Council, Lord Woolf rejected this argument. It presupposed the defendant's guilt for the offence alleged against him, which was of course a matter of fact to be decided by a jury necessarily subsequent to any application to stay. Lord Woolf held that prosecutors could not argue on the strength of Lord Lane's judgment, that in this sense, the defendant had contributed to delay. Lord Woolf held that what Lord Lane was referring to in *A-G's Reference* were acts of the defendant outside the subject of the trial, for example absconding.

(5) *Oral versus documentary evidence cases* – Lord Lane emphasised that a distinction must be drawn between cases which turn largely on contemporaneous documentary evidence and those which do not. Lord Lane perhaps had in mind *R v Buzalek and Schiffer*[3] where the Court of Appeal held that a distinction should be drawn between cases where the prosecution is dependent on available documents, as in most fraud cases, and where it is dependent on a late complaint and oral testimony, as in many sexual offence cases. The Court held that generally-speaking only in the latter may it be inferred from a long delay that a fair trial would not be possible. This approach was followed by Watkins LJ in *R v Central Criminal Court, ex p Randall and Pottle*[4] where the defendants were in 1990 to be tried for offences that they had allegedly committed in 1963. Watkins LJ rejected the defence submission that the delay between the offence and the trial was sufficiently extreme to warrant a stay on the ground of abuse. Watkins LJ held that as the defendants had virtually admitted their offence in a book which they had written in 1989, which the prosecution sought to rely on as part of its case, the trial should proceed.

1 (24 August 1990, unreported), CA.
2 [1994] AC 1.
3 [1991] Crim LR 115.
4 [1992] 1 All ER 370.

1.42 It can be seen from this analysis of Lord Lane's judgment in *A-G's Reference* that the overriding and determinative issue of whether an application to stay on the ground of delay is successful or not should be prejudice to an accused. Furthermore, in seeking to establish a common judicial approach in evaluating such prejudice, Lord Lane emphasised two interrelated and over-lapping principles. First, before a stay should be exercised, the prejudice complained of must be adjudged to be so serious that as a result the defendant can no longer receive a fair trial. Second, the flexibility of the trial process is such that prejudice can often either be eradicated or largely ameliorated, therefore allowing a fair trial to be held.

1.43 It is now necessary to consider how the courts subsequent to Lord Lane's judgment have interpreted and applied these two fundamental principles. While logically and in practice they may overlap, this chapter shall attempt for the sake of clarity to consider them separately and then draw some conclusions common to both.

SERIOUS PREJUDICE TO AN ACCUSED

1.44 Establishing the existence of such prejudice is an evidential burden resting solely on the defence. It must establish to the civil standard, on a balance of probabilities, that the prejudice suffered is so serious that the defendant could not receive a fair trial.

1.45 Since Lord Lane's judgment the courts have been obliged to consider complaints of serious prejudice, typically in cases where the defence have argued that delay-caused recollection deficiencies of witnesses and loss of potential exculpatory evidence has created unavoidable prejudice and unfairness to the accused. As the relevant authorities demonstrate, these arguments have largely been ventilated in cases involving allegations of sexual misconduct by the defendant alleged to have occurred many years previously. In these cases, delay is often to be measured in decades rather than simply in years; the lapse of time between the alleged assaults on the complainant and the complainant thereafter reporting the matter to the police. Importantly therefore most of the authorities subsequent to *A-G's Reference* on serious prejudice and delay have not been concerned with delay, inadvertent or deliberate, by the prosecution but delay by a complainant or alleged victim in reporting the matter.

1.46 While the courts have often repeated that the principles enunciated by Lord Lane are universal and apply equally to all criminal cases it is nonetheless helpful to distinguish into two groups the authorities on serious prejudice. First, those where there has been a substantial delay in the victim coming forward. These authorities represent the overwhelming majority on the subject of serious prejudice. They are all sexual offence cases. Second, those cases concerning delay by the prosecution.

Judicial toleration of massive delay by a complainant in reporting an offence

1.47 It is submitted that a consideration of the authorities, to be conducted below, reveals that the courts' attitude has consistently been, first, to explain and justify a complainant's delay in coming forward, in order that a defence submission that the delay in reporting was unjustifiable or deliberate can be rejected and second, as a consequence, to adopt an attitude of scepticism to submissions made by the defence that this delay has caused proven or likely prejudice.

1.48 Bearing in mind that these authorities concern sexual offences it appears that public disquiet concerning historical allegations of sexual misconduct often committed by persons in a position of authority seems to have influenced and hardened the attitudes of trial judges and members of the Court of Appeal. In *R v Percival*[1] Auld LJ observed: 'A developing concern with and, understanding of sexual abuse, is reflected in a growing experience of cases featuring delays that at one time would have been regarded as intolerable. That experience and the underlying problem of unreported abuse has served to encourage experienced judges to be more liberal in their concept of what is possible by way of a fair trial in the face of delay' (page 13). It is submitted that the judiciary appear to have resolved that persons accused of sexual offences, no matter how antiquated, must be brought to justice unless there is the clearest and most undeniable evidence of serious prejudice. In the words of Lord Lane, the case must be 'wholly exceptional'.

1 (1998) Independent, 8 July.

1.49 A good example of such judicial policy at work is the case of *R v B*.[1] In *B* the accused was tried in February 1995 for sexual offences against two girls. The matters covered by the indictment related to offences which went back to the years 1973 to 1976. One count on the indictment potentially went back to 1970. Before the trial commenced an application by the defence was made for it to be stayed on the ground of delay. This was rejected. Following his conviction, the accused argued before the Court of Appeal that the trial judge should have acceded to this application.

1 [1996] Crim LR 406.

1.50 Hobhouse LJ in rejecting this argument said: 'This was a case where there was a very considerable lapse of time, especially in relation to the girl J. But it is in the public interest that where people are believed to have committed offences, including offences of abuse of young children, they should be brought before the court and, if their guilt is proved, be convicted of the offences. Provided that there can be a fair trial, it is strongly in the public interest and mere lapse of time is not a reason for failing to bring the defendant before the court' (page 4). Hobhouse LJ was thus establishing that the mere fact that there has been a significant delay in the reporting of an allegation is never of itself to be a valid reason for staying a criminal prosecution. Having expressed this general view as to delay, Hobhouse LJ then focused on the causes of delay in sexual offence cases and sought to describe why in his view delay was so often an endemic feature:

> 'There are many inhibitions upon a child complainant making complaints of sexual abuse against a parent or step-parent or some other close member of their family. The offences occur when they are immature and uncertain of their position and maybe even uncertain of the criminality of the conduct to which they have been subjected. They may have been told that no-one will believe them and they may similarly believe that they will never be believed by others if they do make complaints. They may blame themselves, probably totally unjustly, for what has happened to them. Similarly they may have an understandable reticence about speaking to third parties, particularly prosecuting authorities, about sexual matters. They may fear the break-up of the family or distress to innocent members of the family. Similarly, the person who has been abusing them may have in some way corrupted them or may have put them in fear' (page 4).

1.51 It is submitted that the guidance from the Court of Appeal in *B* to trial judges in the context of the defence seeking a stay on the grounds of a complainant's delay is clear. Every allowance is to be made in favour of a complainant in order that their delay in reporting the allegations can be regarded as excusable and justifiable. Furthermore as the second quoted passage from his judgment demonstrates, Hobhouse LJ was suggesting that the fault for the delay could be attributed to the defendant himself. It was he who may have put the complainant in terror for decades and therefore it would be a manifest injustice if having done so, the defendant could then evade justice. Ironically, and without expressly saying so, Hobhouse LJ was seeking to blame the innocent as yet untried defendant for the delay in order to then disentitle him from complaining about it. As Lord Lane had held in *A-G's Reference*, an accused cannot complain about any delay of which he is the author.

1.52 While this judicial policy may be consistent with prevailing public attitudes about persons accused of sexual offences is it consistent with the presumption of innocence? This was an observation forcefully made by Lord Woolf (in a different context) in *Wai-Bun*. To suggest that in dismissing a defence abuse application in a case like *B*, a judge can rule that the defendant is partly or wholly responsible for the delay, means that defendant's guilt for the offences for which he has yet to be tried, is impliedly being assumed.

1.53 The position of course would be entirely different and unobjectionable if there was evidence that the defendant had threatened the complainant with repercussions if she complained. There relevant evidence would show he had contributed to the delay thus properly putting him within Lord Lane's category.

1.54 It is also interesting to observe that the stereotype as described by Hobhouse LJ in *B* about the immaturity and vulnerability of a complainant is undermined, as the relevant cases reflect, by the fact that the complainants do not report their allegations until they are in their mid- to late-20s and only often after animosity has developed, apparently for other reasons, between the complainant and the defendant. In *B* for example, the facts of which have already been recounted, both complainants were in their late-20s. In *Dutton*[1] the complainant alleged that the accused abused him when he was aged 10 or 11 but made no complaint until he was aged 29. However the Court of Appeal attached no importance to the fact that the complainant had waited a long time after he had become an adult and in upholding the appellant's conviction reference was made to Lord Lane's prescription in *A-G's Reference* that a stay should only be employed in exceptional circumstances. In *King*[2] the accused was convicted of sexual offences in 1995, alleged to have been committed between 1964 and 1970 when the complainant was aged between 4 and 11. The Court of Appeal upheld the trial judge's decision to reject an application to stay again justifying the fairness of the trial by referring to Lord Lane's prescription and holding that the delay in this case did not make the circumstances exceptional.

1 [1994] Crim LR 910.
2 [1997] Crim LR 298.

1.55 Other examples of a similar judicial approach employing both assumptions about the frailty of complainants and the exceptional nature of the abuse jurisdiction can be found in *Wilkinson*[1] and *John E.*[2] In *Wilkinson* the delay between alleged offence and the accused's committal for trial ranged between 28 to 17 years: in *John E*, 22 to 17 years. In both cases the Court of Appeal agreed with the trial judge's decision not to exercise a stay despite this lapse of time and the abundance of opportunity open to the complainant to have come forward earlier.

1 (1996) 1 Cr App Rep 81.
2 (1996) 1 Cr App Rep 88.

The problem of delay in sexual offence cases

1.56 If delay itself, even if great, is never to justify the imposition of a stay, what prejudice arising out of the delay have the courts accepted as sufficiently serious to justify this?

1.57 To appreciate how the courts have resolved this question in sexual offence cases it is necessary first to consider the forensic situation which arises in cases of alleged sexual assault where the complainant has delayed making a complaint. The evidence on which the prosecution relies is almost entirely the oral evidence of the complainant who recounts her experiences. The complainant is asked why she delayed coming forward and explains that this is because of the fear or shame. Moreover, such feelings may have been instilled in her by the defendant as a means of trying to cover up his guilt. For its part, the defence suggests that the complainant has fabricated her story and, for whatever motive, is lying. The defence is that: *'I didn't do it.'*

1.58 The common feature to both the prosecution and the defence cases is that the effect of substantial delay has been to deprive both sides of other direct or circumstantial evidence which might support their respective cases. Both sides may allege that, but for the delay, material witnesses who have disappeared or died would have been available, contemporaneous records now disappeared or destroyed would have been found, the locus in quo of the alleged offence would not have changed and medical or scientific evidence could have been discovered. Both sides suggest that the effect of delay is to deprive them of corroborative evidence and furthermore allege that the blame for this delay can be laid against the opposing side. The complainant will say the defendant is responsible for the delay because he put her in terror and the defendant will reply that the complainant is responsible because she deliberately delayed coming forward.

The defence perspective

1.59 The defence perspective can be seen from the reports of the relevant authorities. In *Dutton,* the delay amounted to 20-14 years.

The complainant, who by the time of trial was aged 30, alleged that when aged 10 or 11 he was assaulted by the defendant in a caravan and also at his home where he lived with two relatives. There was no corroborative medical or scientific evidence. When the defence came to prepare their case it was discovered that the caravan had been so significantly altered that it was impossible to reconstruct how it appeared at the time. Second, the two relatives had both died. In *King* a delay of some 33 years (one which the trial judge accepted was '*massive*'), the defence complained that simply no witnesses could be found to deal with any of the incidents in question. In *H*[1] the complainant alleged that generally she was abused by the accused during her school holidays. To rebut this, the defence sought the accused's employment records in the hope of establishing his recollection that he was away at work at times when he was alleged to have abused the complainant. However, the records had been destroyed. In *Percival* (delay of 30 years) relevant witnesses and records had all disappeared and so the defence in denying the allegations of assault were only able to pray in aid of such denial, evidence of the accused's general good character.

1 [1997] Crim LR 409.

1.60 In each of these four cases there were also other examples of specific evidential difficulties arising from the delay, on the basis of which the defence sought to justify their application for a stay. The common defence submission was that the absence of available detail prevented a proper cross-examination by the defence of the complainant and therefore the accused was unable to properly confront his accuser and test her veracity. In *B*, for example, when the two complainants were asked about the surrounding or background detail of various incidents they understandably replied that they could not recollect this. Their cross-examination could not therefore proceed any further as it lacked any factual basis. Furthermore, the defence could not convincingly argue that the complainants had chosen to forget details in order to weaken the efficacy of their cross-examination. At the accused's appeal it was contended that he suffered a disadvantage in being unable to properly test the evidence of his accusers and this constituted a serious prejudice.

1.61 However, in all of the cases mentioned above both the trial judge, and subsequently the Court of Appeal, rejected the defence applications for a stay. The Court held that a sufficient means of negating prejudice suffered by the defence was the ability of a judge to direct a jury during his summing-up. In other words, giving the jury directions as to the effect of delay on the defence case was deemed to be a sufficient compensation or safeguard for any evidential disadvantage suffered by it. The only recent case in which the Court of Appeal has disagreed with the decision of the trial judge not to stay the accused's trial on the ground of delay is *Jenkins*[1] decided in December 1997. The facts and in particular the delay in that case were startling.

1 [1998] Crim LR 411, CA.

1.62 In *Jenkins* the delay amounted to 30 years. The two complainants went to the police in late 1995 alleging offences committed against them by the defendant between 1963 and 1967. There was some evidence that the recollections of both complainants were suspect. In giving her evidence at the trial, complainant S claimed to recall many more matters of detail, which during earlier police statements she could not recall. In relation to the second complainant, complainant J, when she was originally interviewed by the police she had denied that anything abusive had been done to her. In considering the decision of the trial judge not to order a stay when faced with these facts, the Court of Appeal held that the 30-year delay was so substantial as to put the case within the 'exceptional' category propounded by Lord Lane.

1.63 In giving judgment on behalf of the Court Mantell LJ first observed that: 'Our attention has not been invited to any case in which there has been a greater elapse of time between the dates of the alleged offences and the date when complaint was made' (page 7). Second, he added that: 'This is not a case where the offences are alleged to have occurred over many years nor a case where events have occurred in a home shared by the complainants and the defendant' (page 7). In turning to the facts of the case Mantell LJ observed that: 'The case fell to be decided on oral evidence. There was and could be no documentary or physical evidence to assist ... Consequently the ability of witnesses to remember events occurring thirty years ago and more was crucial ... What was crucial was the ability of the appellant on the one side and S and J on the other to remember the detail of visits to the appellant's home more than thirty years ago' (page 8). Turning to the effect of this delay on the defendant's case Mantell LJ observed, 'Certain it is that he could not be expected to remember the kind of detail which, if innocent, might have enabled a skilful cross-examiner on his behalf to confound his accusers. Consequently we are unable to agree that the exceptional delay in this case was not a source of serious prejudice to the appellant and, moreover, we are unable to agree that such prejudice was capable in this case of being cured by the trial process and appropriate directions in the summing up' (page 8).

1.64 It is submitted that this survey of the relevant authorities demonstrates that the hurdle to be surmounted by a defendant seeking a stay in a sexual offence case on the ground of delay is a very high one. A defendant seeking a stay even when there has been an inexplicable and/or inexcusable delay on the part of the complainant which has, on any reckoning, been substantial confronts an almost insurmountable judicial attitude that stays should never be granted in these circumstances. Even when as for example in *Dutton*, the defence can point to specific evidential difficulties occasioned by the delay, which undeniably place it at a disadvantage, the response of the Court of Appeal has been to hold that this is insufficient to discharge the burden of proving that this prejudice is so serious that a fair trial cannot be held as per the test of Lord Lane in *A-G's Reference*. In *Dutton* the Court of Appeal in holding the trial judge was entitled to dismiss the defence application said, 'Judges should be assiduous to ensure there really was evidence of serious prejudice to the extent that a fair trial could not be held before they find that a defendant has discharged, on a balance of probabilities, the burden of proof that lies on him before any power of the sort sought to be invoked could be used.'

Delay by the prosecution

1.65 The principal authority post *A-G's Reference* dealing with prosecutorial delay is *R v Cardiff Magistrates Court, ex p Hole* decided by the Divisional Court in October 1996. In November 1995 at the defendants' committal, the magistrate refused to stay the committal proceedings on the ground of delay. The applicants sought a judicial review of that decision which was decided by Lord Bingham CJ. The delay complained of was the period between August 1991 when complaint concerning the applicants was first made to the police and May 1995 when they were charged. In considering this delay Lord Bingham readily agreed that it had been substantial: 'The court is bound to observe that the lapse of time appears to have been very great ... It may even be that these charges could have been preferred nearly three years before they were' (page 4). Lord Bingham held that the principles to apply concerning delay were those propounded by Lord Lane in *A-G's Reference*. In deciding how they should be applied Lord Bingham observed: 'It is necessary to look at the charges and see exactly what defence it is which they [the applicants] are impeded from advancing' (page 8). A complaint for example of missing documents or lost witnesses, '... must be closely tied to the detail of particular charges so that the court can be told ... that the documents on which the defendant would wish to rely and on which he is prevented from relying relate to a particular charge. Equally with oral evidence it is, in my judgment essential, if the defendant is to satisfy the burden which lies upon him, to identify the witness he would have wished to call and which in the circumstances he cannot' (page 11).

1.66 On the facts of the case before him Lord Bingham decided that the applicants' case was not made out. He added that if the applicants were committed for trial then they could repeat and advance their arguments before the trial judge with direct reference to the specific ingredients of the counts in the indictment.

1.67 The approach of Lord Bingham in *ex p Hole* is, it is submitted, wholly consistent with the approach of the Courts in other similar non-sexual offence delay cases. The case of *R v Grays Justices, ex p Graham*[1] illustrates this. The defendant had been interviewed for offences of theft and obtaining by deception and thereafter had been released on police bail. This bail was subsequently cancelled and then without warning, some 15 months after he had originally been interviewed summonses against him were issued. The prosecution, however, were not ready to proceed to committal with the result that a further delay of six months was occasioned. The defendant complained that because of the two-year delay the continued prosecution of him was contrary to fairness. May LJ (giving the court's judgment) disagreed holding that the delay, while regrettable, did not constitute an abuse. Furthermore there was no instance of mala fides on the prosecution's part.

1 [1982] QB 1239.

1.68 While both in *ex p Hole* and *ex p Graham* the courts were prepared to countenance delay by the prosecution amounting to several years. Nonetheless one is bound to observe the striking difference between periods of delay complained of in prosecutorial delay cases such as these and those in sexual offence cases, considered above. This despite the fact that *Ex p Hole,* for instance, was a case turning largely on documentary evidence in contrast to the sexual offence cases which turned on oral evidence. It is perhaps ironic that in documentary evidence cases where the primary evidence is still available, the court's tolerance of delay appears to be far less than in sexual offence cases where the primary evidence is usually simply the recollection of witnesses.

Judicial faith in the flexibility of the trial process as a means of ameliorating prejudice caused by delay

1.69 In all of the cases considered above except *Jenkins* the Court of Appeal or Divisional Court has held that the trial of the accused was fair and hence the trial judge was correct to refuse the defence application for a stay.[1] The Court has repeatedly endorsed the principles propounded by Lord Lane in *A-G's Reference* in holding that trial judges should, whenever possible, refuse such applications. Reliance has been placed particularly on what Lord Lane held were the more desirable alternatives to a stay:

> 'In asserting whether there is likely to be prejudice and if so whether it can properly be described as serious, the following matters should be borne in mind: first, the power of the judge at common law and under the Police and Criminal Evidence Act 1984 to regulate the admissibility of evidence; secondly, the trial process itself, which should ensure that all relevant factual issues arising from delay will be placed before the jury as part of the evidence for their consideration, together with the powers of the judge to give appropriate directions to the jury before they consider their verdict.'

In this passage from his judgment Lord Lane mentioned three possible measures or safeguards in delay cases to be utilised as alternatives to a stay: first the power of the trial judge to exclude evidence on the grounds of fairness, second the right of the defence during the trial to raise factual issues relating to the delay and third the power of the trial judge to give the jury directions relating to it.

1 *Ex p Hole* and *ex p Graham* are Divisional Court cases.

1.70 There have been few appeals against conviction based on the alleged inadequacy in a trial of the first two measures. This, it is submitted, is not surprising. In relation to the first, the defence difficulty has been an absence of evidence on which the prosecution wish to rely. In relation to the second, invariably the defence has been permitted by the judge, in front of the jury, to fully explore the reasons for the delay in the making of the complaint. Appeals in relation to these measures have instead concentrated on the alleged shortcomings in the trial judge's summing-up, specifically the failure to give adequate directions concerning delay to the jury.

The role and responsibility of the trial judge

1.71 The first case concerning delay, post *A-G's Reference*, and therefore the first time the Court of Appeal had to consider delay in a real case this issue was *Dutton*[1] whose facts have already been recounted in para 1.52. In *Dutton* complaint was made that the trial judge in his summing up only briefly referred to the issue of delay and how this could disadvantage the defence. The appellant contended that when the issue of delay has been raised in extenso during the trial by defence counsel then the jury must be given full and careful directions by the judge about the difficulties faced by the defence in dealing with the evidence. The Court agreed and said:

> 'Lord Lane [in Attorney General's Reference No. 1] referred to the power to give directions. Such would surely be called for in a case in which not only had there been substantial delay but it could be seen that witnesses who might have been able to give relevant evidence had disappeared. This was a case in which it really was incumbent on the judge, having taken the decision he did [ie not to stay the proceedings], to point out to the jury that what was said by the defence about the possible prejudice as a result of the delay was a matter to which they could and should properly have regard. If a judge was silent in relation to a topic such as that when it had been advanced and canvassed extensively by the defence, the very silence of the judge might tend to devalue what was perhaps the most important point which could be advanced from an adversarial point of view on behalf of [the defendant]. [The judge] was wrong not to assist the jury as to the possible adverse affects that the delay could have occasioned the defence and not to refer in the summing-up to the age of the complaint and the difficulties this could well have posed.'

The appeal in that case was accordingly allowed and the conviction quashed.

1 [1994] Crim LR 910.

1.72 After *Dutton* the next opportunity for the Court of Appeal to deal with delay was *Birchall*[1] decided in March 1995. Having held that the trial judge was correct not to accede to an application to stay the proceedings the Court quashed the appellant's conviction and held that the summing-up was again inadequate: 'In our judgment, just as in the case of *Dutton*, so in this case, the failure of the learned judge to make any reference to the difficulties occasioned by the lapse of time or to explain to the jury the way in which they affected the ability of the defence to advance its case was a material misdirection or non-direction and, accordingly, we would conclude on that ground that this appeal must be allowed and the conviction quashed.'

1 (1995) Times, 23 March.

1.73 In *Egan*[1] decided in June 1995 Lord Taylor CJ adopted what had been said supra in *Dutton* and *Birchall*. In relation to the case before him he concluded that the trial judge's summing-up had been inadequate in failing properly and fully to present the defence's predicament to the jury. He said: 'We consider that in a case of this antiquity, where the evidence of the complainant was wholly uncorroborated, it was appropriate of the judge to give a direction of the kind we have indicated' (page 7). Lord Taylor CJ also held that, 'It is not sufficient for the fairness of the trial to be ensured by the issue of delay simply being canvassed, even extensively, by the defence. The judge must refer to it in his summing-up.' A rationale for this requirement was explained by Hobhouse LJ in *B*: 'If counsel have made points which are, in truth, relevant and then the judge fails to refer to them at all in his summing-up, the jury may be led to believe that such consideration can be disregarded' (page 8).

1 (1996) 1 Cr App Rep 88.

1.74 However, Lord Taylor CJ stated in *Egan* that he was not acceding to the suggestion that a direction to the jury concerning delay was mandatory in all cases. He said: 'We are not saying that as a matter of law or as a matter of invariable practice whenever there has been some delay in the case coming to trial the judge must give a jury directions as to the difficulties in which the defence find themselves. Much must depend upon the length of the delay, the cogency of the evidence and the circumstances in the case' (page 7). In other words, the obligation to give directions arises out of the general duty of the trial judge to put the defence case fairly before the jury and not because of some specific obligation in relation to delay.

1.75 Since *Egan* the Court of Appeal has adopted Lord Taylor's view. In *J*[1] there was a delay of approximately six years but the judge did not refer in his summing-up to any evidential difficulties faced by the defence because of this lapse of time. *J* appealed on the basis that this omission rendered his conviction unsafe. The Court of Appeal disagreed and dismissed the appeal, because it held that as the defence had not contended either at the trial or at the appeal that it had suffered any specific evidential disadvantage there was accordingly nothing unfair about the trial. *J* therefore suggests that the judge has no independent responsibility for drawing the jury's attention to delay if the defence have not done so. Presumably this even when the defence ought in the judge's view to have done so and have mistakenly overlooked this relevant issue.

1 [1997] Crim LR 297.

1.76 In *H*[1] the defence again did not argue at the trial that specific difficulties were caused by the delay. However, it was submitted at his appeal that the trial judge should have, of his own motion, directed the jury on difficulties faced by the defence. Potter LJ rejected this argument. He held that in the absence of any complaint from the defence during the trial regarding the impact of delay, there was no obligation on the trial judge to give directions on this issue to the jury. However, having expressed the principle of the judge having only a reactive not a proactive duty, Potter LJ mentioned two sets of circumstances where such a proactive duty might nonetheless arise. First, where there was, despite the defence not realising it, an aspect of prejudice which was apparent to the judge. Second, when a direction was necessary for the purposes of being even-handed between the prosecution and the defence. The approach of Potter LJ in *H* represents, it is submitted, a softening of the harsh adversarial approach expressed in *J* above. The judge has an obligation to ensure a fair trial which may require him to intervene and he should not always remain on the fence.

1 (1998) 2 Cr App Rep 161.

1.77 In *Percival* the Court of Appeal again emphasised the inescapable responsibility of trial judges to give proper directions to the jury concerning delay. In considering the trial judge's summing up, Holland J held that it was not sufficient for the trial judge even-handedly to remind the jury as to the problems confronting the prosecution and defence because of delay, regarding them as 'two sides of the coin'. In this context the judge failed to recognise that the burden of proof lies only on the prosecution and therefore it ought to have been emphasised to the jury that the prosecution may not have discharged this burden in the case of a defendant who is having to conduct his defence at a disadvantage. On the part of the judge there should have been, as Holland J put it, a 'conscientious concern for the burden and standard of proof.'

1.75 According to Holland J: 'The judge did not adequately put the imprimatur of the bench behind such directions as he did give about delay ... These were faithfully reiterated in a balanced way but what, as we think, was lacking was a clear expression as to where he stood as the person seized with the task of securing a fair trial, notwithstanding the delay.'

1.79 In *Hickson*[1] specific aspects of disadvantage caused by delay had been raised by the defence during the trial but the judge had failed to mention such difficulties during his summing up. The Court therefore had to consider whether the absence of proper directions was of itself to be regarded as rendering the appellant's conviction unsafe pursuant to the Criminal Appeal Act 1996. The Court held however, that it did not because, in its view, there was very strong evidence against the appellant so that despite the trial judge's failure, the conviction was safe. The Court was perhaps taking a pragmatic approach. Convictions based on very strong evidence will be regarded as safe even if the judge forgot to give a required direction.

1 [1997] Crim LR 494.

1.80 In *JK*[1] the judge again failed to direct the jury on the difficulties caused to the defendant by the lapse of time and dealt only with the difficulties caused to the complainant. The Court of Appeal held that while it would have been wise for the trial judge to have given directions to the jury concerning difficulties caused to the defence, such a direction was not required as a matter of law or practice. The Court held that the defence were able to put these issue fairly before the jury by calling evidence.

1 [1999] Crim LR 740.

Final observations

1.81 In sexual offence cases the Court of Appeal has repeatedly held that a defendant could have a fair trial even when the allegations against him are of antiquity. While in *Jenkins* the Court held that the delay was so massive as to cross the line into unfairness, in other cases the delay, although massive, has been held not to render the trial unfair. For example, in *Percival* there was a delay of at least 28 years between the alleged offences (indecent assault and buggery) and the making of the complaints. The Court however was prepared to countenance such delay.

1.82 It is submitted that while it is impossible and undesirable to lay down a fixed limitation period, a line has to be drawn reflecting the obvious fact that very substantial delay is likely to cause serious prejudice to the defence. The Court of Appeal has, however, hitherto studiously declined to offer any guidance on this point. In *Jenkins,* while the Court held that the trial judge was wrong and the delay was too great, it was careful to confine its comments to the particular circumstances of the case before it. The Court has therefore declined to inject any meaning in this context into the phrase of 'exceptional circumstances' coined by Lord Lane.

1.83 In allowing trials to continue despite massive delays the Court has emphasised the responsibility on trial judges to ensure that such trials are fair principally by their giving careful directions to the jury. It is interesting to observe that in many cases where the Court of Appeal has held that the trial judge was right to refuse a defence application for a stay it then proceeded to quash the appellant's conviction on the ground of inadequate judicial direction to the jury. The fact that the Court has quashed so many convictions arising out of this failure, in trials which it has held were otherwise fair, demonstrates the importance which it attaches to the giving of such directions. This is because the Court firmly holds to the belief that such directions really can compensate for substantial disadvantages suffered by the defence. However, it must, it is submitted, be questioned whether such strong faith is justified. While a trial judge can mention the defence's predicament and the fact that supporting evidence for the defendant's denials would be unlikely to be available, what more can be said? In reality, it must be doubted whether a summing-up really can compensate for substantial disadvantage suffered by the defence. While there is not even a hint in any of the judgments of the Court where convictions have been quashed, it is perhaps possible that the most persuasive reason for quashing those convictions is not so much that the trial judge failed to give adequate directions but because the appellant should never have been tried at all.

1.84 It may be relevant to appreciate in this context that there has been no encouragement or formulation of a standard direction to assist trial judges and to prevent future avoidable mistakes. Surely if judges are regularly failing to grasp what directions they should be giving to juries about substantial delay, a standard direction propounded either by the Court or Judicial Studies Board is both necessary and desirable.

1.85 In the law on abuse generally it appears that in so far as delay is concerned there is an absolute insistence on positive proof of serious prejudice. This insistence differs markedly from the approach taken in other circumstances, for example misuse or manipulation, where there appears very little emphasis on the requirement to prove prejudice.

1.86 Time will tell whether the current judicial toleration of delay will be abused by prosecutors and complainants. In resource-pressed prosecutorial agencies, a complacency may already have developed that no matter how long it takes to decide to initiate proceedings, the courts will never interfere. A belief of immunity in this regard may in the future lead courts to become more intolerant of delays.

DELAY UNDER THE EUROPEAN CONVENTION OF HUMAN RIGHTS

1.87 Two articles of ECHR are concerned with delay: Article 5(3) which applies only to individuals under arrest and Art 6(1) which applies to all civil and criminal cases irrespective of whether an accused is being held in custody or is on bail. Article 5(3) states, 'everyone arrested or detained in accordance with provisions of para (1)(c) of this Article shall be brought promptly before a judge or other officer authorised by law to exercise judicial power and shall be entitled to trial within a reasonable time or to release pending trial.' In *R v Crown Court at Manchester, ex p McDonald*[1] Bingham CJ carefully considered the provisions of Art 5(3) in the context of custody time limits. Having surveyed the principle ECHR authorities concerned with Art 5(3)[2] Bingham CJ concluded 'we do not find anything in these European cases which in anyway throws doubt on the English law as we have attempted to summarise it. It would appear that the term 112 days prescribed by the regulations imposes what is, by international standards, an exacting standard.'

1 [1999] 1 All ER 805.
2 See especially pages 812-813.

Article 6(1)

1.88 The Article commences with the following words: 'In the determination of the civil rights and obligations or of any criminal charge against him, everyone is entitled to a fair and public hearing within a reasonable time ...' In criminal cases the rationale of this reasonable time guarantee has been explained as being 'designed to avoid that a person charged should remain too long in a state of uncertainty about his fate'.[1]

1 *Stögmuller v Austria* (1969) 1 EHRR 155.

1.89 The reasonable time guarantee runs from the moment that an individual is held to be subject to a 'charge.' The meaning of 'charge' is autonomous in ECHR jurisprudence and has been defined as the point at which 'the situation of a person concerned has been substantially affected as a result of a suspicion against him'.[1] Alternatively the European Court defined a charge as 'the official notification given to an individual by the competent authority of an allegation that he committed a criminal offence'.[2] By reference to the use of 'reasonable' it is immediately apparent that ECHR jurisprudence does not impose any absolute or maximum time limit. The reasonableness of the length of proceedings depends on the particular circumstances of the case. Furthermore no particular fact or circumstance is of itself conclusive, instances of delay must be considered in the round and facts and circumstances assessed cumulatively.

1 *X v Austria* (1967) 24 CD 8 at page 18.
2 *Eckle v Germany* (1982) 5 EHRR 1.

The Human Rights Act 1998

1.90 Section 2 of the Human Rights Act 1998 ('HRA 1998') obliges UK courts and tribunals to 'take into account' the judgments, decisions, declarations or opinions of the institutions established by ECHR when determining a question which has arisen in connection with a Convention Right. The 'Convention Rights' are defined[1] to mean, inter alia, the rights and fundamental freedoms set out in Arts 2 to 12 of ECHR, which obviously includes the Article 6 'reasonable time' guarantee. While the Courts are required to take the above into account, given they are all of potential relevance to the proper interpretation of the Convention rights, they are not however bound to follow the European Courts' judgments.[2]

1 In s 1(1) HRA 1998.
2 See the detailed commentary on the provisions of s 2 HRA 1998, by Lester & Pannick, *Human Rights Law and Practice* (1999) at p 22.

1.91 It is anticipated, that the abuse jurisdiction will only expand as a consequence of the coming into force of HRA 1998. By virtue of Section 6 of HRA 1998, it is unlawful for any public authority, which would include a Court or tribunal, to 'act in a way which is incompatible with a Convention right.' In these circumstances, the rights conferred by the Convention will assume a precedence over existing common law protections and over any relevant protections contained in delegated legislation. Moreover, as both the police and the Crown Prosecution Service fall within the definition of public authority any act by them which is incompatible with a Convention right is unlawful and may therefore prima facie constitute an abuse.

1.92 Section 8(1) of HRA 1998 states: 'In relation to any act (or proposed act) of a public authority which the Court finds is (or would be) unlawful, it may grant such relief or remedy, or make such order, within its powers as it considers just and appropriate.' Where the Crown Prosecution Service or Police, therefore for example, are found to have acted in breach of a given Convention right, this may trigger a trial judge's discretion to stay proceedings for abuse of process. Abuse submissions whether based upon the fact of delay or not are therefore likely to include a reliance on relevant Convention jurisprudence.

The period of time to be taken into consideration

1.93 The reasonable time guarantee has been interpreted as applying only to the period starting from when a person is 'charged' and concluding when a case is fully determined, for example, at the expiry of the appeal proceedings.[1] An individual becomes subject to a charge, within the meaning of the Convention, at such time as he is 'substantially affected' or 'officially notified' of the proceedings taken against him.[2] Complaints about the length of criminal proceedings may even be considered in circumstances where, albeit the proceedings have not yet terminated, it is nevertheless alleged there has already been unreasonable delay.[3]

1 See *Eckle v Germany* (1982) 5 EHRR 1; *Reinhardt and Slimane-Kaïd v France* (1998) 28 EHRR 59, ECtHR.

2 See *Deweer v Belgium* (1980) 2 EHRR 439, at para 46; and *Corigliano v Italy* (1982) 5 EHRR 334.

3 See *Mylnek v Austria* (which was settled before the court) 27 October 1992, Series A, No. 242-C; (1992) 18 EHRR 581.

What is a 'reasonable time'?

1.94 In order to determine whether or not a 'reasonable time' has been exceeded, the court will consider the various phases of the criminal proceedings and their overall time span. The court will have regard to the particular circumstances of each case including, in particular, the complexity of the case, the conduct of the applicant and the conduct of the judicial authorities. Each of these factors can be considered separately.

The complexity of the case

1.95 The Courts' jurisprudence suggests that any manner of different factors may be considered when assessing the complexity of proceedings. Those considered have included the volume of evidence, the number of defendants or charges, the difficulty of the legal issues involved, the necessity of obtaining expert evidence and the international dimensions of a case. When these factors have been accepted as genuine the view of the Court has been to tolerate delay. The Court has, however, determined that there is a moment where irrespective of the proven complexities, the delay is simply too great. In *Ferrantelli and Santangelo v Italy*[1] where the applicants were convicted finally after 16 years and after what the Court accepted were complex and difficult murder proceedings it held that the delay was unreasonable.

1 (1996) 23 EHRR 288, ECtHR.

The conduct of the applicant

1.96 The state is not responsible for delay that is deemed attributable to an applicant. For example, an applicant who stays outside the jurisdiction and fails to respond to an arrest warrant, or who flees, while subject to a 'charge', cannot fairly criticise the length of proceedings, even where they remain pending indefinitely as a result. Such a principle is hardly surprising. However, in *Reinhardt and Slimane-Kaïd v France*[1] the court stated that an applicant's argument on delay should not be prejudiced simply because full use is made of the available procedures to pursue a defence. The Court there found that the applicant was not to be criticised for supplying to the investigators material which he argued established his innocence, or for requesting the investigation of certain matters, or indeed for having employed all available legal remedies, albeit they clearly prolonged the criminal proceedings.

1 (1998) 28 EHRR 59.

The conduct of the judicial authorities

1.97 In a variety of different circumstances, the Court has found states responsible for unjustified delays which were attributable to the prosecution or the Court. Particular examples include delays in relation to the entering of a nolle prosequi;[1] the initiation of court proceedings following the preferment of an indictment;[2] the communication of a judgment to the applicant; the transferring of cases as between courts; the hearing of cases involving two or more defendants together; and with regard to the hearing of appeals.

1 *Orchin v United Kingdom* (1982) 34 DR 5, EComHR.
2 *Eckle v Germany* (1982) 5 EHRR 1, ECtHR.

1.98 Under the Convention the contracting parties must also have regard to their duty, which applies regardless of cost,[1] 'to organise their legal systems so as to allow the courts to comply with the requirements of Art 6(1).[2] This obligation is in addition to their existing duty to ensure the reasonably expeditious conduct of cases. This organisational duty, however, means that states' excuses in relation to backlog or administrative difficulties will not be accepted where there has been a failure to take adequate remedial measures. On the other hand, violations will not normally be found where the backlog is a temporary or exceptional one, provided the authorities have taken 'reasonable prompt remedial action'.[3]

1 *Airey v Ireland* A32 (1979) 2 EHRR 305, ECtHR.
2 *Zimmerman and Steiner v Switzerland* (1983) 6 EHRR 17.
3 *Buchholz v Germany* (1981) 3 EHRR 597, ECtHR.

1.99 Finally, what amounts to unreasonable delay may also be determined by what is 'at stake' for an applicant. This was acknowledged by the Court in *Abdoella v Netherlands*,[1] where it was stressed that a more rigorous standard of urgency applies where applicants are in detention pending the outcome of their case. In *Abdoella*, where the applicant had been convicted of incitement to murder, the Court found a violation of the 'reasonable time' provision in relation to a period of some four years and four months between charge and final disposal, which period had included all domestic appeal proceedings.

1 (1992) 20 EHRR 585.

1.100 While the above-mentioned factors represent the main criteria for deciding on unreasonableness, it is apparent that no particular factor is necessarily conclusive. The European approach is to scrutinise them separately and then to determine their cumulative effect. In these circumstances, whereas particular instances of state led delay may not seem unreasonable, the same conclusion may not be reached when the same instances are viewed together, in terms of the overall picture.[1]

1 *Ruotolo v Italy* A 230-D (1992).

1.101 While there are common features in the criteria for determining delay related abuse in this jurisdiction, on the one hand, and Art 6(1) delay on the other (such as the necessity to consider the conduct both of the prosecution/state and that of the defendant/applicant), there are material differences between the two. The principal difference relates to the period of time under consideration. Whereas, in this jurisdiction the Court normally considers the period from the date of the actual offence to the date of the abuse submission (if not beyond in certain circumstances), under ECHR law the European Court generally holds that time runs from the moment of charge to the time marking the conclusion of all the Court/appellate proceedings.

1.102 In the light of the current UK judicial tolerance of even substantial delays (exemplified in the child abuse cases), it may be that the English Courts would benefit from a broader ECHR interpretation of Art 6(1), so as to encompass pre-charge delay. Whether Art 6 will ever be stretched so far remains to be seen.

Observations

1.103 The reasonable time guarantee of Art 6(1) only begins to run when a person is charged. Accordingly the Convention does not make any discrete or explicit provision for delay between the date of the alleged offence and the moment of charge. In all of the sex cases considered in this chapter, this was the overriding characteristic of the delay complained of. Accordingly it appears that ECHR jurisprudence will not come to the assistance of those who are charged or summonsed for alleged offence which occurred many years previously.

2. Breach of promise

2.1 If in a criminal case the prosecution reneges on a promise it has given to an accused not to prosecute him, does a breach of this promise ipso facto give rise to unfairness and an abuse of process? The law concerned with breach of promise would be easy to state if the answer to this question was an unequivocal yes. However, the Court of Appeal has held that the answer is equivocal. Breach of promise not to prosecute does not necessarily give rise to abuse. It depends on the circumstances and each case should be judged on its merits. All that the Court of Appeal has held is that where a defendant has been induced to believe that he will not be prosecuted, this is capable of founding a stay for abuse.

2.2 The authorities concerned with this head of abuse will necessarily touch on a number of issues which must be resolved in order that the parameters of this head are determined. Furthermore, the parties should know when it is permissible for a prosecution to proceed despite a defendant contending that they received a promise that this would not occur. The issues to be resolved can usefully be outlined in paras 2.3 to 2.5.

2.3 *The promise* – Must a promise not to prosecute be an explicit unequivocal undertaking by the prosecutor? Alternatively can a 'promise' be inferred from something lesser, for example, an indication or statement of intent? Also, to be binding, must the promise come only from the prosecutor direct or can it instead emanate from someone who is simply a member of the prosecution team or from what a prosecutor has said to a third party which is known about or overheard by the defendant?

2.4 *Prejudice* – If a promise has been made, can it nonetheless be withdrawn? For a court to hold the prosecution to its word, is the uttering of a promise enough or must there in addition be some prejudice which would be caused to the defence were the prosecution to be allowed to renege? In other words, using the terminology of the law of contract, must there be an offer, an acceptance and consideration. By 'consideration' is meant prejudice to the defence; the defendant has relied on the promise and as a direct consequence, has done some act or abstained from doing some act, which has prejudiced or been detrimental to his defence.

2.5 The heart of the issue here is the difference of approach between the judgment of Lord Lane CJ in *Attorney General's Reference (No 1 of 1990)*[1] where Lord Lane emphasised the need to prove prejudice before an abuse submission can be sustained versus the approach of the House of Lords in *ex p Bennett*[2] which emphasised prosecution impropriety over prejudice. Quoting Lord Lowry in *Bennett* whether to try the case in a circumstance of breach of promise would 'offend the Courts sense of justice and propriety to be asked to try the accused' (page 74).

1 [1992] QB 630.
2 [1994] AC 42.

2.6 How the courts have resolved these difficult issues will be the subject of this chapter. It will consider the categories of breach of promise in the following sections, namely:

(1) promises not to prosecute;
(2) promises to offer no evidence;
(3) promises on acceptable pleas;
(4) other promises.

PROMISES NOT TO PROSECUTE

2.7 In England the cornerstone of the law on breach of promise is the authority *R v Croydon Justices, ex p Dean.*[1] Before analysing the significance of *Dean*, a brief review of some of the earlier authorities may help to place it in a better context.

1 (1993) 98 Cr App Rep 76.

PRE-DEAN AUTHORITIES

2.8 While some of the most relevant authorities emanate from the Privy Council, and from Hong Kong, it is interesting that the English authority of *Lund v Thompson*[1] was not apparently cited in *Dean.*

1 [1959] 1 QB 283.

2.9 In *Lund* Diplock J giving the judgment of the High Court said, albeit with some reluctance, that a statement by police that they had no intention to prosecute did not nullify a prior notice of intended prosecution which had been issued in relation to a road traffic offence. The Court acknowledged that in certain cases, where the police indicate an intention not to prosecute and subsequently change their mind (as occurred in *Lund*), this may lead to considerable injustice to the person prosecuted. However, strict statutory construction was said to militate against *Lund.* The fact that a citizen was entitled to mount a private prosecution and permitted to act on the basis of the original notice, whatever subsequent representations were made by the police, was deemed to be an overriding factor. For that reason, the suggested concept of some loose form of 'estoppel' binding a police officer to keep another person's promise not to prosecute was dismissed by the Court.

2.10 In *Chu Piu-Wing*[1] the appellant had been subpoenaed to attend a police disciplinary tribunal to give evidence of certain payments of 'protection money' he had made to police officers in respect of gambling establishments. The appellant had refused to do so because of the conditions on which he had given the information in the first place. These conditions were first, that he would give the information only once, second, that he would only provide information and not give evidence against the policeman in court, and third, that the information would not be used against him. In due course, he was assured by the interrogating International Commission Against Corruption officers that, if any information which he gave verified the material which they already had (which it apparently did), he would not be prosecuted. Notwithstanding such promise, he was charged, convicted and sentenced to imprisonment, in respect of the matters on which he had given information. When the appellant was subsequently subpoenaed before the police disciplinary tribunal, he attended but refused to give evidence of the matters concerned. For this refusal he was committed to six months' imprisonment for contempt by the High Court. In the light of the circumstances in which the information had been given to the authorities, the Hong Kong Court of Appeal held that the issuance of the subpoena was an abuse of the process of the court.

1 [1984] HKLR 411.

2.11 McMullin V-P giving the judgment of Hong Kong's Court of Appeal stated that there was:

> 'a clear public interest to be observed in holding officials of the state to promises made by them in the full understanding of what is entailed by the bargain.'

The authorities had reneged on a solemn promise where there was no doubt the appellant must reasonably have believed he had kept his side of the bargain. The theme of holding officials to account for promises or representations runs through the subsequent case law, up to the present day.[1]

1 See *Postermobile plc v Brent London Borough Council*, para 2.32 to 2.33.

2.12 In *Bell v DPP*[1] the Privy Council considered what was ostensibly a 'delay' case but which had a bearing on the principles relating to implicit promises or expectations. The case concerned an appellant who had been arrested in Jamaica and charged, inter alia, with firearm offences. Having been convicted in the Crown Court, and successful in an appeal against conviction, a retrial was ordered. On several occasions thereafter the prosecution were not ready on the due trial dates. Finally, after more adjournments he was discharged by a judge, the Crown having offered no evidence against him. However, three months later he was re-arrested and a retrial was ordered

1 [1985] AC 937, PC.

2.13 The Board allowed his appeal. It held that the Jamaican courts had overlooked the significance of the order of the retrial and of his being discharged, on the basis that further delay would then be unfair to him, his constitutional rights having been infringed (to a fair hearing within a reasonable time). Where the defence submitted that the appellant had been given great hope when no evidence was offered, Templeman LJ said that in a proper case the Court could treat the renewal of charges, even after the lapse of a reasonable time, as an abuse of process of the Court. For, as the Law Lord noted, '... the appellant's complaint is that he was discharged and told to go free ...' before being re-arrested.

2.14 In line with the courts avowed duty to secure 'fair treatment' for those before them, the Privy Council in *Bell* acknowledged, inter alia, the public interest in minimising the '*anxiety and concern of the accused*',[1] in the context of delays awaiting trial. In practice, while there are no doubt many occasions where defendants ought to be aware of the possibility of re-arrest (having been discharged in criminal proceedings), nevertheless, this case illustrates an instance where a legitimate expectation that there would be no further prosecution was foiled.

1 Per Powell J in *Barker v Wingo* 407 US 514 (1972).

2.15 The decisions of *Bell* and *Chu Pui-Wing* were later considered in the 1990 *Harris* decision of the Hong Kong Court of Appeal[1] which court helpfully reviewed the state of the law in relation to the common law jurisdictions on this topic. Harris was a member of the Attorney General's Chambers who, while at the time personally responsible for the section dealing with vice prosecutions, was himself later convicted of procuring a girl for unlawful sexual intercourse. The defendant appealed on the basis, inter alia that, having assured him in May 1989 he would not be prosecuted, the Attorney General should not be permitted to change his mind in October 1989, following what was said to be increased pressure from the mass media.

1 [1991] 1 HKLR at p389.

2.16 In dismissing the appeal, Faud V-P ruled that the Attorney General was quite entitled to change his mind in the light of the changing public interest, notwithstanding that it may entail a possible erosion of confidence in his individual decisions. While Silke V-P found that: 'There was no "promise" made to the appellant other than in the widest of layman's terms,' and albeit that it came from a colleague, can one easily ignore the fact that it came from the Attorney-General himself? Indeed, as a recent commentator well noted,[1] Harris' counsel[2] posed an interesting question which was left unresolved by the Court, counsel perhaps having the facts of *Chu Piu-Wing* in mind, namely, 'Why should the recipient of an unqualified assurance be in a worse position than the recipient of one that is qualified?'

1 Sze Ping-Fat 'Resiling from Assurances not to Prosecute' [1998] Justice of the Peace, Vol 162 at 604.
2 Mr Anthony Scrivener QC acting pro bono.

2.17 In *A-G of Trinidad and Tobago v Phillip*,[1] the Privy Council held that the prosecution of offenders, after a pardon had been granted and an order of habeas corpus made, would constitute an abuse of process even if the pardon was in fact legally invalid. The Island's Acting President had granted the 'pardon' to a group of individuals who had participated in an armed insurrection. In attempting to overthrow the lawful government, they had seized certain buildings and had taken hostages. Having released the hostages on the promise of this 'pardon' they themselves surrendered, only to be arrested and charged with, inter alia, treason and murder.

1 [1995] 1 AC 396, PC.

2.18 The court's policy of holding officials to their promises was shown in extremis in *Phillip*, where this promise was upheld, albeit it was obtained by coercion and in circumstances where a trial could be fairly held. Lord Woolf, in identifying this particular form of abuse of process, stated that: 'The common law has now developed a formidable safeguard to protect persons from being prosecuted in circumstances where it would be seriously unjust to do so.'

R v CROYDEN JUSTICES, EX P DEAN[1]

2.19 The facts were as follows. The applicant, aged 17, along with two other men, were arrested by police in respect of a murder investigation. He denied taking part in the killing but admitted that after it had taken place he had assisted in destroying the victim's car. At the end of a police interview he was informed by the officers that he was regarded as a prosecution witness and had the protection of the police. Five days after the co-defendants had been charged, the applicant further assisted and co-operated and admitted that the co-defendant had driven him to the scene of the crime, and shown him the victim's body. Later, however, after the CPS had taken charge of the prosecution and reviewed the evidence it decided that Dean should be charged. The CPS decided, after a conference with the police, to charge him with assisting in the destruction of the car.

1 See para 2.5.

2.20 Following the committal where the justices rejected an application for abuse, Dean sought a judicial review. The Divisional Court held that the prosecution of a person who had, received a promise, undertaking or representation from the police that he would not be prosecuted earlier was capable of being an abuse of process. On the undisputed evidence the applicant was given to understand, for a considerable time, that he was to be a prosecution witness, from which it almost certainly followed he was not himself to be prosecuted.

2.21 There was a dispute between the parties concerning the number of occasions when more specific assurances were said to have been given by police that there would be no prosecution: such assurances allegedly given when the tape recorder was switched off. A passage in the CPS representative's affidavit, which contradicted the police position, was accepted by the Court as being truthful.

2.21a The CPS argument against the application for judicial review was a constitutional one as the police, in any event, did not have the requisite authority to tell the applicant he would not be prosecuted, therefore such police conduct could not amount to an abuse of process. Staughton LJ however, was not persuaded and held that whether or not the promisor had the power to decide, or whether or not it was a case of bad faith or something akin, these were not essential requirements: 'The effect on the applicant, or for that matter his father, of an undertaking or promise or representation by police was likely to have been the same ... whether or not it was authorised by the CPS.' What was found to be in Dean's mind was adjudged highly significant for, as the Court noted, '... the impression created was not dispelled for over five weeks, during which period he gave repeated assistance to the police'. The timing of the police promise to use him as a witness, and rule him out as a defendant, was also a feature given that the promise (which the Court accepted) was given at an early stage before he provided the important information. Staughton LJ pointed out that the applicant and his father could have taken legal advice as to the binding effect, or not, of such statements by police, but considered it unreasonable to expect that in the particular circumstances of the case (ie the applicant's young age, the nature of assistance he had provided and the length of time involved).

2.22 While no doubt a combination of factors affected the Court's decision, the immense prejudice he inflicted on his own position, which was largely irremediable, must have surely been the greatest consideration before the Court in opting to stay proceedings. In answer to the CPS's constitutional argument, Staughton LJ held that the remedy, 'must surely be a greater degree of liaison at an early state.'

2.22a It is apparent that this case was decided very much on its own particular facts. One can readily foresee a different outcome in circumstances where, for example, an unrealistic promise is either made or implied, by a young police officer to an experienced criminal, who indeed would have realised as much. Further, it is submitted that in practice certain individuals who provide witness statements to the police, having themselves been arrested and charged, expect and/or agree to testify for the Crown not because they expect an immunity but in the hope (or promise sometimes) of a reduced sentence.

2.23 The central importance of *ex p Dean* is that it explored the interrelationship between the police and the CPS and their respective roles in the prosecution of crime. The CPS argument was that if the Prosecution of Offences Act 1985 is to make any sense, then they ought to be unfettered in decision making where prior police action is unauthorised. The Court, while pronouncing that the CPS succeeded, in that they alone are entitled and bound to decide who shall be prosecuted, granted a somewhat hollow victory, given the police's recognised ability to, in effect, tie their hands. While it follows that the police have no authority to tell a suspect that he will not be prosecuted in connection with an offence (save where the CPS authorise such action), nevertheless, police will have to conduct themselves with restraint, for their conduct, even inadvertent or unintentional may lead to a stay of proceedings.

2.24 Police officers will need to be especially wary of having informal unrecorded discussions with the suspect or his solicitor where an impression is conveyed by the officers that if the suspect co-operates as desired, others but not him will be charged. If in reliance on this vague indication, the suspect confesses and/or implicates the others, he will certainly feel aggrieved if not betrayed if charges follow. As this case bears out, informing a suspect that he will be a Crown witness might be construed as an implied promise that no prosecution will take place. Practitioners whose clients complain about being charged, or prosecuted, and who state they genuinely believed they were only to act as witnesses, ought to carefully inquire into the circumstances which led to that belief. Did the client have a legitimate, as opposed to a fanciful, expectation that there would be no prosecution? Was the client justified in holding such a belief or did it simply result from gossip, hearsay or informal observation or comment? Which officer made or implied such a promise not to prosecute? Was the client entitled to reasonably rely on an indication given by an officer only marginally connected to the case, and perhaps of very junior rank? These are perhaps some of the practical questions with which the courts will have to grapple in deciding the bona fides of alleged unfairness. Lessons will hopefully be learnt from *ex p Dean*, which serves well to illustrate that a greater liaison between CPS and police is essential for both branches to function more effectively in the interests of justice.[1]

1 'The Crown Prosecution Service and the Police: A Loveless Marriage?' [1994] LQR 376.

2.25 As Julia Fionda neatly observed, when comparing *ex p Dean* with that of the earlier decision in *Lund*: 'The only possible means of distinguishing that authority (*Lund*) from the circumstances of the recent case (*Dean*) were that in 1958 the Court was seeking to prevent the promises of the police being binding on any citizen as a potential prosecutor (that is, third party), whereas in the present case the promise was merely held to be binding on the CPS, a body acting in its official capacity as public prosecutor to whom the police are obliged to refer cases.'

Post *Dean* authorities

2.26 *Ex p Dean* has been considered and adopted in a number of subsequent cases, most notably *R v Horseferry Road Magistrates' Court, ex p Bennett*[1] and in *Townsend.*[2]

1 [1994] AC 42.
2 [1997] 2 Cr App Rep 540.

2.27 *Townsend* was a case of a suspect in fraud proceedings, being treated as a prosecution witness for a considerable period, before eventually the prosecution deciding to abandon him as a witness and prosecute instead. While being treated as a witness *Townsend* had made a statement implicating a co-defendant. At the trial, however, an abuse submission was rejected, the judge holding that no prejudice had been suffered.

2.28 At the appeal, the prosecution emphasised that in *ex p Dean,* Staughton LJ had made it plain that the facts in that case were exceptional and therefore *Dean* could easily be distinguished. Here, during the period that Townsend was treated as a witness, the CPS were unaware of the true extent of this central role in the fraud. Rose LJ held in the Court of Appeal that, whereas the circumstances where a defendant is induced to believe he would not be prosecuted this is capable of founding a stay for abuse. But such a breach of promise did not necessarily and ipso facto give rise to abuse. Considering the circumstances of this case, the Court held that there had been nothing improper in interviewing the appellant first as a witness and, further, that he had not changed his position in reliance on his treatment as a prosecution witness or volunteered incriminating information. However, the conviction was held to be unsafe given that the appellant had seriously prejudiced his chances of a fair trial. For, while still acting in the capacity qua witness, the CPS had served on the co-defending lawyers the appellant's witness statement (as unused material) which heavily implicated the co-defendant. This led to the co-defendant giving evidence against him at a joint trial, where a severance application had failed, and to a hostile situation which might well have been avoided.

2.29 Situations where witnesses metamorphosise into defendants are obviously fraught with potential problems and the courts no doubt will have to remain on guard as to the bona fides of certain abuse claims. Caution ought to be applied in *Townsend* type scenarios for the reasons astutely noted by a recent commentator[1] as follows:

> 'It is perfectly possible to imagine a case of a dishonest witness who is happy to implicate another; the other may have been content not to implicate the witness as long as the witness did not become involved. But if his attitude were to change on being served with a lying statement made by the witness, it would not only be understandable, but it would be a charter for the dishonest and unscrupulous witness if it were to be held that his "co-operation" had effectively earned him immunity.'

1 See also Professor Birch's commentary, [1997] CrimLR 128.

2.30 The concept of fairness and breach of promise arose in *R v Liverpool Magistrates' Court, ex p Slade*.[1] A dog owner was prosecuted for allowing a pitbull terrier in a public place. Under the relevant legislation this was an offence and if it was proved then the Magistrates' court was bound to order the destruction of the dog. The issue in the case was therefore whether the dog was of this breed or not. At the trial the prosecution dog expert failed to appear and the magistrates accordingly dismissed the charge. The next day the dog owner duly went to the police station to retrieve his dog which was released to him by the police. However, it appears that the police still felt aggrieved at the situation and subsequently chose to bring fresh proceedings seeking to re-prove that the dog was a pitbull terrier.

1 [1998] 1 WLR 531, [1998] 1 Cr App Rep 147; see also *R v Haringey Magistrates' Court, ex p Cragg* (1996) 161 JP 61.

2.31 The dog owner argued breach of promise. His argument was that by releasing the dog to him at the police station, the police had not only created a legitimate expectation in his mind that having the dog in a public place was perfectly lawful, they had also connived with him continuing to commit the offence. In the Divisional Court this argument found favour. Pill LJ, in holding that there was an abuse here, categorised it as falling under the second strand as delineated by Neill LJ in *Beckford*: '... it was unfair to try the accused for the offence and offensive to the Court's sense of justice and propriety'.

2.32 In *Postermobile plc v Brent London Borough Council*[1] the Divisional Court also applied the second strand of *Beckford.* In this case 25 separate informations were laid against the appellants by Brent Council for displaying advertisements without obtaining the necessary planning consent. The appellants did not deny the charges but alleged that at a meeting between a planning consultant employed by the appellants, a director of the appellants and officers of the council, they were told that planning consents would not be required for the advertisements in question. Immediately after the advertisements were erected, the council commenced prosecutions against them.

1 (1997) Times, 8 December (dc); see also *R v Aylesbury Justices, ex p Kitching* [1997] Env LR D16; and see also *R v DPP, ex p Duckenfield* [1999] 2 All ER 873.

2.33 Schiemann LJ held that the prosecutions were an abuse of process, on the basis that it would be unfair for the defendants ever to be tried. He emphasised the importance of citizens being able to rely on the statements of public officials and commented, with wry humour, that it was not as if they requested 'planning advice from one of the council's gardeners'.

PROMISES TO OFFER NO EVIDENCE

2.34 In a handful of decisions, the Courts have found abuse to apply where post-charge the Crown have reneged on promises to offer no evidence.

2.35 *Bloomfield*[1] was an example of a volte face by the prosecution. At a plea and directions hearing at the Crown Court, the prosecution counsel indicated to defence counsel that the Crown wished to offer no evidence. It was accepted that the defendant had been the victim of a set-up. Prosecution counsel confirmed this intention in the trial judge's room. However, it was said that it would be embarrassing to the police and prosecution if no evidence were offered that day, and so the judge was invited, in open court, to adjourn the case and re-list it 'for mention'. The judge duly obliged with the agreement of the defence. However, in the intervening period the CPS arranged a conference with a new prosecution counsel who advised differently and then declared its intention to proceed with the prosecution.

1 [1997] 1 Cr App Rep, 135 CA.

2.36 In the Court of Appeal, the prosecution counsel, save for stating that the first prosecuting Counsel's indication was unauthorised, did not attempt to demonstrate that the original decision was wrong. It would appear that the only hint as to CPS thinking was reference being made first to the fact that the CPS representative was not present in court when the original action was taken and second, that the first prosecutor was 'inexperienced'.

2.37 Staughton LJ, in allowing the appeal on an abuse submission held:

> '... whether or not there was prejudice to the Defendant, it would bring the administration of justice into disrepute to allow the Crown to revoke its original decision without any reason being given as to what was wrong with it, particularly as it was made coram judice ...' Second, 'That neither the court nor defendant could be expected to enquire whether prosecution counsel had authority to conduct a case in court in any particular way and they were therefore entitled to assume in ordinary circumstances that counsel did have such authority.'

2.38 It is clear that what particularly offended the Court's sense of propriety in *Bloomfield*, was the stark manner in which the CPS appeared to treat the Court. Staughton LJ emphasised that the statement by the first prosecution counsel was not merely a statement to the defendant or to his legal representative, it was also been made in the presence of the judge. This point in Staughton LJ's opinion was so significant that considerations of prejudice became immaterial; 'it seems to us that whether or not there was prejudice it would bring the administration of justice into disrepute if the Crown Prosecution Service were able to treat the courts as if it were at its beck and call, free to tell it one day that it was not going to prosecute and another day that it was'.

2.39 Bloomfield was applied by Auld LJ in *Wyatt*[1] where prosecuting counsel informed the judge that, 'depending on the results of the DNA evidence the Crown may be in a position to take a different view which would be in the defendant's favour'. In other words, prosecuting counsel had made plain that if the DNA evidence was found not to incriminate the defendant, the case would be dropped. Eventually, the DNA analyses was forthcoming which was not incriminatory. However, the CPS decided that rather than discontinue the proceedings against the defendant, a new but less serious count to the indictment should be added. The trial judge held that the proceedings should not be stayed because there was no evidence that the defendant could not have a fair trial in relation to the new lesser charge.

1 (1997) 3 Archbold News 2, CA.

2.40 In his judgment, Auld LJ emphasised that an abuse of process may arise, 'even though it may not effect the fairness of the trial, but is so unfair or wrong that the court should mark it by not allowing the prosecution to proceed'. Applying the facts of the case to this principle, Auld LJ held, 'it seems to us in the circumstances that the prosecutions very late change of tack when the matter came before the court was very unfair to the defence ... we take the view that the intervention by the Crown Prosecution Service at that late stage, prevailing over counsel for the prosecutions better judgment, was unfortunate.'

2.41 In *Mahdi*[1] a stay was deemed appropriate where a change of judge on the adjourned hearing of a trial left a defendant to face a trial, which he should not have had to do, because of some confusion as to certain indications previously given to counsel. The assistant recorder, before whom the trial was re-listed, was not fully and properly informed as to the case history. Two senior judges had previously made plain their firm views as to whether the trial should proceed. Lord Taylor CJ in quashing the conviction, found that '... an injustice was inadvertently done to this appellant by reason of the lack of accurate information placed before the assistant recorder'. It should be added that the Court of Appeal stated, per curiam, that the case did not fall within the scope of the well-known authorities on abuse of process.

1 [1993] Crim LR 793.

2.42 In contrast to the principles embodied in *Bloomfield* it is, at first blush, difficult to reconcile the Divisional Court judgment in *R v DPP, ex p Burke*,[1] where an applicant was refused an application for judicial review of the DPP's decision to reinstate a prosecution, the CPS having expressly discontinued proceedings. In *Burke* the applicant had been charged with indecent assault on a 13-year old child. After the Senior Crown Prosecutor, the Principal Crown Prosecutor and a further prosecutor reviewed the case and agreed that there should be no prosecution, the CPS informed the applicant's solicitor that they had decided to discontinue the prosecution, albeit that the formalities of preparing a Notice of Discontinuance would take a little while. This information was passed on to the applicant, on or about March 1996.

1 [1997] COD 169, DC.

2.43 In April 1996 the Senior Crown Prosecutor received a complaint from the complainant's mother, about the decision to discontinue. While the Branch Crown Prosecutor, to whom the matter had been referred, concluded that the Senior Crown Prosecutor had made the wrong decision, nevertheless it was decided to issue a Notice of Discontinuance, given that the applicant had already been so informed. The standard form discontinuance letter included the words: 'Exceptionally, if further significant evidence were to become available at a later date this decision may be reconsidered.' While no further significant evidence apparently came to light, significant further discussions took place. The complainant's mother complained to the Prime Minister and her complaints were passed on to the Attorney General and then the Director of Public Prosecutions. The outcome was that the DPP decided to reinstate the prosecution, the applicant was informed, and a fresh summons issued. While no submissions as to abuse of process were made, the applicant sought judicial review of the DPP's decision, inter alia, on the grounds that he had a legitimate expectation that the prosecution would not be reinstated unless fresh evidence emerged (which it had not).

2.44 While Phillips LJ acknowledged that 'legitimate expectation' was an aspect of fairness, he concluded that the terms of the discontinuance letter were not designed to lead the applicant to believe that he was free of jeopardy. A simple question arises however. What would any ordinary person conclude on receipt of such a letter? Leaving aside a new evidence situation, would one not reasonably conclude that that was the end of the case? Should one be expected to anticipate that the Crown Prosecution Service may well, as occurred here, take a different decision at a later date? It is a moot point whether the same decision would have been reached had unfairness been considered in the context of the abuse of process authorities, as opposed to the administrative law ones which were apparently argued before the Court. One suspects that the applicant may have been more successful had he argued the public interest in holding the CPS to account for, in effect, a broken promise, where they failed to keep their side of the bargain. It was not an ill-considered notice of discontinuance, served by some administrative error. It resulted from a conscious decision by a high ranking prosecutor.

2.45 Finally, the recent case of *R v Horseferry Road Magistrates' Court, ex p DPP*[1] serves to highlight the fact that not all broken promises will be sufficient to justify a stay. In that case, a 'relatively junior' police officer told a representative of the defendant's solicitors (so the magistrate found) that he would not be charged in relation to an alleged fraudulent conspiracy. A year later, he was told he would be charged. The magistrate stayed the proceedings as an abuse of process, in apparent reliance on the principles of *ex p Dean*. However, the Divisional Court subsequently concluded that she had been wrong so to do. The Court held that it was not possible to say that a breach of an assurance not to prosecute necessarily justified a stay. Earlier cases were distinguished on the facts by reason of their special features, such as the youth of the defendant, and the assistance he had given to police in *ex p Dean* and in *Bloomfield*, the fact that the assurance had been given in the presence of a judge.

1 Archbold News, Issue 7, 13 August 1999; QBD No CO/3832/98, 8 March 1999.

2.46 In the course of their respective judgments in *ex p DPP* Kennedy LJ and Blofeld J emphasised the exceptional nature of the abuse jurisdiction. Blofeld J quoted Lord Lowry's judgment in *ex p Bennett* where he said, 'the jurisdiction to stay must be exercised carefully and sparingly and only for very compelling reasons. The discretion to stay is not a disciplinary jurisdiction and ought not to be exercised in order to express the courts disapproval of official conduct' (page 74).

2.47 In the course of his judgment, Kennedy LJ, clearly implied that, for a breach of assurance type abuse submission to succeed, the defence must pass the high hurdle of 'special circumstances' or 'special features', which were found to be lacking in that particular case.

PROMISES ON ACCEPTABLE PLEAS

2.48 While formal plea-bargaining is not part of our system, it is an everyday licit practice by the prosecution and defence to broker pleas in order to 'carve the indictment' and so avoid a trial. A considerable amount of time and money is no doubt saved as pragmatic considerations impact on the criminal justice system. Judges are routinely asked to provide sentence indications for specific guilty pleas. It is a practical balancing task, carried out in the public interest, where consideration is keenly given to sentencing levels in respect of various different offences.

2.49 For this informal system to work, of course, it is expected that the prosecution will keep their bargains, particularly where they agree on acceptable pleas. *R v Thomas*[1] is one such case where the Crown failed to keep their side of a bargain. In *Thomas* at a pleas hearing, the defendant pleaded not guilty to offences of s 18 Wounding, ABH and Affray, but pleaded guilty on a qualified basis to the alternative s 20 charge. Prior to such a hearing the CPS had indicated, in response to a letter from defence solicitors, in unequivocal terms that such a proposed plea was acceptable to the Crown. At the Crown Court hearing, the plea having been so entered, the counsel for the Crown then told the Court that the plea was not acceptable to him and that he sought a trial.

1 [1995] Crim LR

2.50 In this first instance decision the Court, in holding that there was an abuse, re-emphasised the principle of holding officials of the state to promises made. Whether or not the CPS indication was justifiable, the fact was that the defendant had seriously prejudiced his position by tendering a guilty plea to the s 20 offence. The defendant, of course, may not have tendered a guilty plea at all were it not for the CPS correspondence.

OTHER PROMISES

2.51 In addition to the three above-mentioned areas, where this category of abuse has been deemed applicable, there are a number of miscellaneous areas worthy of attention:

(1) raising expectations of a non-custodial sentence;
(2) the prosecution code for 're-starting a prosecution';

(3) the *Hayter* case;
(4) Crown Divisibility.

Raising expectations of a non-custodial sentence

2.52 While this is a part of the law on sentencing principle, and not of abuse, nevertheless a study of the sentencing authorities reveals much of interest to the abuse jurisdiction. Most of the abuse authorities, of course, relate to the question of fairness within the trial process, whether or not there can be a fair trial, or whether it is fair to try the accused in the particular circumstances of a case. But does abuse stop there? Can abuse of process be extended to the sentencing arena?

2.53 The leading sentencing authority on this topic, that of *Gillam*,[1] has much in common with the abuse concepts of fairness. In *Gillam*, the sentencing judge, having previously adjourned a case for sentence to determine the appellant's suitability for a community service order, proceeded to sentence the appellant to immediate imprisonment, although he was deemed suitable for such an order. Lord Justice Watkins, giving the Court of Appeal's judgment, found there to be an important principle of sentencing law.

1 *R v Gillam* (1980) 2 Cr App Rep (S) 267 (CA).

2.54 In so adjourning the case, Watkins LJ held:

> 'There was, therefore, created in the applicant's mind an expectation not unnaturally, of performing that service if the probation officer and others ... were disposed to recommend such a course to the court. It was recommended. When a judge in these circumstances purposely postpones sentence, so that an alternative to prison can be examined, and that alternative is found to be a satisfactory one in all respects, the court ought to adopt the alternative. A feeling of injustice is otherwise aroused.'

2.55 Where the judge had left the applicant with a legitimate expectation of avoiding custody, the Court deemed it unfair to defeat the expectation. In *Rennes*,[1] following *Gillam*, Lloyd LJ spelled out, in similar circumstances, that a Defendant could well suffer a sense of injustice where his legitimate expectations were defeated. The Court emphasised that everything depended on what a particular defendant had been led to believe.

1 *R v Rennes* (1985) 7 Cr App Rep (S) 343 (CA).

2.56 In more recent authorities, such as *Chamberlain*[1] and *Norton and Claxton*,[2] the Court of Appeal have made it clear that the better practice for judges, in dealing with sentencing or bail, is to indicate that (if it be the case) all options are open to the court, and consequently no promises are being given or should be inferred. This more realistic and prudent approach will doubtless help some judges avoid falling foul of this important sentencing principle. The rationale behind this policy, that defendants should not be misled as to their fate, has much to commend it to the development of the abuse jurisdiction.

1 *R v Chamberlain* (1994) 16 Cr App Rep (S) 473 (CA).
2 *R v Norton and Claxton* (1989) 11 Cr App Rep (S) 143 (CA).

The prosecution code for 're-starting a prosecution'

2.57 A new edition of the code for Crown Prosecutors was issued in 1994, pursuant to s 10(1) of the Prosecution of Offences Act 1985. The code, as was pointed out by Staughton LJ in *Bloomfield*, is not law, nor is it delegated legislation. It is simply a code which gives guidance on general principles for Crown Prosecutors, issued by the Director of Public Prosecutions. Part 10 is entitled 're-starting a prosecution', which reads as follows:

> '10.1 People should be able to rely on decisions taken by the Crown Prosecution Service. Normally if the Crown Prosecution Service tells a suspect or defendant that there will not be a prosecution, or that the prosecution has been stopped, that is the end of the matter and the case will not start again. But occasionally there are special reasons why the Crown Prosecution Service will re-start the prosecution, particularly if the case is serious.
>
> 10.2 These reasons include:
> (a) rare cases where a new look at the original decision shows that it was clearly wrong and should not be allowed to stand;
> (b) cases which are stopped so that more evidence which is likely to become available in the fairly near future can be collected and prepared. In these cases the Crown Prosecutor will tell the defendant that the prosecution may well start again;
> (c) cases which are stopped because of a lack of evidence but where more significant evidence is discovered later.'

2.58 The tenor of the code appears to indicate that a decision to re-start proceedings will most likely only occur in rare and exceptional cases, of some gravity. For a defence lawyer who is considering whether an abuse point arises, and who seeks to challenge the reinstitution of proceedings, the first step must be to consider the circumstances in which the case came to a halt, albeit temporarily. Were proceedings discontinued in court, or in writing, or in both? Was the client discharged in the magistrates' court after a contested hearing where evidence had been called, or submissions had been made and argued, or after a review hearing where committal or transfer papers were not prepared in time? If there was a formal notice of discontinuance in writing from the CPS, it is submitted that the terms of it are crucial to the consideration of an abuse point.

2.59 Where the CPS discontinue on the basis of a particular stated reason, and then on some occasion thereafter seek to restart proceedings on the basis of a different reason altogether, an abuse question may well arise. If, for example, a defendant is told that proceedings are being discontinued due to lack of evidence (with a warning that they may reinstate if more evidence emerges later) and then, after several months, he is told they have no additional evidence but they have decided the first decision was in error, a feeling of injustice may well lead to a successful abuse submission.

2.60 While the terms of the discontinuance letter did not assist the applicant in *Burke*, nevertheless Phillips LJ, in the Divisional Court, expressed his own view that it would be more satisfactory if the CPS standard letter of discontinuance annexed para 10 of the code 'by way of explanation of the circumstances in which the prosecution might be reinstated'. While this suggestion has much to commend it, and might reduce the number of potential abuse cases, it is submitted that such quasi 'exemption clauses' cannot necessarily prevent unfairness to an accused. Indeed, it is submitted that if the CPS are discontinuing for a particular reason they should say so whenever possible. It may well be argued that to allow the CPS the use of a standard discontinuance letter, which warns of every eventuality (whereby proceedings may be resurrected) is a carte blanche to encourage them to restart in circumstances where it would be unjust.

The Hayter Case[1]

2.61 In this case the police took the view that two 16-year-old defendants, who had been arrested for threatening unlawful violence and assault, could properly be cautioned for the offences, as a means of disposing of the prosecution. Each defendant received legal advice, admitted his involvement in the offences, signed a form indicating that a caution did not preclude the commencement of proceedings against him by an aggrieved party, and was then duly cautioned. The victim's father proceeded to bring a private prosecution against the defendants in the youth court. In due course, the youth court ordered that the proceedings be stayed as an abuse of process and dismissed the informations. The prosecutor appealed by way of case stated to the Divisional Court. It was held, allowing the appeal, 'that it was not an abuse of process to prosecute a defendant after he had been cautioned by the police unless the particular circumstances of a case disclosed an abuse'.

1 *Hayter v L*, sub nom. *H v L* [1998] 1 WLR 854 (1998) Times, 3 February, QBD.

2.62 While one can contemplate some cases where a caution is accepted leading to a successful abuse submission, this is not one of them. Such an example would be where a caution is accepted on the clear understanding that such a course would dispose of the matter altogether, where promises (from persons in authority) are made to that effect. In *Hayter* the defendants were apparently well aware that further criminal proceedings were not precluded, and the Court found no unfairness to result from the private prosecution. Indeed, Poole J pointed out that the trial process contained sufficient 'common law and statutory mechanisms to ensure fairness' in reference to the defence's opportunity to apply for exclusion of the evidence of the caution, in the event of the Crown seeking to admit it as evidence of an admission. This was a reference to the Court's discretion, at common law, and under s 78 of the Police and Criminal Evidence Act 1984, to exclude evidence.

2.63 While one can understand why the appellants failed in this particular case, one can equally envisage a different outcome where there was no legal advice prior to the acceptance of the caution, where an unrepresented defendant was not advised by police that a private prosecution could still take place, or where a defendant did not sign or read a form which explained the correct position, that is, that they may still be in jeopardy on a private prosecution.

Crown divisibility

2.64 The concept of 'the Crown' or of 'the prosecution' has been in a state of evolution. The ambit of the concept became important in the area of criminal law in connection with the prosecution's common law duty of disclosure. Here the courts were concerned in particular cases to expand the concept so that, for example, forensic scientists were covered. In *R v Liverpool Crown Court, ex p Roberts*[1] Glidewell LJ referred to the 'total apparatus of prosecution'. In *Blackledge*,[2] Lord Taylor CJ referred to the Crown as an 'indivisible unity.'

1 [1986] CrimLR 622.
2 [1996] 1 Cr App Rep 326.

2.65 The concept of an indivisible Crown or, in reality, an indivisible state has not taken route in criminal law. Perhaps recognising that the state is composed not only of separate Government departments with their separate and possibly conflicting aims and policies, but also composed of an increasing variety of semi-autonomous bodies and agencies. These bodies are the Crown Prosecution Service, Customs and Excise, the Inland Revenue and so on, all of which carry out the public function of criminal investigation and prosecution. Even within these bodies, however, there may be a disparity of function: for example the Inland Revenue is not primarily a prosecutorial agency and the investigation and prosecution of tax fraud is not one of its highest priorities.

2.66 In *R v W*[1] the two applicants were facing trial for conspiracy to defraud. At a preparatory hearing the defence submitted that the Crown was not empowered to prosecute and, further, that the proceedings were an abuse of process. The applicants appealed to the Court of Appeal to challenge the trial judge's first preparatory ruling that the Crown were so empowered. The prosecution case alleged a time-share fraud whereby large amounts of Corporation and Income Tax were said to have been evaded. While the criminal proceedings commenced in 1996, in 1997 the Inland Revenue agreed to accept a large settlement in relation to the Company's tax liability.

1 [1998] STC 550, Transcript No 9800559/52, 12 March 1998, CA.

2.67 The defence argued that if the Crown, through the Inland Revenue, had elected not to prosecute for tax evasion but instead to accept tax, penalties and interest, then it followed that the Crown through the CPS were not empowered or entitled to ignore that election. The defence sought to stress the apparent fact that the Inland Revenue, in deciding not to prosecute, had liaised with the DTI, the Police Commercial Fraud Squad and the CPS. At some stage, however, whereas the Inland Revenue took the view that a £3.5m transfer on bogus invoices could be regarded as a loan, the CPS took the view that the transfers gave rise to theft!

2.68 The question posed was whether, given that two linked Government departments took different views, a criminal prosecution could proceed. Rose LJ, while dismissing the appeal for jurisdictional reasons, gave a ruling on Crown divisibility, albeit obiter. The Court held that the Crown was divisible, in essence, because both branches were pursuing separate agendas and policies.

2.69 While this was not an abuse case on the facts, Rose LJ commented:

> 'Of course, Crown indivisibility may well be pertinent to a claim for abuse of process if, for example, the CPS were to prosecute when the Revenue, in accepting settlement from a taxpayer, had told him with the concurrence of the CPS, that he would not be prosecuted by anyone.'

2.70 In so commenting, Rose LJ was rightly acknowledging that, in certain cases, one can readily contemplate the Revenue binding the CPS, in the same way that police officers bound the CPS in *Dean*: see paras 2.19 to 2.24. On the facts, it is submitted that the Court adopted a realistic approach, given that the applicants had not been misled. Grey areas will no doubt continue to flourish, however, particularly in relation to cases of suspected serious tax fraud where the Inland Revenue's 'Hansard' policy comes into play.[1] For, as was recently commented on:[2]

> 'Although the statement makes it clear that the Board reserves to itself full discretion as to which course of action it takes, and the statement does not guarantee immunity from prosecution, in practice, once the Hansard statement is given, prosecutions are rare.'

1 The Hansard policy being the system whereby where serious fraud is suspected, the Board may in certain circumstances, accept a money settlement instead of instituting legal proceedings in respect of fraud alleged to have been committed by a taxpayer.
2 See Elwes and Clutterbuck 'Tax and Criminal Prosecutions' [1999] CrimLR 139.

2.71 Where taxpayers have co-operated with the Revenue, perhaps having made confessions or declarations against their interest, only to find themselves being prosecuted, practitioners ought to carefully consider whether any express or implied assurances are evidenced, or even legitimate expectations breached. Where no argument lies as to abuse of process, consideration ought to be given to an application for Judicial Review in the rare circumstances where the decision of the CPS, to bring criminal proceedings, may be attacked on the basis that it was both unfair and contrary to the legitimate expectations of the taxpayer.[1]

1 See in particular the decisions of *R v IRC, ex p Mead* [1993] 1 All ER 772, and *R v IRC, ex p Allen* [1997] STC 1141; see also *R v IRC, ex p MKF Underwriters Agents Ltd* [1990] 1 WLR 1545. See also *R v IRC, ex p Unilever* [1994] STC 841 and the *Postermobile* case in paras 2.32 and 2.33.

CONCLUDING REMARKS

2.72 For the practitioner, who is considering the question as to whether or not a breach of promise point arises, there are a number of practical steps to follow. The first, logically, is to determine whether there is, or is not, a 'promise'. It need not simply be a promise in the strict sense, for an 'undertaking' or 'representation' will also suffice. The promise may either be a clear, unequivocal, express promise or one which is implied and inferred from the particular circumstances of a case.

2.73 The second step is to identify whether there is any evidence of a breach of the said promise. Needless to say where there is no breach, there is no abuse.

2.74 Third, the practitioner may wish to determine whether any significant prejudice has been suffered by the accused. If such prejudice has been sustained that may well go to the fourth question, which relates to 'fairness'. In certain abuse cases, however, the absence of prejudice will not be fatal to a successful submission. Evidence of prejudice to the individual has been declared unnecessary in cases involving unfairness, in the sense of the prosecution process bringing the administration of justice into disrepute, per Staughton LJ in *Bloomfield*.

2.75 The fourth step is to identify whether or not significant 'unfairness' has resulted. Indeed, by no means every breach of an assurance or promise will satisfy the test of unfairness. In order to attain the threshold of unfairness, practitioners will have to demonstrate that the circumstances are sufficiently special or particular to justify a stay. In drawing together the strands identified in the case-law, it is submitted that the courts have defined 'unfairness' from three particular perspectives, albeit there is a degree of overlap.

Unfairness to the accused

2.76 Was the act (or breach) manifestly unfair to the particular defendant or party to litigation? Was his position seriously prejudiced? These questions relate directly to whether or not a fair trial is possible.

Unfairness in the public perception

2.77 Would the act (or breach) bring the administration of justice into disrepute among right-thinking people? Is doubt cast on the bona fides of the prosecution? Lord Oliver, in the House of Lords decision in *Bennett,* considered this an important point when considering the *ex p Dean*[1] authority (at page 132).

1 See page 112 F-H of the judgment of Lord Oliver in *ex p Bennett* [1993] 3 WLR 90.

Unfairness from the judicial perspective

2.78 Does the act complained of offend the Court's own sense of propriety and injustice? This view of unfairness is directly connected to the second strand of abuse identified by Neil LJ in *Beckford.* For in that second strand an abuse of process was said to relate to occasions where it would be unfair to try an accused, albeit a fair trial was yet possible.

2.79 Where the promise, breach, prejudice and unfairness come together, so comes about the makings of a submission with moral integrity. Promises are meant to be kept.

3. Double jeopardy

3.1 The rule against double jeopardy can be summarised as 'a defendant in criminal proceedings should not be tried twice on the same general allegation'. Alternatively, a defendant in criminal proceedings should not be put in peril of conviction more than once for the same or substantially the same offence. The rule is designed, in a general sense, to prevent re-litigation of similar factual issues and, in a particular sense, to prevent over-zealous prosecutors seeking to maximise the prospects of a conviction against the same defendant against whom a previous prosecution has failed. It also prevents a prosecutor seeking to correct the perceived failure by a second attempt or where proceedings have resulted 'successfully' with a conviction but one that is perceived as only being a precursor or dummy-run to subsequent more grave allegations. If a court holds that the rule has been violated then pursuant to its obligation to prevent an abuse of its process, it has power to stay the prosecution.

3.2 The arguments underpining the rule against double jeopardy have been succinctly explained by Choo: 'to put a person in double jeopardy may increase the chances of his or her being convicted even though innocent, and will also undermine the moral integrity of the criminal process. The accused may, as a result of having revealed his complete defence at the first trial, be at a greater disadvantage at the second trial and thus less able to defend him or herself effectively. Irrespective of this, it is in any event morally objectionable to subject someone to the embarrassment, expense and anxiety of a second prosecution, with the possibility that a verdict might be returned which in inconsistent with that reached the first time. Considerations such as these ought to be borne in mind when considering stays of proceedings in the double jeopardy context'.[1]

1 AL Choo 'Halting Criminal Prosecutions' [1995] CrimLR at 866.

3.3 In *Green v US*[1] Black J explained the principle in the following terms:

> 'The underlying idea, one that is deeply ingrained in at least the Anglo-American system of jurisprudence, is that the State with all its resources and power should not be allowed to make repeated attempts to convict an individual for an alleged offence, thereby subjecting him to embarrassment, expense and ordeal and compelling him to live in a continuing state of anxiety and insecurity, as well as enhancing the possibility that even though innocent he may be found guilty.'

1 355 US 184.

3.4 The origins of our jurisprudence concerning double jeopardy lie in the ancient remedies of Autrefois Acquit ('AA') and Autrefois Convict ('AC'). Both remedies are collectively known as 'pleas in bar' which are available to a defendant in criminal proceedings and constitute an alternative plea to one of guilty or not guilty. A defendant who pleads either AA or AC challenges the validity of the indictment or seeks to bar it against him. Logically therefore, this plea precedes one of guilty or not guilty which is an answer to the subject matter of the indictment and presupposes its validity. A plea in bar is always aimed at staying the trial of the defendant altogether even before it has begun. If upheld by the court, if gives the defendant an absolute right to relief. Blackburn J in *Wemyss v Hopkins*[1] said it is 'a well established common law principle that where a person has been convicted and punished for an offence by a court of competent jurisdiction ... the conviction shall be a bar to all further proceedings for the same offence, and he shall not be punished again for the same matter' (page 381).

1 (1875) LR 10 QB 378,

3.5 The scope of both AA and AC was considered at great length by the House of Lords in *Connelly v DPP.*[1] For present purposes, *Connelly* can safely be considered as the root of modern law on double jeopardy and it is not necessary to peer back in history behind it.[2] The speeches of all five Law Lords in *Connelly* evidence a vigorous debate between them, first as to the exact legal scope of those pleas. Second, as to whether a court's power to stay a prosecution was restricted to those narrow sets of circumstances where on established principles, either plea could be validly claimed or whether in addition, there existed a wider discretionary power to stay proceedings where a situation of double jeopardy was recognised as occurring but which was not within the scope of either plea. At the heart of all the speeches delivered in *Connelly* was a consideration of these two interrelated issues. It was also appreciated by the Law Lords that if the debate between them was to be resolved in favour of the view of there being a wider discretionary power, then this led to a consideration of a third issue. Whether in a situation of unfairness caused by double jeopardy, the response of the courts should be to expand the scope of the pleas in bar so as to allow them to cure unfairness using the doctrine of AA or AC. Alternatively, the pleas in bar should be narrowly constrained and the courts embrace a wider and more discretionary jurisdiction based on the concept of abuse of process. Finally, if the abuse of process route was to be preferred, then what constraints should be imposed to preserve the separate functions of the judiciary and the prosecution?

1 [1964] AC 1254.
2 For a history of double jeopardy, see J Hunter 'The Development of the Rule Against Double Jeopardy' (1984) Journal of Legal History.

3.6 As Viscount Dilhorne perceived this final question in *DPP v Humphrys*,[1] 'the functions of prosecutors and judges must not be blurred. If a judge has power to decline to hear a case because he does not think it should be brought, then it may soon be thought that the cases he allows to proceed are cases brought with his consent or approval.'

1 [1977] AC 1.

3.7 In other words, if one allows a power that allows trial judges to stop prosecutions before any evidence has been heard, how is its exercise to be constrained to really exceptional and deserving cases? How to ensure that courts proceed only with the greatest caution or reluctance?

3.8 In *Connelly*, as will be considered below, the House resolved decisively in favour of the abuse of process jurisdiction as the principal means to cure unfairness caused by double jeopardy. Thus, it relegated the importance of the pleas in bar. Since *Connelly* all the leading authorities on double jeopardy have consistently adopted the same approach. In *Humphrys* Lord Salmon recognised the existence of judicial power to intervene: 'if the prosecution amounts to an abuse of the process of the court and is oppressive and vexatious' (page 46) Lord Edmund-Davies took a similar view, 'in my judgment, *Connelly* ... established that they [Judges] are vested with the power to do what the justice of the case clearly demands' (page 55). More recently, for example, in *R v Beedie*[1] the Court of Appeal confirmed that the general rules against double jeopardy should not be regarded as subsumed within the doctrine of AA or AC, but should instead be conceived as part of the Court's wider discretionary power to stay proceedings which constitute an abuse of process. Rose LJ held in *Connelly* the majority had 'identified a narrow principle of autrefois, applicable only where the same offence was alleged in the second indictment' (page 360).

1 [1998] QB 356.

3.9 The Court held that whereas the remedy of pleas in bar subsists, its scope has been narrowly construed with the result that in practice it is available only in strictly defined and highly exceptional circumstances. Conversely, where the courts have in any other circumstances recognised an unfairness caused by double jeopardy they have sought to utilise and, if necessary, expand their abuse of process jurisdiction in order to stay the prosecution.

3.10 This chapter can conveniently be divided into two parts: first, relating to the scope and availability of the pleas in bar, AA and AC and second, the scope and availability of the abuse of process jurisdiction in relation to double jeopardy.

AUTREFOIS ACQUIT AND CONVICT

The Scope of the Pleas as Determined in *Connelly*

The Factual Situation

3.11 The factual situation in *Connelly* was briefly as follows: an armed robbery took place at a dairy in south London during which an employee of the dairy was shot and killed by the robbers. Subsequently Connelly was arrested and charged with the murder. The prosecution did not contend that he was the killer but contended that as he was part of the gang that had committed the murder, he had the requisite criminal intent to be legally responsible for it. At his trial before Roskill J, Connelly's defence was essentially two-fold; first he claimed alibi – that he had not been involved in any way with the robbery and had not been present at the scene of the crime. Second, and alternatively, that in any event the prosecution had not proved that he had the requisite intent even if he had been a member of the gang and had been present. Connelly was tried only for murder, not for robbery in the alternative. This was because of a then practice rule laid down by the House of Lords in *R v Jones*[1] which stated that an indictment containing a count for murder should not be combined with any other count alleging a different offence.

1 [1918] 1 KB 416.

3.12 When it retired to consider its verdict, the jury at Connelly's trial had three options available to it, guilty or not guilty of murder but if not guilty of murder, then guilty of manslaughter. Even though the prosecution did not concede the possibility that Connelly was guilty only of manslaughter and, similarly, the defence did not propose this as an alternative verdict to murder, the law nonetheless allowed the jury to return this verdict. In the event, the jury convicted Connelly of murder. His subsequent appeal to the Court of Appeal was grounded on important misdirections committed by Roskill J during his summing up. Albeit with great reluctance, the Court of Appeal agreed and accordingly quashed Connelly's conviction for murder. In law therefore, at this point, Connelly stood acquitted of murder and manslaughter, the latter because the jury could have convicted him of this offence if it chose, but did not do so.

3.13 However, immediately after this appeal hearing, the prosecution then proceeded with the leave of the Court of Appeal, to lay a second indictment against Connelly, this time only alleging robbery at the dairy.

3.14 At the opening of his second trial Connelly pleaded AA, a plea which was rejected by the trial judge. However, while the trial judge rejected Connelly's plea of AA he also declared that the prosecution ought not, in his opinion, to proceed against Connelly for the count of robbery. This was because the factual issue of whether he had taken part in the robbery had already been decided in the first trial in Connelly's favour. The trial judge opined that the quashing of his conviction for murder by the Court of Appeal surely meant that it had been determined by that court that he was not present at the crime. The prosecution, however, disagreed and chose to press ahead with the trial. Subsequently, Connelly was convicted by the second jury for robbery and sentenced to imprisonment. Unsurprisingly, he appealed alleging that the dismissal by the trial judge of his plea of AA was erroneous.

3.15 The case duly came before the House of Lords for its consideration. The House was unanimous in the view that the plea of

AA had properly been rejected by the trial judge and upheld Connelly's conviction. The House also set aside the practice direction given in *R v Jones* and held that the situation which had occurred in *Connelly* should not recur, ie that in future an indictment could be framed containing counts of both murder and, for example, robbery. What, however, has made *Connelly* a landmark case is the debate which divided the Lords, as demonstrated by their respective speeches, concerning the scope and availability of the pleas in bar.

The governing principles underlying the availability of AA or AC

3.16 In his exhaustive judgment spanning 34 pages, Lord Morris considered all the authorities known to him concerning pleas in bar in order to formulate a set of what he termed 'governing principles' which ought to determine in future the availability of either AA or AC. While Lord Morris' formulation was to a limited extent queried by others in *Connelly*, and has been qualified subsequently, it largely remains valid law today. For example it was revisited and approved by Ackner LJ in *R v Basingstoke Justices, ex p Howard.*[1] Bearing this in mind, each of these principles and their subsequent refinements should be considered.

1 QBD CO 1562/84 (18 March 1985, unreported).

3.17 A person cannot be tried for a crime in respect of which they have previously been acquitted or convicted. In other words, where the later proceedings are for the same offence with which a court was concerned in the earlier proceedings. This principle can be summarised as the 'same offence' test. As Lord Devlin in *Connelly* put it, 'it must be the same offence both in fact and in law' (page 449). The narrowness of this test means that a person can be tried a second time for the same conduct where the offence charged is different from that charged at the earlier trial (see also Lord Reid's speech at page 419). The effect of this rule is now circumscribed by ss 54-56 of the Criminal Procedure and Investigations Act 1996, dealing with tainted acquittals, see para 3.96.

3.18 A person cannot be tried for a crime in respect of which they could in previous proceedings have been lawfully convicted; where the offence tried in the earlier proceedings, of which the defendant was either convicted or acquitted, constituted an alternative to the offence now proposed to be tried. In other words, where there is an implied conviction or acquittal arising out of the earlier proceedings.

3.19 The principle is not whether the evidence relied on to prove the offences in both sets of proceedings is the same but a purely legal test of whether the person's acquittal in the first proceedings necessarily in law involves an acquittal in the second. An implied alternative acquittal would be where the jury could lawfully have convicted the defendant on an alternative charge to the one being tried but have returned no verdict on it. An express acquittal arises when there are alternative charges, for example, theft and handling which are expressly averred in the indictment but are alternative to each other. Where a jury returned a verdict on one charge this would allow a defendant to plead autrefois to the other.

3.20 This principle, difficult to comprehend, can be best explained by two examples. In *Connelly*, as mentioned in para 3.5, the defendant could in his first trial have been convicted by the jury of murder or manslaughter. Accordingly, once he was acquitted of murder by the Court of Appeal this also constituted in law an acquittal of manslaughter. This was an implied acquittal. However, the defence argument in *Connelly* was that there was also an implied acquittal in relation to a charge of robbery. As the killing occurred at a time when four people were committing the robbery, Connelly's conviction for robbery would also involve him being guilty of manslaughter. This offended the autrefois principle because, as accepted, he stood acquitted of manslaughter. Hence he should not be tried for robbery. The House, however, disagreed. It held that the evidence relied on by the prosecution to charge robbery would not have been sufficient to procure a conviction for manslaughter. His acquittal for murder and implied acquittal for manslaughter therefore did not prevent a subsequent trial for robbery.

3.21 In the more recent case of *Velasquez*[1] the defendant was tried for two offences, rape and attempted rape in relation to the same victim. In delivering its verdicts, the jury acquitted Velasquez of attempted rape but then went on to convict him of rape. With perhaps a degree of resourcefulness, he appealed his conviction for rape arguing that once he was acquitted of the attempt, the plea of AA was then immediately available to him in relation to preventing his conviction for the rape. As he was acquitted of the attempt, the prosecution should then have been barred from seeking his conviction for the substantive offence. The Court of Appeal rejected this argument, holding that there was no implied acquittal in relation to the substantive offence said to arise out of the actual acquittal in relation to the attempt. It held that it did not offend the autrefois principles for a defendant where the facts were exactly the same to be not guilty of the attempt but guilty of the substantive offence. The charges were logical alternatives.

1 (1996) 1 Cr App Rep 155.

3.22 The rule in para 3.18 also applies if the crime, in respect of which a person is tried, is in effect the same or substantially the same as the crime in respect of which they have in previous proceedings been acquitted or convicted (or could have been convicted by way of alternative verdict). This rule is subject to one proviso; the offence charged in the second indictment must have been committed at the same time of the first alleged offence

3.23 In Lord Morris' view the best test of whether the second charge is the same or substantially the same as the earlier is whether the evidence which is necessary to support the second charge would have been sufficient to prove a legal conviction on the first (see pages 1310-11). An example of this would be where it is shown that an offence of which the accused has already been convicted is a necessary step towards proving the offence now charged. As Lord Hodson put it in *Connelly*, 'whether the acquittal of the first charge necessarily involved an acquittal on the second' (page 1332). This principle can be illustrated by the two cases following:

(1) In *Dabhade*[1] the defendant was first charged with obtaining property by deception contrary to s 15(1) of the Theft Act 1978. He pleaded not guilty and the prosecution decided to offer no evidence leading to the charge being dismissed. A new charge based on the same facts, theft contrary to s 1 of the Theft Act 1968 was then preferred. Dabhade pleaded AA in relation to the theft charge submitting that the two charges were, in the circumstances of his case, the same or substantially the same (even though theft is not an alternative verdict on a charge of obtaining by deception). The Court of Appeal rejected the plea of AA holding that it did not come within the requirement that the evidence supporting the theft charge would have sufficed to secure a conviction of the obtaining by deception charge. It held that, although in some cases because of the evidence theft is an alternative verdict to obtaining by deception, the evidence in this case to support a charge of theft would not suffice alone to support a charge of obtaining by deception.

(2) In *Valasquez*[2] the Court of Appeal was minded to apply Lord Hodson's proposition quoted above and hold that an acquittal on

an attempt should bar a conviction for the full offence on a later indictment. The two crimes charged, rape and attempted rape, were arguably substantially the same. However, it held on the facts before it that there was no necessary inconsistency between the verdicts delivered in that case. In its discretion, therefore, the Court, it is submitted, declined to follow this principle. In *Velasquez* the Court of Appeal were in fact applying its discretion to refuse relief believing that no injustice was done to the defendant by the verdicts.

1 (1992) 96 Cr App Rep 146.
2 See para 3.21.

3.24 The judgment of the Court of Appeal in *Valasquez* is, it is submitted, a vindication of the view of Lord Devlin who, in *Connelly*, disagreed with Lord Morris that this third principle should properly form part of the Autrefois doctrine. Lord Devlin's view was that this principle belonged more to courts' inherent discretionary power pursuant to an abuse of process rather than to Autrefois: 'I have no difficulty about the idea that one set of facts maybe substantially, but not exactly the same as another. I have more difficulty with the idea that an offence may be substantially the same as another in its legal characteristics; legal characteristics are precise things and are either the same or not. If I had felt that the doctrine of Autrefois was the only form of relief available to the defendant I should be tempted to stretch the doctrine as far as it would go. But as that is not my view I am inclined to favour keeping it within limits that are precise' (page 1340).

3.25 In *Beedie*[1] the Court of Appeal opined that this principle should not be viewed as part of the doctrine of Autrefois at all but should instead, in the absence of special circumstances, lead to the exercise of the wider discretionary power to stay proceedings on the grounds of abuse. In the light of *Beedie* it may be that the decision in *Dabhade* should be reclassified as falling under the abuse jurisdiction rather than that of *Autrefois.*

1 See para 3.8.

3.26 An illustration of the proviso in relation to this principle of *Salvi*[1] is where the defendant, after being acquitted of a charge of wounding with intent to murder was, after his victim's death, indicted for murder and convicted. His plea of AA failed in the Court of Appeal. It held that a person can be convicted in law for murder without an intention to murder being proven. Therefore the evidence on the indictment for murder would not necessarily have supported a conviction on the first, wounding with intent to murder.

1 (1857) 10 Cox CC 481n.

3.27 It is immaterial that the facts under examination or the witnesses being called in the subsequent proceedings are the same as those in the earlier proceedings. Instead, what matters is whether the crime or the offence charged in the later indictment is the same or substantially the same as the crime charged in the earlier indictment.

3.28 This principle can be illustrated by the facts in *Connelly* and *DPP v Humphrys*.[1] In *Connelly*, the facts of which have already been outlined in paras 3.5 and 3.8, the evidence called and the facts relied on by the prosecution at the trial for robbery were the same as they had relied on in the earlier trial for murder. However, the House of Lords were unanimous in holding that the coincidence of factual evidence at the two trials did not form the basis of a successful plea for AA.[2]

1 [1977] AC 1.
2 See also *Thomas* [1950] 1 KB 26, where a plea of AC failed in circumstances where the defendant had been convicted of wounding and was subsequently following the death of the victim charged with murder.

3.29 In *Humphrys*, which was the first occasion after *Connelly* when the House of Lords considered issues relating to double jeopardy, a plea of AA was similarly rejected. In that case the defendant had been charged with driving a motor vehicle while disqualified. He pleaded not guilty and in his defence gave evidence asserting that not only had he not driven on the date in question but that he had also not driven for a period of one year prior to that date. The jury acquitted Humphrys obviously believing his testimony. Subsequently fresh evidence concerning the veracity of Humphrys' evidence came to light suggesting that he had driven at times during that preceding year and he was charged with perjury in relation to his evidence given at the first trial. He pleaded AA partly on the basis that the main witness against him, a police officer at the first trial who claimed to have observed Humphrys driving would be giving the same evidence at the proposed second trial: evidence which the jury at the first trial must have rejected. The House rejected the plea of AA holding that the offence of driving while disqualified and of perjury were different and separable. What mattered was not that similar facts would be under scrutiny in both trials but whether similar crimes or offences would be under scrutiny. The plea of AA related only to offences not also facts and was therefore unavailable.[1]

1 It should not be overlooked that H had pleaded guilty to forging an MOT certificate in relation to the car he had denied driving. This admission may have jaundiced the view of H's protestation of innocence.

3.30 The House in *Humphrys* also approved a Scottish case of *HM Advocate v Cairns*.[1] Here the defendant had been acquitted of murder and then subsequently confessed that he was guilty to a newspaper. On the strength of this confession he was subsequently tried for perjury despite the fact that the evidence would in effect be that he had committed the murder for which he had been acquitted. Lord Grant held that this did not bar a second trial, 'identity of the charges and not of the evidence is the crucial factor.'

1 1968 JC 37.

3.31 In relation to this principle the House also held in *Connelly* that the fact that a count or an indictment has been marked 'not to be proceeded with without leave of this Court or the Court of Appeal' will not per se bar subsequent proceedings on that count or indictment if the necessary leave is obtained.

3.32 The earlier adjudication of a defendant's guilt or innocence subsequently relied on in later proceedings by the defendant to plead either AA or AC must have been in regard to his guilt or innocence and also have been made by a court of competent jurisdiction. In other words, there must be a valid acquittal or conviction.

3.33 The meaning of 'adjudication' was defined in *DPP v Nasralla*[1] as the occurrence of any of the following events: a jury's express verdict, a plea of guilty being entered and accepted or a verdict of not guilty having been directed pursuant to s 17 of the Criminal Justice Act 1967.[2] Outside of these events, it is submitted, the courts have consistently adopted a narrow view of what constitutes adjudication. For example in *Connelly* the House of Lords held that the quashing of Connelly's conviction for murder by the Court of Appeal did not prevent his subsequent trial for robbery, in part because the issue of his guilt or innocence in relation to that specific offence was never adjudicated on by the jury in the first trial.

1 [1967] 2 AC 238.
2 In reciting this list, the court should have included s 27 Magistrates' Court Act 1980; a magistrates' dismissal of a prosecutor's information under s 15 constitutes an acquittal.

3.34 Another example of this narrow interpretation of adjudication is where a court has acted ultra vires and the accused could never have been legally convicted. It has been held that the accused was never therefore technically in peril or in jeopardy. See for example *West*[1] where magistrates purported to acquit the accused of the offence which was triable only on indictment. Having realised this error the prosecution then recharged the accused who then pleaded AA in order to resist his committal for trial. This was rejected: as the summary proceedings were a nullity, the subsequent committal and trial were unobjectionable.[2]

1 [1962] 1 QB 15.
2 For a more complete consideration of this principle see paras 3.36-3.49.

3.35 In seeking to prove the validity of either AA or AC, a defendant is not confined to a comparison between the latter and the earlier indictment or to the records of the Court. Evidence can be called from other sources in relation to the identity of the persons, dates and facts as is required. In other words the test is one of substance not form. In *West* this principle was interpreted as entitling a later court to inquire into the validity of an earlier court's jurisdiction and hold that the initial proceedings were a nullity (see para 3.34).

Instances that do not form a basis for a plea of AA or AC

3.36 The cases considered in paras 3.37 to 3.41 are all concerned with proceedings in the magistrates' court. As a matter of legal semantics, the pleas of AA and AC are not available in that court as they are strictly only pleas in answer to an indictment. However, in practice they are recognised there in all but name. Generally such pleas are referred to as examples of the rule against double jeopardy.

3.37 *Discharge of an accused at committal proceedings (ruling of no case to answer)* – In *R v Manchester City Stipendiary Magistrate, ex p Snelson*[1] the accused was discharged at his committal following the offering of no evidence by the prosecution. Subsequently, the prosecution initiated fresh proceedings in relation to which the accused asserted AA. His plea was that as the magistrates had already discharged him for the offence in question, they were unable to reconsider it. The magistrate disagreed and committed the accused at trial and the accused sought judicial review of this finding. Lord Widgery CJ upheld the magistrate's decision holding that pursuant to the principle in para 3.32, a plea of AA was not available to a defendant by reason of his earlier discharge in committal proceedings. (But see also limits imposed as a matter of discretion on the prosecution's right to pursue charges basically the same as those already dismissed, *R v Horsham Justices, ex p Reeves*[2] considered in para 3.65).

1 [1977] 1 WLR 911.
2 (1980) 75 Cr App Rep 236n.

3.38 *Withdrawal of a summons by the prosecution in the magistrates' court prior to the accused having pleaded to it* – In *R v Grays Justices, ex p Low*[1] the prosecution issued a summons for ABH against the accused which was subsequently withdrawn once the accused accepted a bind over. Subsequently, the alleged victim of the assault who felt aggrieved at the prosecution's decision to accept a bind over launched a private prosecution and a second summons was issued. The accused pleaded AA in relation to this second summons. The magistrates disagreed and the accused sought judicial review. Lord Nolan upheld the magistrates' refusal to recognise a plea of AA. He held that the withdrawal of a summons did not operate as a bar to the issuance of a further summons for the same charge because there had been no adjudication by the court on the merits of the allegation contained in the first summons and the defendant had not been put in peril of conviction on it. (However, on the ground of abuse of process the Court set aside the summons – the alleged victim had not told the court, as he should have done, when he applied for the issuance of the second summons about there being a first trial and what had happened then.)

1 [1990] 1 QB 54.

3.39 The same point was also made in *R v Liverpool Magistrates, ex p Slade*. If a summons is withdrawn before a trial and therefore as a result the case is dismissed, a plea of AA cannot be made in relation to a subsequent summons for the same offence because there has been no earlier trial on the merits. See also *Brookes*[2] where acceptance by the prosecution of a plea of not guilty to GBH (s 20 Offences Against the Person Act 1861) did not establish a plea of AA to bar a subsequent charge of GBH with intent (s 18).

1 [1995] CrimLR 630.

Notices of Discontinuance

3.40 In the same vein, a plea of AA cannot arise in relation to proceedings which are begun for the same offence charged in earlier proceedings but which are terminated by the prosecution pursuant to it serving a Notice of Discontinuance under s 23 of the Prosecution of Offences Act 1985. There is no inhibition in principle on the prosecution who may wish later to restart proceedings against the same defendant in respect of whom earlier they were discontinued.

3.41 Where 'the accused was, as a matter of fact, never in peril or in jeopardy because the earlier proceedings against him were irregular and/or without jurisdiction' this rule can be broken down into three sub-categories as follows:

(1) Where the summons or charge against the accused has been dismissed before he has pleaded to it: this concerns what was conceptualised by Roujier J in *Williams v DPP*[1] as a 'temporal question'. In *Williams*, a motorist was charged with driving with excess alcohol in his breath. When he was called on to plead at court, before he did so his advocate took a legal objection to the charge, which because of an error in procedure committed by the police was bound to succeed. The prosecution realising their mistake applied for an adjournment to enable the bringing of an amended summons but this was refused by the court who then dismissed the summons. However, subsequently the prosecution having corrected the legal error brought a fresh summons which was now legally unanswerable by the defendant motorist. The defendant pleaded AA contending that because the earlier summons had been dismissed he could not be tried again on a charge based on the same facts. The prosecution conceded that the offence charged in the second proceedings was the same or substantially the same offence as that charged in the first, ie driving on a road after ingesting an excess of alcohol. The issue, however, was whether the defendant had been in jeopardy at the time when the justices dismissed the original charge. Roujier J concluded, pursuant to his 'temporal question', that the first set of proceedings had not reached such a stage that the defendant had been in danger of conviction. He held that this would only have arisen once he had actually pleaded, and only then would he have been in jeopardy or in peril. To support this view, Roujier J quoted with approval the remarks of Lush J in *Haynes v Davies*[2] who held in relation to the expression 'acquittal on the merits' that 'in my view the expression is used by way of antithesis to a dismissal of the charge upon some technical ground which had been a bar to the adjudicating upon it' (page 340).

(2) Dismissal of proceedings against an accused following the withdrawal of a charge by the prosecution on the grounds of its legal defectiveness. The case of *Dabhade* has already been considered in para 3.23. The accused was originally charged with obtaining property by deception but the prosecution offered no evidence and the charge was dismissed. A new charge of theft was subsequently preferred. The accused claimed AA and sought judicial review. The court held that because of the manifest defects in the original charge the accused had in fact never been in danger of conviction in relation to it. The court established as a principle of law that if the summary dismissal of a charge is because it is apparent that it is defective for any reason then the defendant has never been in danger of conviction and so cannot claim AA. There was '*no real sense*' in which it could be said that the defendant was in jeopardy on the first charge. To support this view, the court stated that it would be absurd to prescribe a situation whereby the prosecution keep alive a charge it has no intention of pursuing, merely to defeat a feared attempt of a plea of AA '*in circumstances which are both technical and without merit.*'

If a new charge, which was more appropriate to the facts was substituted, then a consensual dismissal of the original charge and the substitution of a new one does not give rise to AA.

(3) Where the proceedings are a legal nullity, a plea of AA arising from them cannot be pleaded in relation to subsequent proceedings. This rule can be illustrated by two authorities, *Pressick*[3] and *R v Dorking Justices, ex p Harrington*.[4] In both cases the prosecution, at a hearing which was listed for a trial sought an adjournment of it, but this application was refused by the magistrates who also dismissed the charges. Subsequently, the prosecution initiated fresh proceedings in respect of which the accused pleaded AA. In *Pressick* the Divisional Court held that the magistrates had acted within their jurisdiction to refuse the adjournment and to dismiss the charge. They had, therefore, both dismissed on the merits and had acted as a court of competent jurisdiction which subsequently properly founded a plea of AA. The court speculated that only if the proceedings before the magistrates had been a complete nullity would the prosecution properly be able to re-charge the accused.

1 [1991] 1 WLR 1160.
2 [1915] 1 KB 332.
3 [1978] CrimLR 377.
4 [1978] CrimLR 377.

3.42 The possibility of a hearing in this context being adjudged to be a complete nullity, that somehow magistrates could wrongly dismiss a charge and that this could prevent a plea of AA was taken up by Lord Roskill in *ex p Harrington*. He held that the magistrates had acted in a grossly unfair way towards the prosecution, so that their dismissal of the prosecution's summonses was without jurisdiction and was a legal nullity. Lord Roskill held that the magistrates had a duty under the Magistrates' Court Act 1980 to hear the evidence before adjudicating but that they had ignored this. He held, 'the decision of the Justices to dismiss on information is a decision which they have no jurisdiction to take because they were declining to adjudicate upon a matter upon which it was their duty to adjudicate and thus was a nullity' (page 754). Insofar as the defendant was concerned, even though he was blameless for what had occurred at the first trial, he was in Lord Roskill's view never in peril or jeopardy at this trial and therefore double jeopardy would not occur if the trial restarted. (Lord Roskill therefore granted a remedy of mandamus to the prosecution with the effect that the case would be remitted to the magistrates for re-hearing.)

3.43 This decision, it is submitted, appears harsh on the defendant. He could not be held responsible for the magistrates' decision to dismiss and, presumably, he had arrived in court in the expectation (and possibly apprehension) of a trial. For him then to face a complete retrial because of magistrates' misbehaviour seems a prospect which the rules relating to AA and AC were intended to prevent. These rules are defendant-orientated. Furthermore, in *Harrington*, the court cut the link between a defendant's sense of ordeal of being subject to trial and successive legal proceedings against him: the former appearing to have no relevance to the latter. In *Holmes v Campbell*[1] for example, the Divisional Court held that although the magistrates were entitled to dismiss the charges against the defendant, the first hearing was not therefore a nullity as per *Harrington*. Nonetheless, because for legal reasons he could not have been convicted, there was no acquittal on the merits. In *Campbell* the prosecutor did not appear at the trial following a mistake over dates and the summonses were dismissed.

1 QBD CO/776/98 (1998) 162 JP 655.

Instances that do not form a basis for a plea of AC

3.44 *A finding of contempt of court in relation to similar facts in respect of which the accused was subsequently convicted* – In *Sherry*[1] the defendant was convicted of an offence of conspiracy to abduct a child. However, prior to his trial he had been committed to prison for contempt for a violation of a civil court injunction banning him from removing the child from its mother. The defendant claimed that the finding that he was in contempt this consequent punishment constituted a valid plea of AC in relation to his subsequent trial for conspiracy. However, the Court of Appeal disagreed on two grounds:

(a) AC did not arise because the defendant had never previously been charged with the offence of conspiracy and there were no previous proceedings where he could possibly have been convicted of this offence.
(b) In any event, the proceedings for contempt were civil not criminal proceedings and therefore AC could not arise. In *Green*[2] it was held that although a plea of double jeopardy is available in civil as in criminal proceedings, such a plea cannot jump the boundary between those different types of proceedings.

1 [1993] CrimLR 536.
2 [1993] CrimLR 46.

3.45 *A finding of a foreign court of competent jurisdiction that the accused is guilty of the same offence for which he has been tried by an English court but where there is no prospect of the accused being punished by the foreign court in relation to the conviction awarded* – In *Treacy v DPP*[1] Lord Diplock held that AA and AC was 'a doctrine which has always applied whether the previous conviction or acquittal based on the same facts was by an English court or by a foreign court' (page 562). This view was expressed obiter and was not followed subsequently in *Thomas.*[2] Thomas was tried in England for the same conduct for which he had already been convicted in absentia by a court in Italy. He pleaded AC in relation to the English trial. The court rejected this plea holding that the mere fact of a foreign conviction is not, of itself, sufficient to found a plea of AC unless the accused had genuinely been in jeopardy which in this case meant being in jeopardy, of punishment post conviction. On the facts of this case however, Thomas had fled to England and could not subsequently be extradited back to Italy. In view of this, the Court of Appeal held that he was in no real risk of danger of punishment in Italy and therefore had not, in relation to the Italian proceedings, ever been in peril or in jeopardy. The court also took into account the fact that the defendant had been convicted in Italy in absence and had taken no part in his trial there.

1 [1971] AC 537.
2 [1985] QB 604.

3.46 The principle enunciated in *Thomas* concerning the necessary connection between jeopardy or peril and punishment was followed by the Privy Council in *Richards v R.*[1] The Board held that a finding of guilty alone is not a sufficient condition for a plea of AC, that finding has to be accompanied by the infliction of an actual penalty in order for the plea to succeed. Lord Bridge held that the underlying rationale of AC was to prevent double punishment and could therefore only be based on a complete adjudication against the accused which as a matter of definition must include the final disposal of the case by the passing of a sentence.

1 [1993] AC 217.

3.47 *The taking of an offence into consideration when passing sentence for other offences of which the offender has been convicted* – In *Nicholson*[1] the accused was convicted of an offence and at his sentencing he asked for the other offences to be taken into consideration. This occurred. Subsequently his conviction was quashed and the prosecution decided to proceed on those offences. The accused pleaded AC by this was rejected on the ground that he had not been 'convicted' in respect of them. The Court of Appeal, however, also held that the practice of trying a person for such offences was generally undesirable.

1 (1947) 32 Cr App Rep 98.

3.48 *A finding of guilt in disciplinary proceedings, even where that finding is followed by the imposition of a penalty* – In *Hogan*,[1] prison escapees were punished by justices with loss of remission pursuant to the Prison Rules. Subsequently, they stood trial for an offence of escaping by force and pleaded AC. This was rejected.

1 [1960] 2 QB 513.

3.49 This issue also arose in *Secretary of State for Trade and Industry v Baker.*[1] Baker was a director of the Barings Group which collapsed following the discovery of unauthorised trading on a massive scale by Nick Leeson. Subsequently, at the suit of the Secretary of State, a Company Directors Disqualification Act action was launched against Baker. He argued that these proceedings infringed the principle against double jeopardy because he actually had already had to face disciplinary proceedings brought against him by his regulator, the

Securities and Futures Authority (SFA). Those proceedings had been based substantially on the same conduct as that on which the disqualification proceedings were founded. This claim was rejected, the Court of Appeal finding that the SFA proceedings were concerned with whether Baker had professional competence (and was therefore a fit and proper person to run a bank) whereas the CDDA action was concerned with whether acting as a director of a company, he was unfit to be concerned with its management.

1 (1998) Times, 6 July.

Procedure on Autrefois Pleas

3.50 The most obvious moment for pleading autrefois is at arraignment but before the indictment is put to the accused. If the accused is legally represented the conventional procedure is for the plea to be entered in writing and signed by Counsel using the following form of words: '[Name of Accused] says that the Queen ought not further to prosecute the indictment against him/her because he has been lawfully acquitted/convicted of the offence charged therein. Having made the plea the prosecution must either admit it is good or join issue. Pursuant to s 122 of the Criminal Justice Act 1988 it is then the role of the trial judge sitting without a jury to determine whether the plea is correctly made or not.'

3.51 In *Coughlan*[1] the Court of Appeal held that if a person enters a plea of AA/AC they must establish their plea on a balance of probabilities pursuant to the sixth principle formulated by Lord Morris in *Connelly* (see paras 3.5 and 3.9). Evidence can be called in support of contentions made by either side as if the hearing were a voir dir. The court can also consider the validity of the earlier court's jurisdiction, see *West.*[2] If the plea succeeds it bars any further proceedings in relation to the Indictment. If it fails, the indictment must then be put and the accused can then plead guilty or not guilty in the normal way.

1 (1976) 63 Cr App Rep 33.
2 See para 3.34.

3.52 A plea can be made at any time during the currency of the criminal proceedings even after the accused has pleaded guilty. In *Cooper v New Forest District Council*[1] the accused pleaded guilty to various breaches of planning enforcement notices and was sentenced by the magistrates. Subsequently, the accused was advised that a plea of autrefois was available and he appealed to the Crown Court acting in its appellant capacity. The Crown Court refused the appeal because of the previous unequivocal plea of guilty before the magistrates. The accused sought judicial review of this refusal and the Divisional Court held that despite the plea of guilty, a plea in bar was so fundamental to the fairness of the proceedings and was a special plea that the Crown Court should accept the plea and consider it.

1 [1992] CrimLR 877.

STATUTORY EXCEPTIONS TO THE AUTREFOIS RULE

1. Case stated

Pursuant to s 111 of the Magistrates' Courts Act 1980 the prosecution may appeal to the Divisional Court in the case of a summary acquittal on the ground that the acquittal 'is wrong in law or is an excess of jurisdiction'. If the prosecution appeal succeeds, the Divisional Court can substitute its own finding or order a re-hearing.

2. Appeal to the House of Lords

Pursuant to the Administration of Justice Act 1960 ss 1, 2 when the Court of Appeal quashes a conviction, the prosecution can appeal to the House of Lords.

3. Re-trial following successful appeal against conviction

Pursuant to s 1 Criminal Appeal Act 1964, the Court of Appeal has the power to order retrial whenever it allows an appeal against conviction if this is in the interests of justice.

4. Tainted acquittals

Pursuant to the ss 54-56 Criminal Procedure and Investigations Act 1996. A procedure has been created whereby a person can be retried for an offence for which he or she has already been acquitted so long as that acquittal is judged to be 'tainted'.

These sections were inserted into the CPIA as a result of fears concerning the practice of 'jury nobbling'. Such was the concern that major criminals were evading justice by corrupting or intimidating jurors that Parliament created an unprecedented procedure whereby a valid acquittal could be quashed by the High Court if it was satisfied that four conditions set out in s 55 were satisfied. The first condition, the most significant for present purposes, is as follows: 'that it appears to the High Court likely that, but for the interference or intimidation [of a juror or witness], the acquitted person would not have been acquitted.'

No application has yet been made to quash an acquittal.

5. Section 33 Army Act 1955
Person tried by a court martial shall not subsequently retried by a civil court.

6. Section 27 Magistrates' Court Act 1987
'Where on the summary trial of an information for an offence triable either way the court dismissed the information, the dismissal shall have the same effect as an acquittal on an indictment.'

7. Extradition
Pursuant to s (3) of the Extradition Act 1989, 'a person accused of an offence shall not be returned or committed or kept in custody for the purpose of return if it appears to be appropriate authority that if charged with that offence in the United Kingdom he would be entitled to be discharged under any rule of law relating to this acquittal or conviction.'

It therefore follows that extradition will be prohibited by s 6(3) in circumstances where had the conduct alleged by the requesting state been committed in the United Kingdom and the Crown sought a trial on charges arising from that conduct, either a plea of AA or AC would available or the indictment would be stayed as an abuse of process.

Bearing in mind that the direction of European criminal law is for ever increasing co-operation in cross-border fraud,[1] this issue was one of increasing importance. If one state decides to prosecute in respect of an overall fraud and another stay its hand, the question arises whether the state which has stayed its hand can later obtain extradition in respect of substantially the same matters as those in which there have been an acquittal or a decision not to pursue prosecution has been taken.

1 See the Shengen Convention Title III, Chap 11. Also, an authoritative analysis of European conventions on mutual assistance which contain references to double jeopardy in Van den Wyngaert, *International Criminal Law* (1997) Kluwer.

ABUSE OF PROCESS

3.53 The starting point for any consideration of the law of abuse of process in relation to double jeopardy is the House of Lords decision in *Connelly.*[1]

1 See para 3.5.

3.54 In *Connelly*, one of the grounds of appeal was that the trial judge in the second trial was wrong to hold that he had no discretion to stay the proceedings even if he held that they were unfair. Before the House, Connelly contended that a court possessed an inherent power to protect an accused against abuses of criminal procedure. Notwithstanding the narrowness of the availability of the pleas in bar, the court could, pursuant to this power, stay the proceedings if it felt the trial would be unfair. The issues of whether a criminal court possessed such power beyond the scope of the pleas in bar and whether a court had any overall responsibility to ensure the fairness of the proceedings before it preoccupied the speeches of all five Law Lords.

3.55 Lord Morris contended that a court did not have the power to stay a prosecution because it judged it to be unfair unless this unfairness came within the scope of a plea in bar. His view can be encapsulated from the following short extracts from his speech:

> '... that generally speaking a prosecutor has as much right as a defendant to demand a verdict of a jury on an outstanding indictment, and where either demands a verdict a judge has no jurisdiction to stand in the way of it ... It would in my judgment, be an unfortunate innovation if it were held that the power of a court to prevent any abuse of its process or to ensure compliance with correct procedure enabled a judge to suppress a prosecution merely because he regretted that it was taking place. There is no abuse of process if to a charge which is properly brought before the court and which is framed in an indictment to which no objection can in any way be taken there is no plea such as that of autrefois acquit or convict which can successfully be made'(page 1304).

3.56 However, Lord Morris did concede that: 'There is inherent in our criminal administration a policy and a tradition that even in the case of wrongdoers, there must be an avoidance of anything that savours of oppression ... The power to prevent abuses of its own process and to control its own procedure must in the criminal court, include a power to safeguard an accused from oppression or prejudice' (page 1301).

3.57 Lord Devlin expressing the majority view disagreed with Lord Morris. He held that the courts did possess an inherent jurisdiction to enforce rules in order to ensure that the court's process was used fairly. He stated '... a general power, taking various specific forms, to prevent unfairness to the accused has always been a part of the English criminal law, and I shall illustrate this with special reference to the framing of the indictments. Secondly, if the power of the prosecutor to spread his case over any number of indictments was unrestrained there could be grave injustice to defendants. Thirdly, a controlling power of this character is well established in the civil law' (page 1347).

3.58 Later Lord Devlin added in a passage which has now become famous for both its statement of principle and its prescience: 'The fact that the Crown has, as is to be expected, and that private prosecutors have (as is also to be expected, for they are usually public authorities) generally behaved with great propriety in the conduct of prosecutions, up till now avoided the need for any consideration of this point. Now that it emerges, it is seen to be one of great constitutional importance. Are the courts to rely on the Executive to protect their process from abuse? Have they not themselves an inescapable duty to secure fair treatment for those who come or are brought before them? To questions of this sort there is only one possible answer. The courts cannot contemplate for a moment the transference to the Executive of the responsibility for seeing that the process of law is not abused' (page 1354). Lord Devlin argued that the courts have always possessed a general power to prevent any unfairness to an accused, this after all was the basis for the development of the Judge's Rules and the common law duty of prosecution disclosure.[1]

1 Rules were formulated in various cases concerned with the questioning of suspects in police detention. They were superceded by the codes of practice created by PACE.

3.59 With particular regard to the possibility of sequential trials, ie where a defendant faces separate proceedings arising out of the same events albeit that different offences are alleged, Lord Devlin held that these were normally to be regarded as oppressive; 'a second trial on the same or similar facts is not always and necessarily oppressive and there may be in a particular case special circumstances which make it just and convenient in that case.' Once special circumstances are absented, then the rule is that sequential prosecutions or trials are to be stayed.

3.60 Lord Pearce agreed with Lord Devlin, that a court must possess an inherent power to ensure the fairness of its proceedings. Furthermore, he observed that this power could not be constrained within the limits of extant pleas in bar. He concluded: 'It is clear that the formal pleas [in bar] which a defendant can claim as of right will not cover all such cases. Instead of attempting to enlarge the please beyond their proper scope, it is better that the courts should apply to such cases and avowed judicial discretion based on broader principles which underlie the pleas' (page 1364). Lord Reid, in his speech, of only one page, agreed with the speeches of Lord Devlin and Lord Pearce holding that: 'There must always be a residual discretion to prevent anything which savours of abuse of process' (page 1296).

Issue Estoppel

3.61 One of the issues considered by the House of Lords in *Connelly* was whether the doctrine of issue estoppel applied to criminal cases and whether it was available as a plea in bar to an indictment. The doctrine can be defined as follows: if in the course of deciding a total cause of action, one specific issue is determined, then if that issue arises as an essential ingredient in subsequent proceedings between the same parties, that issue cannot be re-litigated.

3.62 In *Connelly* the defence contended that the doctrine did apply and operated in favour of the accused which should have prevented his second trial for robbery. On the facts (see para 3.11) the defence contended that the quashing of the murder conviction must constitute a finding in favour of the defendant on the essential issue of alibi, ie the court must have held that his alibi was correct and therefore vis-à-vis the second trial, and that the prosecution could not seek to argue that he was present during the robbery. While this submission was rejected, the availability of the doctrine was not decided by the House in *Connelly*, the matter being left to the consideration of the House in *Humphrys*.[1] There the House held that the doctrine had no place in English criminal proceedings. The House held that as it cannot be known how juries arrive at their verdicts, reasons never being given, it would be an exercise fraught with both speculation and uncertainty in a particular case as to what issues a jury had determined in favour of the defence and what in favour of the prosecution.

1 See para 3.6.

3.63 It is submitted, however, that the doctrine does still survive, albeit in a rudimentary form. In *Hay*[1] the defendant was alleged to have made a statement to the police admitting two unrelated offences, burglary and arson. He was tried first on the arson charge and having asserted that his admissions were fabricated, was acquitted. Oddly perhaps, the prosecution then decided to press ahead with a second trial for burglary. The defendant wished to assert that his burglary admission was also fabricated and, in support of that claim, to rely on his previous acquittal. The trial judge refused to admit evidence of the acquittal in the first trial. The Court of Appeal disagreed with this refusal holding that the jury's acquittal was conclusive evidence that the defendant was not guilty of arson and his confession to that offence was untrue. They should, therefore, have been made aware of this and directed that in deciding the issue in relation to the burglary they should bear in mind that the admission in relation to the arson made at the same time as that appertaining to the burglary, had to be regarded as untrue. As the editors of Archbold state, 'there is a fine distinction between the principle in this case and the principle that issue estoppel has no place in criminal proceedings' (para 4-331 1999 edition).

1 (1983) 77 Cr App Rep 70. See also *R v B* (unreported, 3 December 1999).

3.64 This distinction was somewhat exploded by Lord Lane CJ in *H*[1] who stated that fairness, rather than any remote or abstruse legal principle, was the basis upon which a judge's reasoning should be based. Lord Lane clearly believed that issue estoppel was unnecessary in view of the availability of the abuse of process discretion in a double jeopardy context.

1 (1989) 90 Cr App Rep 440.

3.65 The effect of this rejection of issue estoppel from our jurisprudence on abuse of process can also be illustrated by *ex p Reeves.*[1] Here, the accused's submission of no case to answer in respect of various charges against him was upheld by the magistrates at the committal and he was discharged in respect of them. Subsequently, the prosecution effectively restarted its case and recharged the same offences. The accused pleaded both AA and issue estoppel and the case went to the Divisional Court. Ackner LJ dismissed both pleas: AA did not arise because, as had been held in *Snelson,*[2] AA does not lie in respect of a discharge at committal proceedings. In relation to issue estoppel, despite the fact that the magistrates had already explicitly and directly considered and dismissed the charges against him, it could not be asserted, because of the decision in *Humphrys* which rejected the applicability of the doctrine. Ackner LJ, however, held that the court was not powerless to stymie repeated attempts by the prosecution to have the accused committed for trial. If following scrutiny of all the circumstances such attempts were vexatious and/or oppressive and therefore constituted an abuse of process, the case could be stayed.

1 See para 3.37.
2 See para 3.37.

3.66 Bearing in mind this wholesale rejection of issue estoppel, a doctrine which ironically is regarded as a fundamental part of US jurisprudence concerned with double jeopardy, three observations can be made:

(1) In accepting that abuse of process should be the principal remedy against situations of double jeopardy, the House in *Humphrys* in effect decided that the court's approach would be based on discretionary concepts of fairness and not on doctrinal and abstruse concepts of estoppel. See paras 3.62 to 3.65.

(2) In determining whether proceedings were fair or unfair, a court of review should avoid being drawn into an assessment of how for example the jury arrived at its verdict. To avoid any temptation of creating a notional but fictional rational jury in order to then decide how such a jury would have arrived at its verdict upon a particular issue which the defence would seek to foreclose from consideration in subsequent proceedings.

(3) In considering pursuant to its abuse jurisdiction whether a second trial for the defendant would be unfair or oppressive, a court can certainly consider what issues were aired in the first trial and whether they were resolved in favour of the defence. If so, then this is highly relevant to a consideration of whether in relation to the same general allegations or issues, a defendant should be in danger of being tried twice. See para 3.86 for consideration of the ruling of Buckley J in *Maxwell*.[1]

1 CCC (September 1996, unreported).

AUTHORITIES POST CONNELLY

3.67 The House in *Connelly* having held that courts had an inherent jurisdiction to stay prosecutions on the grounds of unfairness created by double jeopardy, it was then left to the courts to apply it whenever necessary. The first post, Connelly authority was *Riebold*.[1] In *Riebold* the two accused were indicted on 29 counts, the first two being counts of conspiracy. The remaining 27 related to overt acts which were relied on by the prosecution as acts in furtherance of the conspiracy and therefore probative of the conspiracy counts. At the first trial the prosecution proceeded only on the second count of conspiracy. The defendants were acquitted. The prosecution then sought leave to proceed on all the remaining counts. Barry J refused leave on the ground that the prosecution was effectively seeking to secure a retrial of the whole case. He held that the subject matter of counts 3 to 29, 'did in fact constitute the whole of the overt acts of conspiracy on which the prosecution relied, and there were no additional facts or evidence on which the prosecution relied in order to secure a conviction on the conspiracy charge' (page 656). It is submitted that *Riebold* is an important authority. It establishes that it is not permissible for prosecutors to enjoy a free licence to have, using a colloquialism, a 'second bite of the cherry'. In *Riebold*, the defendants having been acquitted in circumstances where the Prosecution had carefully chosen which count to proceed on in the first trial, were entitled to expect that a second trial would not commence against them based on the same evidence given in the first trial. The prosecution's desire to maximise the chances of a conviction needed to be constrained by the values of both fairness and avoidance of oppression.

1 [1967] 1 WLR 674.

3.68 Post-*Riebold*, double jeopardy was reconsidered by the House in *Humphrys*. It is apparent from reading of the speeches delivered in that case that the Lords were concerned that their decision in *Connelly* would be interpreted by lower courts as tantamount to a near unbridled discretion to stop prosecutions if the tribunal felt that they were unfair or oppressive. The Lords sought to correct this perceived error and make plain that a judge should only intervene where there is, on the clearest grounds, an abuse. For example, Lord Salmon said: '... a judge [has no] power to refuse to allow a prosecution to proceed merely because he considers that, as a matter of policy, it ought not to have been brought. It is only if the prosecution amounts to an abuse of process of the Court and is oppressive and vexatious that the judge has the power to intervene' (page 46). Viscount Dilhorne echoed similar sentiments warning that the power to stop a prosecution should only be used 'in the most exceptional circumstances'. He continued, 'a judge has no power to quash a properly preferred indictment because he thinks that the prosecution of the defendant for the defence should not have been instituted' (page 509). Further, 'the judge must not appear to have any responsibility for the institution of a prosecution' (page 511).

1 See para 3.6.

3.69 Courts have since *Humphrys* intermittently felt it necessary to restate similar principles, perhaps perceiving that various tribunals have shown an undue willingness to stay prosecutions. A recent example would be the judgment of Bingham CJ in *Enviroment Agency v Stanford*[1] who, in that case, felt that a magistrate had improperly refused to commit a defendant for trial in view of a perceived abuse. Lord Bingham stated that even if on reasonable grounds a court considers that a prosecution should never have been brought, such views are only to be reflected in mitigation of the sentence imposed. Furthermore, it was of no benefit to the defendant if a stay was granted by the magistrate if this were only to be reversed on appeal.

1 [1998] COD 373.

3.70 Post *Humphrys*, the main authorities concerning double jeopardy can be considered.

'Same activity' cases

3.71 Cases concerned with this theme are largely road traffic cases. In *Moxon-Tritsch*[1] the defendant was convicted of driving without due care and attention and driving with excess alcohol. Subsequently, a private prosecution was instituted for causing death by reckless driving. The defendant applied for a stay which was successful. It was clear that the proposed prosecution arose from the same facts as those on which the defendant had already been convicted. In essence the case was concerned with whether the court should countenance a situation where one conviction is followed by a prosecution for a greater and encompassing offence, where the defendant's careless driving necessarily being subsumed into the question of whether such driving was also reckless. Faulks J was satisfied that it would be an abuse to allow the private prosecution to continue. It would be oppressive for the defendant to be tried twice for a more aggravated form of the same offence to which she had already pleaded guilty and she had suffered enough.

1 [1988] CrimLR 46.

3.72 A similar situation arose in *R v Forest of Dean Justices, ex p Farley*[1] where there was a clear overlap of fact between two charges of driving with excess alcohol and causing death by reckless driving. The defendant was charged with both offences but was brought before the Justices first only for the offence of driving with excess alcohol. His application for an adjournment of this charge until after the determination of the graver charge, causing death by reckless driving, was resisted by the prosecution. The prosecution submitted that the summary offence should be dealt with as it was important to ascertain in relation to the graver offence whether the defendant had driven with excess alcohol. Furthermore, so the prosecution contended, a conviction for this offence would then mean that at the trial of the graver offence, the defendant would have the burden of proof establishing that his driving was not reckless. In other words, the prosecution were making plain that their wish was to have a trial in the magistrates' court for the purpose of obtaining evidence to use against the defendant at a later trial in the Crown Court for a more serious offence.

1 [1990] RTR 228.

3.73 The defence argued that this was unfair and was an abuse, particularly because the defendant would be forced to give evidence at two separate trials and would be open to cross-examination at the second trial on any discrepancy between these two sets of evidence. The prosecution riposte to this submission was that the prosecution enjoyed a discretion of how to proceed with cases, and in any event, the unfairness could be dealt with by the trial judge under s 78 of PACE.

3.74 The Divisional Court held that the prosecution's attempt to reverse the burden of proof constituted an abuse. Neil J relied on the general 'rule' that after trial on a lesser charge, a person should not be tried again on the same facts for a more serious offence.

3.75 These cases can be contrasted with the situation in *R v Thomson Holidays Ltd.*[1] Here, the defendants pleaded guilty to an offence under the Trade Descriptions Act 1968 in relation to the making of false statements in a travel brochure. The statements related to a particular hotel in Greece and its amenities. One year later they were charged with the same provision in relation to the same statement. Both prosecutions had arisen from separate complaints made by people who had booked separate holidays at the hotel. The defendants submitted that the second proceedings constituted an abuse. The Court of Appeal however, disagreed holding that the Trade Descriptions Act contemplated that more than one prosecution could be brought in respect of the same course of conduct, the Act was designed to protect the public as individuals.

1 [1974] QB 592.

Separate prosecutions by different prosecution agencies: Sequential trials and special circumstances

3.76 The diversity of statutes creating criminal offences had led to a diversity of separate and independent prosecutors. An important example of lack of co-ordination leading to the finding of an abuse was *R v Beedie*.[1] In *Beedie* a tenant died of carbon monoxide poisoning caused by defects in a gas fire in premises owned by the defendant landlord. The death was investigated by a variety of agencies including the Health and Safety Executive (HSE) and the police. Before the police reported to the Crown Prosecution Service concerning a prosecution by it, the landlord had already been charged and convicted at the behest of the HSE in relation to offences against the Health and Safety at Work Act. Furthermore, the local authority had also prosecuted him in relation to dangerous gas fires. Only after these two convictions and an inquest was the landlord charged with manslaughter by the police and the case taken up by the CPS.

1 [1998] QB 356.

3.77 At the trial the landlord pleaded both AC and argued for a stay. The judge rejected both grounds. The defendant's appeal was principally based on whether the judge should have stayed the prosecution because of the rule established in *Connelly* that apart from special circumstances, there should be no sequential trials on an ascending scale of gravity.[1] In recognising this rule and applying it in this case, the Court of Appeal held that the rule is not part of the doctrine of autrefois but it should, in the absence of exceptional circumstances, give rise to the exercise of the wider discretionary power to stay proceedings as an abuse. Here, the charge of manslaughter should have been stayed because of the previous sets of proceedings and, in the Court's view, there were no special circumstances which should have persuaded the judge not to have done this. Rose LJ opined that, for example, the rule might be overruled where a charge of murder or manslaughter was brought where the victim has died after proceedings for assault. The additional fact of the death means that exceptional circumstances would exist.

1 See page 3.17 for Lord Devlin's judgment in this regard.

3.78 Another illustration of 'special circumstances' is the decision of the Court of Appeal for Gibraltar in *A-G for Gibraltar v Leoni.*[1] In that case the Court held that the discovery of new evidence may amount to be special circumstance.

1 Criminal Appeal No 4 (1998).

3.79 An instance of the rule against sequential trials not being applied was in *R v South Hampshire Magistrates' Court, ex p Crown Prosecution Service*[1] where the defendant was tried in December 1995 and acquitted. In January 1996 along with others he was re-arrested and charged with a series of connected but different offences. He argued that the failure of the prosecution to consolidate all their charges against him in one indictment and in one trial was an abuse. At committal the magistrates agreed but the Divisional Court on a judicial review application brought by the DPP, disagreed. A second trial on the same or similar facts was in the view of the court, not necessarily oppressive and in this case there were special circumstances which made it just and convenient for there to be two trials: for example the lack of a significant evidential overlap between the two proceedings and the delay to the first trial which would have occurred had it not proceeded but been consolidated with the second.

1 [1998] CrimLR 422.

Repeated committal proceedings cases

3.80 In *R v Manchester City Stipendiary Magistrate, ex p Snelson*[1] it was held that a discharge at committal proceedings did not prohibit fresh committal proceedings for the same offence. The doctrine of AA did not apply neither was it an abuse. However, in *R v Horsham Justices, ex p Reeves*[2] it was held that the second set of committal proceedings should be stayed as an abuse. The court held in this case that the prosecution had treated the first set of proceedings as a 'dummy run' and having learned lessons had brought the same proceedings albeit in a simplified form. Ackner LJ began his judgment stating that the case provided a cautionary tale 'the moral of which is do not overload a prosecution with unnecessary charges' (page 236). He held that to allow the prosecution to proceed would be wrong, 'to grant such an indulgence would in my judgment, encourage poor preparation with a resultant waste of time and money ... the prosecution must direct its energies to the simplification of cases they desire to proceed' (page 240). In a call for such simplification Ackner LJ said: 'All too often juries, and to a lesser extent magistrates, are treated like computers into whom superfluous and ill-digested material is fed in the over-optimistic hope that somehow or another they will produce the right result' (page 240).

1 (1977) 66 Cr App Rep 44.
2 (1980) 75 Cr App Rep 236n.

3.81 *Reeves* was, however, distinguished in *R v Willesden Justices, ex p Clemmings.*[1] Here the first set of committal proceedings had been dismissed by the magistrates for failure to serve the advance information on time. A fortnight later the defendant had been recharged and the advance information properly served. The defendant relying on *Reeves*, argued that this was an abuse. Bingham LJ disagreed. In refusing a stay Bingham LJ said: 'The ultimate objective of this discretionary power is to ensure that there shall be a fair trial according to law which involves fairness both to the defendant and the prosecution, for as Lord Diplock said in *Sang* "The fairness of the trial ... is not all one sided".' In his view, the decision to recharge the defendant was not manifestly unreasonable, there was no evidence that the second proceedings would unfairly prejudice the defendant and finally there was no evidence of a prosecution desire to deprive the defendant of any lawful protection.

1 (1987) 87 Cr App Rep 280.

Sequential trials in complex trials arising out of severance of the indictment

3.82 Particularly in the area of serious or complex fraud, the courts have repeatedly emphasized the need for severance of an indictment so as to ensure manageable and not unduly long trials.[1] The best example of a prosecutor's failure to heed this exhortation was the *Blue Arrow* case. The Serious Fraud Office's (SFO) prosecution of *R v Cohen*[2] where the Court of Appeal criticised both the trial judge and the SFO for failing to exercise the power of severance to ensure a fair and manageable trial. The consequence of severance, however, must be more than one trial.

1 See for example *R v Novac* (1976) 65 Cr App Rep 107 and *R v Kellard* (1995) 2 Cr App Rep 134.
2 Court of Appeal (28 July 1992, unreported).

3.83 In the context of double jeopardy, the interplay between severance and abuse arose in the proposed second trial of Kevin Maxwell following his acquittal in the first. Prior to the first trial, with the consent of all concerned, the SFO had severed the indictment accepting that not all counts could be tried together. At the first trial, Kevin Maxwell and the other defendants were tried on only two counts (counts 4 and 10) of the original ten-count indictment on which they were arraigned. Following the acquittal on these counts the prosecution proposed a second trial of counts 1, 2 and 9. The prosecution contended that these counts were in a separate category from 4 and 10 and factual issues in the first trial would not need to be relitigated in the second.

3.84 In answer to the defence contention that it would be oppressive for Kevin Maxwell to be tried again the prosecution contended that the second trial was a result of the earlier severance of the indictment which the defence had agreed to. Furthermore, the prosecution had agreed to this respecting the courts' entreaties to avoid long trials. Were a second trial to be stayed it would mean that mere complexity of the issues would result in the prosecution being unfairly and permanently deprived of presenting a significant part of its case to a jury. How then could it be unfair and an abuse of the court's process for it to proceed with the second trial?

3.85 The defence fundamentally disagreed arguing that all along the prosecution's case had been presented as one continuing offence of fraud and that in any event, it would be impossible to separate the factual issues raised in the first trial from those to be raised in the second. For example Kevin Maxwell's honesty or dishonesty was a central feature in the first trial and it would again be in the second trial.

3.86 Buckley J ruled that a second trial would constitute an abuse. He held that a central theme in the first trial was Kevin Maxwell's alleged dishonesty and that there would be a significant overlap of factual issues between the first and the proposed second trial. Furthermore, he held that the counts, 4 and 10, tried at the first trial, 'constituted a fair presentation of the real dishonesty or fraud alleged by the prosecution ... I have no doubt that those were clearly the most serious examples the prosecution had of the fraudulent course of conduct alleged doubtless that is why they were put forward as a basis for the first trial' (page 22). Buckley J also took cognisance of the fact that 'I have not been referred to any long fraud case in which after an acquittal a further trial has proceeded. Mr Lissack drew my attention to several instances of retrials following abortive first trials or appeals. I do not consider those analogous. In such cases there have been either no acquittal on the merits or determination at all' (page 23). In the most significant passage of his judgment dealing with both the prosecution and the defence submissions Buckley J said:

> 'I wish to make it plain, I am not suggesting that an acquittal even after a long trial necessarily means that severed counts cannot be tried. Each case will turn on its own particular circumstances; there are many factors to be considered as I have already observed. I am suggesting that if all parties have played their part and the essential criminality alleged has been placed before a jury who have acquitted, it should be unusual for a second trial to take place. The reason is that it would be very likely to appear to the public that the authorities were not prepared to accept the verdict of a jury and were determined to pursue the defendant at whatever cost to the public purse, or time, or disruption of the defendant's personal life, business or professional career. But that must not happen' (page 23).

DOUBLE JEOPARDY UNDER EUROPEAN HUMAN RIGHTS LAW

3.87 Bearing in mind that that the rule or prohibition on double jeopardy has been an elemental principle of the English common law for a long period and that English jurists played a major role in the drafting of the European Convention on Human Rights, it is therefore surprising that the Convention itself does not contain any explicit prohibition on double jeopardy. Recognising this omission in the case of *X v Austria*,[1] the Commission held that such a prohibition may be implicit within the terms of Art 6.[2] However, in *S v Germany*[3] the Commission took a contrary view holding that the prohibition was 'neither expressly nor by way of implication' included within Art 6 guarantees.

1 (1970) 35 CD 151.

2 On occasions the Court has been willing to imply into Art 6, guarantees which are not mentioned within its text, eg *Funke v France* (1993) 16 EHRR 297 (Protection against self-incrimination).

3 (1983) 39 DR 43.

3.88 The Seventh Protocol to the Convention is generally concerned with additional fair trial guarantees in criminal cases. Article 2 of the Protocol for example is concerned with the granting of a right to a review of a criminal conviction or sentence. Article 4 is directly concerned with double jeopardy. Before reciting this article, however, it is important to bear in mind that the Protocol has not yet been formally ratified by the United Kingdom and therefore does not form part of the Convention implemented in our domestic law by the Human Rights Act 1998. The Government has indicated an intention to ratify this Protocol, in its White Paper 'Rights Brought Home'[1] it stated that, 'in general, the provisions of Protocol 7 reflect principles already inherent in our law.' Pursuant to the 1998 Act, the Protocol can be made enforceable via an order under s 1(4). This is expected to occur.

1 Cm 3782, page 18.

3.89 Article 4 of Protocol 7 provides:

(1) 'No one shall be liable to be tried or punished again in criminal proceedings under the jurisdiction of the same state for an offence for which he has already been finally acquitted or convicted in accordance with the law and penal procedure of that state.

(2) The provisions of the preceding paragraph shall not prevent the re-opening of the case in accordance with the law and penal procedure of the state concerned, if there is evidence or new or newly discovered facts, or if there has been a fundamental defect in the previous proceedings, which could affect the outcome of the case.

(3) No derogation from the Article shall be made under Art 15 of the Convention'.

In Convention jurisprudence, the rule against double jeopardy is known as the principle of non bis et idem.

3.90 Article 4(1) speaks of 'final acquittal or conviction' and this being 'in accordance with the law and penal procedure of that State.' The Explanatory Report to Protocol 7 states that an acquittal or conviction is only to be regarded as final, 'if, according to the traditional expression, it is has acquired the force of res judicata. This is the case where it is irrevocable, that is to say when no further ordinary remedies are available or when the parties have exhausted such remedies or have permitted the time limit to expire without availing themselves of them'. This in other words means that there is no prohibition on an appeal against acquittal per se, so long as the appeal did not constitute fresh proceedings.

European Court of Human Rights ('ECtHR') authorities

3.91 There are only two authorities concerned with the application of Art 4(1) and unfortunately these are mutually inconsistent. In *Gradinger v Austria*[1] the applicant was convicted of causing death by negligent driving. Subsequently, an administrative penalty was imposed on the applicant for driving with excess alcohol, evidence of alcohol presumably not being available at the original trial. The applicant asserted that the subsequent penalty was a breach of Art 4(1). ECtHR agreed, both charges were based on the same conduct although the offences were different. ECtHR was also persuaded that the administrative authorities who imposed the penalty were 'criminal' for the purposes of this Article. (Had the ECtHR been persuaded that the authorities were in fact 'civil', it would not have found a violation.)

1 (1995) Series A/328-C.

3.92 In *Oliveira v Switzerland*[1] ECtHR held that successive prosecutions were not necessarily via Art 4 if they related to separate offences arising out of the same act. The applicant was originally convicted of a lesser offence of failure to control a motor vehicle and then subsequently for a more serious offence of negligently inflicting personal injury. The applicant complained that she had been prosecuted twice in respect of the same offence but this was rejected. ECtHR held that Art 4, 'does not preclude separate offences, even if they are all part of single criminal act, being tried by different courts especially where, as in the present case, the penalties were not cumulative, the lesser being absorbed by the greater' (para 27).

1 [1998] – V page 1990.

3.93 *Oliveira* therefore suggests that a breach of Art 4(1) occurs only when the offence with which the applicant is charged is, in law, the same offence as that with which he was previously acquitted or convicted. In other words the ambit of Art 4(1) is no further than the autrefois rule considered above.

3.94 It is submitted that there is a conflict between *Gradinger* and *Oliveira*; the former preferring a substantive over a formalistic approach to the principle of double jeopardy whereas the latter preferring the opposite.[1]

1 See the dissenting judgment in *Oliveira* of Repik J.

3.95 Article 4(2) allows for the re-opening of a case after a final decision has been made, when a decision is res judicata. Re-opening in this sense can be contrasted to a fresh prosecution; what is envisaged by Art 4(2) is a way of challenging an acquittal by persuading a higher court to re-open it. Article 4(2) allows for this to occur only on two specified grounds; discovery of new evidence or acceptance that there was a fundamental defect in the original proceedings.

3.96 In relation to tainted acquittals which can now be quashed by the High Court pursuant to ss 54 and 56 of the Criminal Procedure and Investigations Act 1996, it is submitted that as this is consistent with Art 4(2) it must surely be the case that if jurors or witnesses have been intimated or interfered with, this must amount to a 'fundamental defect' in the proceedings.

1 See statutory exceptions to the Autrefois rule after para 3.52.

3.97 It is submitted that based on the above overview of ECtHR authorities, the English law on double jeopardy is consistent with ECtHR law.

3.98 The law concerned with double jeopardy, previously a relatively placid backwater of English criminal law has been disturbed by the outcome of the Lawrence Inquiry which recommended that consideration be given to permitting prosecutions after acquittal where fresh and viable evidence is presented. In July 1999 the Home Secretary referred this issue to the Law Commission who reported back in October 1999 (consultation paper no 156). The Commission will set out its final views on the law in Spring 2000. In relation to discovery of new evidence, the Commission provisionally proposes that the rule against double jeopardy should be subject to an exception where new evidence is discovered after an acquittal. Various safeguards are suggested, for example that the new evidence should only be admissible if the prosecution can establish that it could not, through diligence, have been adduced at the first trial. Overall, the Commission recommended that the rule against double jeopardy should be stated in a statutory form and therefore, in effect, all the jurisprudence concerned with *Connolly* would be abolished.

4. Pre-trial publicity

Knock Knock
Who's there?
Kevin Maxwell
Kevin Maxwell who?
You're on the jury!

4.1 Judicial anxiety concerning the prejudicial effect of pre-trial publicity on criminal trials is not of a recent vintage. A cursory glance at nineteenth century newspapers suggests that coverage of the same sort of crimes that are newsworthy today, for example hooliganism, sexual violence and homicide, was lurid and sensational then. The earliest reported authority of judicial concern on this subject is the judgment of Lord Ellenborough in *R v Fisher*[1] which concerned a rape trial where a newspaper reported that the defendant was guilty of the offence charged. Lord Ellenborough said: 'if anything is more important than another the administration of justice, it is that jurymen should come to the trial of those persons on whose guilt or innocence they are to decide, with minds pure and unprejudiced. Is it possible that they should do so, after having read for weeks and months before, ex parte statements of the evidence against the accused, which the later have no opportunity to disprove or to controvert?' Similar nineteenth century judicial anxiety was expressed in *A-G v Parnell*[2] and by Lord Alverstone CJ in *R v Tibbits*.[3]

1 (1811) 2 Camp 563.
2 (1880) 14 Cox CC 474.
3 [1902] 1 KB 77.

4.2 Traditionally, the responsibility for ensuring that defendants do not suffer 'undue' prejudice from media reported comment is not that of the individual defendant but that of the state itself. A public interest has always been recognised in ensuring that conduct in any form which tends to interfere with the course of justice in particular legal proceedings should be deterred and, if necessary, punished. This has spawned the jurisprudence of criminal contempt of court whereby the state in the personage of the Attorney General has issued proceedings, especially against newspapers where it is felt that reportage has interfered with or perverted the course of justice. While a full consideration of the law relating to criminal contempt is beyond the scope of this chapter, it is important to appreciate that this jurisprudence was the forerunner to that relating to abuse of process. Furthermore, the interrelationship is more than just historical. In seeking to understand the court's abuse of process jurisdiction in the context of pre-trial publicity, it is vital to appreciate that the law on criminal contempt has both shaped and promoted the law relating to pre-trial publicity.

4.3 The law on abuse as it relates to pre-trial publicity is relatively new. Only since the early 1990s have there been decisions on the power and responsibility of the courts, as part of their abuse jurisdiction to stay criminal proceedings on the ground of prejudicial pre-trial publicity. Previously, in the absence of proceedings brought by the Attorney General for such contempt, the courts were unwilling to intervene and accept on the basis of submissions made by the defendant alone that even before the criminal proceedings had begun, there was a risk of unfairness arising out of prior publicity. Why this sudden development or willingness? This is perhaps the result of first, an acceptance that modern media is able to create and orchestrate an unprecedented level of hostility towards a particular defendant, media 'abuses' thus becoming more powerful and insidious. Second, a perception that the state can no longer be relied on exclusively to deter and punish such abuses via actions for contempt or by other means: this perception perhaps going hand in hand with the development of new remedies by the courts especially in the field of public law recognising that the state alone cannot any longer be regarded as the sole guardian of individual rights. Third, in view of the high evidential threshold for contempt introduced by the Contempt of Court Act 1981 and in particular the requirement that each allegedly contemptuous item of publicity be judged in isolation from any others, which together have probably created a climate of prejudice, the test for contempt has increasingly been regarded as less relevant or helpful in an abuse context.

PUBLICITY AND JURY DECISION MAKING

4.4 In our jurisdiction all serious criminal cases are decided on by a jury and not by professional judges. Juries are never asked to provide reasons for their verdicts and indeed it is a criminal offence under the Contempt of Court Act 1981 for individual jurors to be interviewed after a verdict has been delivered as to how it was arrived at. This absence of reasons or inscrutability is in stark contrast to jurisdictions where a judge sits as the tribunal of fact, for example under the Diplock Court regime in Northern Ireland where a High Court Judge sits as the tribunal of fact. If a defendant is convicted, the judge always provides reasons which, furthermore, are directly appealable.

4.5 In proceedings against a particular defendant which has attracted substantial, predominantly hostile publicity and where he is convicted, one can readily appreciate why that defendant may feel he did not receive a fair trial or hearing by the jury. The inscrutability of the jury verdict can do nothing to alleviate this grievance. However, against this is the stark fact that public confidence in the criminal justice system would surely be undermined if notorious defendants accused of horrific crimes could escape justice, not even stand trial, because of adverse publicity.

4.6 Confronting this dilemma the courts have tenaciously grasped the axiom that in criminal trials a jury of ordinary and randomly selected people can be empanelled to try the case objectively. Time and again, English judges have vouchsafed the objectivity and robustness of the traditional English jury where the danger of undesirable 'bias' is excluded.[1] This traditional and endemic view of the English jury is so entrenched by our system that attempts in highly publicised trials to exclude potentially biased jurors by means of questionnaires and so on, have almost always been rejected by trial judges holding that the jury system untouched can be relied on to act dispassionately. Nonetheless, since the early 1990s this conventional wisdom has come under direct attack. There have been cases, to be considered later, where proceedings have been halted or convictions been quashed, at least in part, because of a judicial acceptance that pre-trial publicity rendered a fair trial impossible.

1 Interestingly, the original jury system comprised people from the area where the defendant lived who were expected to use their local knowledge, including their knowledge of the defendant, to judge the plausibility of the prosecution and defence cases.

CONTEMPT OF COURT IN THE CONTEXT OF PRE-TRIAL PUBLICITY

4.7 It has long been recognised by the common law in the realm of contempt that adverse pre-trial publicity can inhibit a fair trial. Perhaps the most famous judicial statement of this is the judgment of Lord Diplock in *A-G v Times Newspapers Ltd*[1] which was concerned with pre-trial reportage by the Sunday Times of the thalidomide scandal. That newspaper intended to print a full story about the scandal and the consequent litigation between the manufacturers, Distillers, and the affected children. Distillers complained about this to the Attorney General who then sought an injunction banning publication. Lord Diplock in granting the Attorney's application said: 'the due administration of justice requires ... that all citizens ... should be able to rely upon obtaining in the courts the arbitrament of a tribunal which is free from bias against any party and whose decision be based upon those facts only that have been proved in evidence and deduced before it in accordance with the procedure adopted in courts of law; and ... that, once the dispute has been submitted to a court of law, they should be able to rely upon there being no usurpation by any other person of the function of the court to decide it according to law' (page 309). Lord Diplock was therefore of the view that if the due administration of justice is hindered or usurped then the result must be that the trial will be unfair.

1 [1974] AC 273.

4.8 In a later case *A-G v English*[1] Lord Diplock said: 'trial by newspaper, or as it should be more compendiously expressed today, trial by the media is not to be permitted in this country ... the true course of justice must not at any stage be put at risk' (page 141). In the same case, but sitting in the Divisional Court Watkins LJ expressed the issue in more florid language, 'everyone surely agrees that the well of justice must remain clear. Thus, by one means or another the poison of prejudice must be kept away from it. If it is not, then the possibility of a miscarriage of justice inevitably accompanies prejudice. No-one will know what harm is done except the jury whose verdict, whatever it be, will not inform others as to whether or not it is tainted by prejudice' (page 125).

1 [1983] 1 AC 116.

4.9 The courts' power to prevent or punish instances of prejudicial pre-trial publicity is now governed by the Contempt of Court Act

1981. Pursuant to s 4(2) a judge seised of active proceedings is empowered to make an order banning publication for a defined period of those proceedings. Section 4(2) provides: 'in any such proceedings the court may, where it appears to be necessary for avoiding a substantial risk of prejudice to the administration of justice in those proceedings ... order that the publication of any report of the proceedings be postponed for such period as the court think necessary for that *purpose.*'

4.10 There must therefore be a substantial risk of prejudice which would be caused by publicity. In relation to the jurors being affected by prejudice, in *R v Horsham Justice, ex p Farquhason*[1] Lord Denning MR held that the risk really must be substantial: 'in considering to make an Order under Section 4(2), the sole consideration is the risk of prejudice to be the administration of justice. Whoever has to consider it should remember that at a trial judges are not influenced by what they may have read in the newspapers. Nor are the ordinary folk who sit on juries, they are good sensible people ... the risk of them being influenced is so slight that it can usually be disregarded as insubstantial – and therefore not the subject of an order under s 4(2)' (page 794).

1 [1982] QB 762.

4.11 In cases concerned with the application of a s 4(2) order, and in particular with the meaning of a substantial risk of prejudice, the appellate courts have emphasised the need for judicial restraint. Such restraint has been encouraged first, by emphasising in general terms the competing public interests involved, in particular the desirability of ensuring freedom of expression and open justice. Second, as the quote from Lord Denning MR in para 4.10 shows, the courts have also evinced a belief that judges and jurors are able to discard from their thinking, prejudicial publicity. Eleven years after Lord Denning's views in *Farquhason, ex p Telegraph plc*[1] Lord Taylor CJ in this context said: 'In determining whether publication of matter would cause a substantial risk of prejudice to a future trial, a court should credit the jury with the will and ability to provide by the Judge's direction to decide the case only on the evidence before them. The court should also bear in mind the staying power and the detail of publicity, even in case of notoriety, are limited and that the nature of the trial is to focus the jury's minds on the evidence before them rather than matters outside the courtroom' (page 987).

1 [1993] 1 WLR 980.

4.12 However, the courts have on occasions accepted that a banning order under s 4(2) is required, otherwise the anticipated publicity would imperil the fairness of future criminal proceedings. For example, in *A-G v Steadman*[1] Bell J granted an injunction against any performances of 'Maxwell; the Musical' a satirical and disparaging play about the life of the late Robert Maxwell on the grounds that it would prejudice the forthcoming trial of his sons, Kevin and Ian.

1 (February 1995, unreported).

4.13 In addition to giving the courts a preventative power pursuant to s 4, the Act also provides a 'strict liability' rule of contempt. An intention to cause prejudice is not an essential element of the contempt. What matters is the effect of the publicity on active proceedings. By s 2(2) this rule, 'applies only to a publication which creates a substantial risk that the course of justice in the proceedings in question will be seriously impeded or prejudiced'. There has been a great deal of jurisprudence on the meaning of the terms 'substantial risk' and 'serious prejudice.' In *A-G v Hat Trick Productions Ltd*[1] Auld LJ said: 'Serious prejudice is not capable of useful paraphrase save possibly as something which puts the course of justice at risk, as, in a criminal trial, by affecting its outcome or necessitating the discharge of the jury' (page 5). In that case Auld LJ held that a broadcast from an episode of 'Have I Got News for You' which denigrated Ian and Kevin Maxwell six months before their trial did create a substantial risk of serious prejudice against them. During the programme Angus Deayton had said: 'The BBC are in fact cracking down on references to Ian and Kevin Maxwell just in case programme makers appear biased in their treatment of these two heartless scheming bastards.'

1 [1997] EMLR 76.

4.14 In a *A-G v Associated Newspapers*[1] a contempt was held arising out of prejudicial publicity in the Evening Standard against various defendants who were, at the date of publication, on trial for serious offences. The newspaper correctly informed its readers that those defendants currently on trail for prison escape, were convicted IRA terrorists. The trial judge held this disclosure was very prejudicial to the defendants and stayed the trial. Subsequently the High Court in effect upheld this view by holding pursuant to s 2(2) that the newspaper had committed a contempt.

1 31 October 1997, unreported.

4.15 These cases demonstrate the existence of a concern which the courts have regarding the prejudicial effects of media coverage. Using the test of s 2(2), the courts have on occasions been satisfied beyond reasonable doubt that pre-trial publicity has created a serious risk of substantial prejudice.

ABUSE OF PROCESS

4.16 The courts power to halt criminal proceedings on the grounds of publicity is a sub-species of its overall 'abuse of process' jurisdiction. This jurisdiction provides both a duty and a power to protect a defendant from having to undergo a trial which for any reason is unfair. In *R v Horseferry Road Magistrates' Court, ex p Bennett*[1] Lord Lowry succinctly explained the jurisdiction as follows: 'either (1) because it will be impossible (usually because of delay) to give the accused a fair trial or (2) because it offends the courts sense of justice and propriety to be asked to try the accused in the circumstances of a particular case' (page 116). In other words Lord Lowry recognised that if a fair trial cannot be held the proceedings should be stayed, no matter what causes the unfairness.[2]

1 [1994] AC 42.
2 All the members of the House of Lords in *Bennett* agreed with Lord Lowry's opposition in this regard. The dissenting judgment of Lord Oliver was concerned with a different point.

4.17 In the abuse context, just as in the cases on contempt considered in paras 4.7 to 4.14, judicial faith in the will and the ability of jurors to ignore any potential prejudicial effect of publicity has always been expressed. This is hardly surprising in view of it being a fundamental tenet of our system that jury trial provides the fairest and most reliable method of determining guilt or innocence. It must be presupposed that the jury will try the case according to the evidence. Perhaps the most frequently quoted reference of this faith in the jury is the robust judgment of Lawton J in *R v Kray*[1] where the notorious Kray twins were on trial only one month after they had been convicted for murder, that first trial having attracted massive media publicity. In rejecting the Kray twins application for a stay of the second trial against them arising out of this publicity Lawton J said:

> 'I have enough confidence in my fellow-countryman to think that they have got newspapers sized up just as they have got other public insti-

> tutions sized up, and they are capable in normal circumstances of looking at a matter fairly and without prejudice even though they have to disregard what they may have read in a newspaper ... it is, however, a matter of human experience, and certainly a matter of the experience of those who practice in the criminal court, first, that the publics recollection is short, and, secondly, that the drama, if I may use that term, of a trial will most almost have the effect of excluding from recollection that which went before. A person summoned for the case would not, in my judgment, disqualify himself merely because he had read any of the newspapers containing allegation of the kind I have referred to; but the position would be different if, as a result of reading what he had, his mind had become so clogged with prejudice that he was unable to try the case impartially' (page 414-5).

1 (1969) 53 Cr App Rep 412.

4.18 Later as Lawton LJ in *R v Coughlan*[1] he expressed a similar view: 'it is our experience that juries in general understand the responsibility which rests upon them ... Juries are capable of disregarding that which is not properly before them. They are expected to disregard what one accused says about another in his absence. If they can do that, which is far from easy, they can disregard what is *said in the newspapers*.'

1 (1976) 64 Cr App Rep 11.

4.19 The views of Lawton LJ have, it is submitted, have been followed by the courts thereafter. In *ex p B*[1] for example Scott Baker J held that Lawton J's observations in *Kray* about juries are as true as in 1994 as they were 25 years ago. Similar sentiments have been expressed in a contempt of court context by Lord Denning MR and Taylor CJ in the cases reported in paras 4.7 to 4.14.

1 (17 February 1994, unreported).

Proximity to trial – the fade factor

4.20 In *A-G v News Group Newspapers*[1] Sir John Donaldson MR said: 'proximity to the trial is clearly a factor of great importance and this trial will not have taken place for another ten months, by which time many wickets will have fallen, not to mention much water having flowed under many bridges, all of which would blunt the impact of publications' (page 16). The courts, as this quotation explains, have adopted the belief that a 'fade factor' is an effective diluter of prejudice. Part of this belief is how juries behave especially in longer complex trials: a gradual focusing of the jury's mind on the evidence before it to the exclusion of all information which has been communicated outside the courtroom. Sir John Donaldson MR said: 'the fact is that for one reason or another a trial by its very nature, seems to cause all concerned to be become progressively more inward looking, studying the evidence given and submissions made to the exclusion of all other sources of enlightenment. This is a well known phenomenon' (page 16). A similar view was expressed by Taylor CJ in *Ex p Telegraph plc*[2] quoted in para 4.11.

1 [1987] 1 QB 1.
2 [1993] 1 WLR 980.

4.21 Belief in this fade factor was confidently asserted by Scott Baker J in *Ex p B*;[1] 'in most cases, one days headline news is the next days fire lighter. Most members of the public do not remember in any detail what they have seen on television, heard on the radio or read in the newspaper except for a very short period of time ... In this country public trust and confidence is placed in juries to decide the facts in all serious criminal cases, and jurors are well able to put out of their minds extraneous material and try the case on the evidence they hear in court' (page 16).

1 [1994] AC 42.

4.22 Based on this line of authorities, there is clearly a widespread judicial scepticism in the context of abuse of process as to pre-trial publicity having any lasting or corrupting effect on the fairness of criminal trials. Such scepticism for reasons described in this chapter already, is unsurprising. Furthermore, until the 1990s it appears that no criminal trial was stayed on this ground. This disbelief in a criminal context as to the effect of publicity after it has occurred, created a disjuncture with the approach of judges in a contempt context the authorities considered in paras 4.7 to 4.15, did recognise this. It is, however, submitted that since the early 1990s this disbelief has been superseded by a more flexible and pragmatic approach.

RECENT LEGAL DEVELOPMENTS ON PRE-TRIAL PUBLICITY

4.23 It is submitted that since the early 1990s there has been an increased judicial willingness to recognise that, in criminal trials, pre-trial publicity can cause a risk of substantial prejudice. The earliest case was *R v McCann*[1] where the Court of Appeal quashed the conviction of alleged Irish terrorists because of the trial judge failed` to discharge the jury following a sudden wave of publicity as it retired to consider its verdict. In *McCann* the alleged target of the terrorist plot, Tom King MP, and also Lord Denning made widely publicised comments suggesting that people who refuse to answer police questions are probably guilty. *McCann* and others had refused to answer such questions. In his judgment Beldam LJ stated that: 'we are left with a definite impression that the impact which those statements and the television interviews may well have had on the fairness of the trial could not be overcome by any direction to the jury' (page 253). Notice, however, that *McCann* is concerned with publicity from senior or authoritative figures occurring at the crucial moment when the jury was about to retire. *McCann* is therefore easy to distinguish on its facts.

1 (1991) 92 Cr App Rep 239.

4.24 A case of far greater significance is the judgment of the Court of Appeal in *R v Taylor and Taylor.*[1] In that case the court took special notice of the adverse publicity which in its view rendered it, 'quite impossible to say that the jury were not influenced in their decision by what they had read in the press' (page 19). While the court did not quash the convictions of the defendants simply on the publicity ground alone it is significant to note that it declined to order a re-trial because, 'by reason of the view taken of the way in which this case was reported, we do not think that a fair trial could now take place' (page 369). In his description of the pre-trial publicity itself McCowan LJ said this: 'in giving leave to appeal, the single judge described that coverage as "unremitting, extensive, sensational, inaccurate and misleading". Having had the opportunity of reading a substantial selection of the newspaper reports in question, we see no reason to dissent from that view' (page 368).

1 (1993) 98 Cr App Rep 361.

4.25 The Court of Appeal's judgment in *Taylor* was followed by the ruling of Garland J in *R v Reade.*[1] Garland J stayed the trial of police officers who were accused of extracting false confessions from members of the Birmingham Six in 1974. Again, as with *Taylor,* the judge in part stayed the trial on the grounds of pre-trial publicity. Two aspects of Garland J's judgment are worthy of special note. First, Garland J accepted that the volume intensity and continuing nature of the publicity against the defendant had a 'snowball effect'.

This snowball effect was the antithesis of the fade factor because in the view of Garland J, each extra bit of added adverse publicity served to fuel and continue the effect of past adverse publicity. Second, because of the enormous publicity concerning the quashing of the convictions of the Birmingham Six, it would be impossible to avoid a jury from having the impression that in quashing those convictions, the Court of Appeal was, as a matter of fact, finding the police officer defendants guilty of conspiracy and perjury.

1 (1993) Independent, 19 October.

4.26 One further aspect of this judgment which deserves mention is the acceptance by Garland J that the prejudice need not be specifically directed at the actual defendants personally. Garland J accepted that the identities of the Birmingham Six police officers was of itself unimportant because the prejudice was generalised and aimed at whichever police officers it was who had allegedly beaten confessions out of the Birmingham Six. Garland J's acceptance of generalised prejudice in this regard can be contrasted with the view of Turner J in *R v Alcindor*[1] which concerned publicity arising out of the capsize of the 'Herald of Free Enterprise'. Here, Turner J held that because the publicity was generalised there was no serious risk of prejudice against the individual defendants.

1 (11 June 1990, unreported).

4.27 Perhaps the most elaborate attempt ever made to persuade a judge to stay proceedings on the grounds of pre-trial publicity was that of Kevin and Ian Maxwell in May 1995. In addition to placing before the trial judge, Phillips J, evidence of allegedly prejudicial newspaper reports and videos of television programmes, the defendants also sought to adduce direct evidence of prejudice by means of findings gathered by opinion polls which they had commissioned from a polling organisation. They commissioned three separate polls in an effort to gauge the public's attitude and depth of prejudice. This was the first time in criminal proceedings that evidence of opinion polls was admitted (although in trademark and passing-off cases such evidence is routinely admissible).[1]

1 See for example *Customglass Boats Ltd v Sorthouse Bros Ltd* [1976] RPC 589 and *Lego System A/S v Lego M Lemelstrich* [1983] FSR 155. Phillips J was not persuaded by the evidence of the opinion pollsters: 'I do not believe I would have reached a significantly different conclusion as to the effects of publicity without the assistance of these [opinion polls] and I hope that their use in this case will not be taken as a precedent in future.'

4.28 After an extensive hearing of the abuse application Phillips J rejected it, holding that the Maxwell brothers could receive a fair trial.[1] However, Phillips J took the opportunity to consider jurisdiction to stay proceedings on the grounds of pre-trial publicity. He first held that: 'I am satisfied that the effect of pre-trial publicity alone can constitute a valid ground for ordering a stay of proceedings' (page 60). Turning to how the courts should approach the question of whether pre-trial publicity has made a fair trial impossible Phillips J said: 'it seems to me that the court will only be justified in staying a trial on the ground of adverse pre-trial publicity, if satisfied on balance of probabilities that if the jury return a verdict of guilty, the effect of the pre-trial publicity will be such as to render that verdict unsafe and unsatisfactory' (page 72). In considering the role of the trial judge faced with an application to stay in these circumstances Phillips J commented that: 'the defendant is likely to have a hard task in establishing that a fair trial is not possible' (page 73). The point Phillips J was making here was that in a case like *Taylor* the trial had concluded and so the Court of Appeal was well placed to evaluate the effect of the publicity and consider the case in its entirety, something which could not be done before the trial had concluded.

1 In the event, Phillips J was proved right because, of course, the brothers were both acquitted.

4.29 On a more general point concerning the Maxwell case it would, it is submitted, be overly simplistic to deduce from the acquittal of the Maxwell brothers that the views of, for example, Lawton J considered in paras 4.17 to 4.19, have been vindicated; ie that the jury can be trusted to exclude all kinds of prejudice. While refusing the application for a stay in Maxwell it is to be recalled that Phillips J did allow the use of an extensive questionnaire, consisting of 40 questions, in order to sift out from the jury panel those persons who invinced any prejudice. The eventual jury was therefore only drawn from the 'survivors' of the much larger panel. How efficacious this highly unusual exercise really was is of course unknown.

POST MAXWELL AUTHORITES

4.30 In *R v Knights*[1] HH Judge Sanders granted a stay of proceedings against the defendant. The judge held that: 'the reporting was unlawful, misleading and scandalous ... certain reporters were determined to run a hate campaign against Knights unchecked by their editors and without any regard to the interests of justice. I have absolutely no doubt that the massive media publicity in this case was unfair, outrageous and oppressive.' Interestingly, following this determination of the criminal proceedings the Attorney General consequently brought contempt proceedings against five newspapers whose reportage had been denounced by the judge. However, the High Court dismissed all the actions holding that they had not caused a substantial risk of serious prejudice.

1 Unreported, Harrow Crown Court.

4.31 In *R v Hassan and Caldon*[1] HH Judge Colgan stayed the proceedings. This case arose out of a 'sting' operation carried out by the News of the World. That newspaper gave wide prominence to its article concerning the defendants in September 1994. It described the defendants as 'veteran villains' with 'long criminal records' etc. At the start of the trial in July 1995 the trial was stayed. The judge held the article was grossly prejudicial, 'especially in attributing criminal records to the accused.' Subsequently, the Attorney General cited teh News of the World for contempt which was upheld by the Divisional Court, who imposed a fine of £50,000.[2] To avoid the problem of being held so liable again, the newspaper publishes story about crime before any proceedings or investigations are undertaken by police. This, therefore, prevents the test of 'active proceedings in the Contempt of Court Act 1991 being triggered.

1 (July 1995, unreported), Isleworth Crown Court.
2 *A-G v News Group Newspapers*, Independent, 17 July 1997.

4.32 In January 1997, in *R v Magee*[1] Kay J stayed proceedings against six defendants arising out of newspaper reports concerning their criminal backgrounds. The case is noteworthy because Kay J held that a dichotomy could be created distinguishing publicity in the advance of the trial and publicity which arises during a trial. He held that there was 'a real difference between pre-trial publicity and publicity which comes to the attention of the jury after they have been selected'. Consistent with his dichotomy Kay J refused applications to stay the proceedings based on publicity which occurred before the trial had which he accepted was prejudicial because it had publicised the criminal past of the defendants. In this regard he held that the jury could be expected to disregard such publicity. However, when it again occurred during the trial this faith was undermined. With respect to Kay J it is submitted that this dichotomy seems more pragmatic than principled if it is accepted that the prejudice was engendered by publicity of the defendant's backgrounds. Surely it is naïve to believe that a juror would forget this or put it out of his mind if he knew of this before the trial commenced but would not do so if he learnt of it after the trial had commenced.

1 (January 1997, unreported), Woolwich Crown Court.

4.33 Perhaps the most prominent and recent case concerned with this aspect of abuse is *R v Andrews*.[1] The defendant was convicted of murder but alleged unfairness because of the pre-trial publicity. The Court of Appeal rejected this as the prosecution's case in its view was strong and the defendant had herself contributed to the publicity.

1 [1999] CrimLR 156.

ALTERNATIVE TO A STAY – REMEDIES TO REDUCE THE RISK OF PREJUDICE

4.34 There are remedies available to a trial judge short of exercising a stay which can dilute or remove the risk of prejudice. Such remedies include:

(1) Moving the trial venue to a different geographical location if the risk of prejudice has predominately been caused by local publicity. Of course if the publicity is national, there is nowhere to go.

(2) As in *Maxwell*, questioning potential jurors to weed out the most prejudiced. It is submitted that there are two difficulties with this remedy, one principled and the other practical. The principled objection is that questioning a potential jury for the purpose of weeding out members constitutes a derogation from the principal that members of the jury should be selected at random, this to ensure fairness and that the jury is a cross-section of society. Second, it creates the insoluble problem of determining how prejudiced a potential juror should be before he is removed from the panel, on what empirical basis is the court to decide that one level of prejudice is acceptable but another not? As Phillips J said in *R v Maxwell*, 'the fact that a juror may have read or heard prejudicial matter about a defendant, and even formed an adverse opinion of him on the basis of it, does not of itself disqualify the juror on the ground of bias.' The view of the Ontario Court of Appeal in *R v Hubbert*[1] is also constructive, 'in this era of rapid

dissemination of the news by the various media, it would be naïve to think that in the case of a crime involving considerable notoriety, it would be impossible to select 12 jurors who have not heard anything about the case, information about a case, and even the holding of a tentative opinion about it, does make partial juror sworn to render a true verdict according to the evidence.' The exercise, it is submitted, is entirely speculative. Moreover, the questioning process may of itself create further problems. First, will the prejudice in fact be identified or elicited as a result of the screening process? As Mason CJ and Toohey J in *Murphy v R*[2] put it, 'the challenge for cause based on partiality run into an obvious difficulty; it seems unlikely that a prejudiced juror will recognise his own personal prejudice, or, knowing it, would admit it' (page 103). Second, the process may be self-defeating in that it brings to the attention of a juror those matters which the parties would wish him to disregard.

(3) Delaying the start of the trial to allow feelings of prejudice to subside. However, this remedy is only likely to succeed if it can be safely assumed that during the 'cooling-off' period no further prejudicial publicity occurs. To ensure this would require widespread use of publication bans which would conflict with the rights of free expression. In a case of notoriety, it is submitted, that this remedy would be prone to fail.

(4) This is the most commonly used remedy whereby at any time during the course of the trial, probably more than once, the judge directs the jury to base its verdict on the evidence it hears in court and nothing else. Depending on the nature of the prejudicial publicity and its specificity a judge is also able to comment in detail informing the jury that various allegations made in the media are, for example, totally false and to be disregarded. In *R v Andrews*[3] the trial judge directed prosecution counsel, before opening his case to the jury, to inform it that certain allegations made in newspapers were entirely bogus and formed no part of the Crown's case. While it is unknown as to whether such directions have the desired effect, based on the presupposition that juries do act fairly, it is presumed that they do so.

1 (1975) 29 CCC (2d) 279.
2 (1989) 167 CLR 94.
3 See para 4.33.

EUROPEAN CONVENTION FOR THE PROTECTION OF HUMAN RIGHTS

4.35 Article 6.1 states that '... everyone is entitled to a fair and public hearing within a reasonable time by an independent impartial tribunal ...'

4.36 As a general principle the Strasbourg Court holds that pre-trial publicity can adversely effect the fairness of criminal proceedings, particularly were such publicity is instigated or encouraged by those in authority. Accordingly, the Court has accepted that press freedom may be curtailed in order to ensure a fair trial and protect members of the jury from exposure to prejudicial influences.[1] Furthermore the commission has accepted that publicity which creates an atmosphere of animosity or a virulent press campaign can prejudice a fair trial.[2]

1 See *Hodgson v United Kingdom* (1987) 10 EHRR 503.
2 See *Berns and Ewart v Luxembourg* (1991) 68 DR 137.

5. Loss or destruction of relevant material by the prosecution

BACKGROUND

5.1 At the cornerstone of our adversarial system is a belief that 'the search for the truth' in any criminal trial is best procured by combat between the two sides. The role of the criminal justice system through the provision of the various codes of practice, and availability of legal aid for example, is to ensure that such combat is fair to both sides. If, therefore, the police enjoy a virtual monopoly over the investigation stage of a criminal offence, this advantage is to be ameliorated by an onerous obligation of disclosure to the defence post-charge. In ECHR jurisprudence the need to ensure a level playing-field, is summed up by the 'equality of arms' principle: despite unequal resources, no party should be allowed an unfair advantage over the other.

5.2 In the English system we strive to achieve the right balance between the opposing sides in order that the wrongly accused are acquitted and the guilty are convicted. This elusive balance and optimum state is ultimately the responsibility of judges who, in a concrete case, are obliged to do justice and serve fairness. An awareness of the recent celebrated miscarriage of justice cases, however, reveals that often judges are prevented from securing such noble objectives, prior to the trial, because evidence has been suppressed, destroyed or perverted. This has the inevitable consequence that a trial which in all appearances is scrupulously fair and dignified is reduced to a charade where the search for the truth is an unachievable goal.

5.3 This chapter will analyse circumstances where, owing to loss of material by the prosecution, the preparation and conduct of the defence is said to have been so seriously prejudiced that questions relating to abuse of process arise.

5.4 It will be within the experience of many practitioners, when preparing a case for trial, that they discover something is 'missing' from the case. Whether it is a witness who becomes untraceable, an exhibit which disappears, or an item of unused material one discovers has been destroyed, all manner of things can, and do, go wrong within the system. The simple question then arises, as to what to do? More often than not, a solution will be at hand, or at least a feasible damage limitation exercise will arise, which will not compromise a fair trial.

5.5 If the problem is remediable, that is the end of the matter. If it is not, the practitioner logically should go on to question what damage, if any, it will necessarily cause to the client's case. If, for example, the damage related to the prosecution's accidental destruction of a prosecution exhibit (of vital importance to the defence case), the question then arises as to the extent of any prejudice this may result to the defence:

- Does it seriously prejudice the preparation and conduct of the defence?
- Is the problem remediable within the trial process?
- For example, by suitable judicial directions or by the regulation of admissibility of evidence.
- Or is the dilemma so exceptional that the practitioner considers an abuse of process has been identified?

5.6 This chapter is concerned with *accidental* loss or destruction of evidence by the prosecution. The cases to be considered do not refer to allegations made by the defence that, out of bad faith, the prosecution has intentionally destroyed or tampered with the relevant material. The relevance of the abuse jurisdiction in relation to such allegations is considered in Chapter 7.

CONTEXT

5.7 One concomitant of the prosecutions' duty of disclosure of both evidence and unused material is an obligation to preserve such material so that in due course it can be served or disclosed to the defence. An obligation of disclosure which did not also presuppose an obligation to retain material would be rendered otiose. This obligation to retain material also arises as a matter of practical necessity. It is the police who invariably conduct the first investigation into the circumstances of the alleged offence, gathering witness statements and collecting forensic samples and so on.

5.8 Our criminal justice system has not adopted the European model of an independent judge or magistrate supervising and directing a police investigation in an inquisitorial and even-handed manner. Accordingly, in most criminal cases, by the time the defendant has instructed lawyers and such lawyers have become familiar with the issues in the case, the evidential trail has gone cold. This virtual monopoly enjoyed by the police over the gathering and retention of material, however, also carries with it a problem when the question of the obligation to retain material is considered. Clearly, bearing in mind for example the rights of third parties to retain their property, the police cannot be expected to seize and retain everything that might possibly be of relevance and therefore judgments of relevance in the field during the course of an inquiry are inescapable. The practical problem, therefore, is always to determine on the basis of limited information what ought to be preserved, even seized, and what need not. A legal obligation of preserving relevant material is easy to accept and understand in the abstract but relevance in a concrete case may be very hard to determine.

5.9 Inevitably, from time to time, instances have occurred whereby the police/prosecution have lost or failed to preserve material which could have had a bearing on a defendant's case at trial. It can easily be understood how this lapse can lead to prejudice being caused to the defence. The line of cases, to be considered below, traces how the common law has grasped this problem in an abuse context. Increasingly, over the last 15 years both the Court of Appeal and the Divisional Court have had to consider a number of cases where the defence has, at first instance, made a failed abuse application relating to the destruction or loss by the prosecution of allegedly material evidence. On appeal, it has been contended that the trial judge wrongly refused the application and because of the loss of potentially exculpatory material, the defendant did not receive a fair trial. Unsurprisingly however, these courts of review have been concerned to ensure that unscrupulous and opportunist defendants are prevented from either successfully making false claims concerning the purported prejudice suffered because of the loss by the prosecution or constructing false defences ex post facto based on knowledge of the unfortunate loss. This attitude of scepticism towards defence complaints of prejudice in these circumstances is consistent with that concerning defence complaints arising out of prosecutional delay.

In the first chapter the approach of Bingham CJ in *R v Cardiff Magistrates' Court, ex p Hole* was considered.[1] There Bingham CJ insisted that the defence, in arguing abuse, would have to establish precisely how in relation to the defence(s) to be advanced at trial prejudice was suffered, '... it is necessary to look at the charges and see exactly what defence it is that they are impeded from advancing.'

1 See paras 1.65 to 1.66.

5.10 At the end of this chapter the provisions of the recent CPIA code of practice are considered. It is perhaps surprising that such a code covering basic issues like retention of material took so long to be introduced into our system. With the advent of this code, however, it is to be hoped that the obligations of the prosecution are more clearly defined and also that the approach of the court when such an obligation is breached is more easy to predict. However, as the code is relatively new and the cases concerning breaches of it are relatively few, the law on this area is far from settled.

THE COMMON LAW AUTHORITIES

5.11 The relevant authorities can conveniently be separately considered.

R v Sadridin

5.12 In *R v Sadridin*[1] the appellant had been convicted of a shoplifting offence and appealed on the basis of a failed abuse submission, having allegedly been deprived of vital evidence at trial, namely certain till rolls (which had been routinely destroyed by the store in question). The day after his arrest for theft he handed certain receipts to his solicitor and claimed he had found them subsequent to his arrest in a shopping bag. The receipts, which were in evidence at trial, were for the correct amount of the goods, but did not indicate either the type of goods or the identity of the purchaser. The defence asserted that in order to establish that these receipts really were for the allegedly stolen goods, the till rolls were required.

1 (11 July 1985, unreported).

5.13 In dismissing the appeal Hirst J held that, on the evidence at trial, it was clear the till rolls were only of limited value and, in effect, could not have authenticated the receipts produced by the appellant, which point the appellant's appeal had depended on. The

Court also found that there was ample other evidence supporting the prosecution case. However, Hirst J stated that:

> 'If at sometime it had become clear that the absence of the destroyed documents was palpably of such crucial significance that a fair trial could not be conducted without them, it would always have been open to the judge, in the exercise of his discretion, to direct an acquittal.'

5.14 The above dicta is a reminder to practitioners to be ever vigilant of an abuse submission emerging into a position of significance as proceedings continue. The fact that the submission fails on a pre-trial hearing, or at the outset of trial may not necessarily be the end of the matter for, of course, during a trial the significance of an exhibit can vary as the evidence emerges.

R v Sofaer

5.15 In *R v Uxbridge Justices, ex p Sofaer*[1] the applicants were alleged to have attempted to export parts of aircraft, assembled or dismantled, to South Africa in 1983 at a time when such export was forbidden by the Export of Goods (Control) Order 1981. When interviewed, the applicants had claimed they were not in contravention of the export ban, for they had attempted to export scrap, as opposed to usable or serviceable parts. By the time of the committal proceedings, the customs officers, albeit acting within their powers, had disposed of the seized goods, in what was described by Pain J as 'a somewhat clumsy manoeuvre.'

1 (1986) 85 Cr App Rep 367.

5.16 Having made a failed abuse submission at the committal the applicants applied for judicial review, alleging a breach of natural justice, by stating they had been prejudiced in their defence by the disposal of the parts. The application was refused largely on the basis that there was in existence a full set of detailed photographs of the destroyed parts. Croom-Johnson LJ held that the photographs, as secondary evidence, were sufficiently adequate for the jury to reach a conclusion as to whether the aircraft parts were in fact usable parts, or scrap, as the applicants had asserted. A further difficulty which the applicants faced was that their own defence expert on committal proceedings made a damaging concession under cross-examination. While the expert stated that, in his view the parts did not appear to be serviceable ones, nevertheless he conceded that, given the availability of all the photographs, an actual inspection of the parts would not have taken the matter any further! A considerable doubt was thus cast on the weight which might have attached to any examination, had one been possible.

5.17 On the principle of preserving evidence Croom-Johnson LJ cited with approval the case of *R v Lushington, ex p Otto*,[1] wherein Wright J said:

> '... it is undoubted law that it is within the power of, and is the duty of "constables" – and for "constables" here read "Customs"– to retain for use in Court things which may be evidences of crime, and which have come into the possession of the constables without wrong on their part.'

1 [1894] 1 QB 420.

5.18 In commenting on the above, Croom-Johnson LJ noted: 'That indeed is a general and very desirable standard which should be maintained and almost always is maintained. Unfortunately it is not always possible to apply it. Exhibits which are part of the evidence do go astray. Sometimes they are tested to destruction. In some cases it is only by testing them to destruction that you obtain the evidence in the first place ... but where you cannot produce the original, you rely on secondary evidence...'

R v Sunderland Magistrates' Court, ex p Z

5.19 In *R v Sunderland Magistrates' Court, ex p Z*[1] in 1988 the applicant Z was committed for trial on a charge of rape: the allegation being that he raped 'X' in 1979. At the committal hearing Z made an abuse application submitting that first, the delay in proceeding with the charge against him was excessive and second, that this delay had resulted in prejudice to him. Examples of such prejudice were the destruction of various documents, clothing and vaginal swabs which made it impossible for the defence to have them forensically examined. However, the magistrates rejected the submission and indicated their intention to proceed with the committal. In response, the defence sought an order of prohibition to prevent the committal taking place.

1 [1989] CrimLR 56.

5.20 The Divisional Court granted the application agreeing that in the circumstances, a fair trial was no longer possible. The Court also held that the delay in bringing proceedings against Z was also unacceptable. This was on the grounds first, that the applicant had not contributed to the delay and second, the police had decided in 1979 not to proceed against Z on the grounds of insufficient evidence.

R v Birmingham

5.21 Following *ex p Z* came the most celebrated case on this subject, *R v Birmingham.*[1] The significance of *Birmingham* over, say, that of *ex p Z* is that for the first time a successful abuse submission was based solely on the ground of destruction of evidence by the prosecution. It was not, for example, bound up with a submission relating to unconscionable delay in bringing the prosecution. While *Birmingham* has undoubtedly become an often-quoted authority on this subject it is important to bear in mind that it was a first instance decision made by HH Judge Bromley sitting at Wood Green Crown Court.

1 [1992] CrimLR 117.

5.22 The facts in *Birmingham* were briefly as follows: seven defendants were charged with violent disorder at or outside a nightclub and also with various assaults on police officers who were called to the scene. Before the jury was sworn, the judge agreed to a voir dire in order to hear 'evidence from two of the prosecution witnesses on the existence and whereabouts of evidence believed to have been in existence at the time and of relevance to the case and possible use to the defence'. This evidence was a video recording of the locus in quo which had been created by an operational camera within the nightclub. After the incidents in question, the recording had been seized by the police and subsequently viewed by them. However, after having done so the recording was then returned to the nightclub and apparently then lost (thrown into a skip). At the voir dire it was discovered that the recording video tape had been viewed by the officers in the case but that its existence had not been revealed to the defence even after specific requests for unused material. To make matters worse, the officers candidly admitted that they had taken no steps to preserve the recording because they had decided that it would not be helpful to the prosecution's case (although this was later corrected and said to mean not to help either side's case).

5.23 Sensibly, in order to attain a full understanding of the likely relevance of the recording, the judge attended the nightclub and surveyed the locus in quo for himself.

5.24 The reasons given by the judge for staying the prosecution were as follows:

(1) The prosecution had breached its duty of disclosure in relation to the recording which should have been disclosed to the defence.

(2) The recordings would have been relevant to the defendants' case. The fact that the police had apparently decided otherwise was not only erroneous but also misguided.
(3) In relation to the defence of alibi run by some of the defendants, the recording would have been relevant to this issue.
(4) The recordings could have assisted the defence in tracing potential defence witnesses.

For these reasons the judge concluded that a fair trial was now impossible.

5.25 For its part, the prosecution had contended that the defence submission of abuse was in reality a matter to be determined by a jury and hence the trial should not be stayed. The judge, who was initially attracted to this view, held that the defence had been wrongfully deprived of material which should have been available during the course of defence preparation. Furthermore it did not, in the final analysis, relate to issues of guilt or innocence of the defendants but to whether they could be fairly tried. Accordingly, the trial judge declined to follow *Heston-Francois*[1] as prosecution counsel had suggested.

1 For a full consideration of that case see paras 8.110 to 8.116.

R v Gajree

5.26 Following *Birmingham* was the case of *R v Gajree*[1] where the appellant was convicted in 1994 of raping a 14-year-old girl, the offence allegedly having been committed in 1987.

1 (20 September 1994, unreported).

5.27 The appellant and the victim worked together at a shop. The victim alleged that after the shop closed she was taken by the appellant to the rear of the shop and there raped. She alleged that after being raped by the appellant, he then ejaculated onto the floor which was carpeted. The victim did not make any complaint about this assault for a period of three weeks and when she reported the matter to the police, there was a dispute between her and the police as to what exactly she told them. In any event, the police did not carry out any investigation of the locus in quo. There the matter remained undisturbed until 1991 (four years later) when an investigation commenced leading to the trial of the appellant. At the trial an abuse application was made which was rejected.

5.28 The Court of Appeal held that the abuse application should have succeeded in the Crown Court because of the destruction of evidence, in this case the shop premises where the alleged rape occurred. During the intervening period there had been a fire at the shop and there was substantial damage to the premises and the carpet in question had also been destroyed. It was also important that a proper plan of the layout of the shop be taken but owing to the fire and lack of recollection this could not now be done. Sachs J stated:

> 'Was it possible for this Appellant, at the time he stood trial, to obtain a fair trial?' In quashing the conviction, Sachs J went on to add: '*We* are satisfied that because of the passage of time and the inertia of the police officers, this Appellant was deprived of evidence that might have otherwise been available to him and that ... renders the verdict unsafe and unsatisfactory.'

R v Beckford

5.29 Our attention can now turn to what is currently regarded as the leading case on this subject, the judgment of Neil LJ in the Court of Appeal in *R v Beckford*.[1]

1 [1996] 1 Cr App Rep 94.

5.30 The facts were that the appellant was charged with causing death by careless driving when under the influence of drink or drugs. The appellant who was driving crashed his car into a concrete block killing his passenger. In terms of the cause of the accident the principle of res ipsa loquitur seemed to apply, the driver being to blame. Following this fatal accident, police examined the scene and the car, apparently finding no evidence of anything which might have caused the accident. Subsequently, the car was examined by a police forensic expert who also found nothing defective with the car. By a process of elimination therefore, the police reached the conclusion that the driver must be to blame. When questioned about what had happened the appellant refused to provide an explanation. Seven months after the accident the appellant was summonsed. However, during the intervening period the car had been scrapped, the police having given no instructions for it to be preserved.

5.31 At the trial an abuse application was made on the ground that if the car had not been scrapped it might have provided vital evidence for the defence. The defence complained it had had no opportunity to examine the car and to discover whether there was any defect in it which caused the accident. It submitted abuse but the trial judge said this was a matter for the jury and rejected the application.

5.32 During the trial the defence also called an expert whose evidence was to the effect that the cause of the accident was probably due to mechanical failure (steering-wheel lock) and not as the prosecution contended, that the appellant fell asleep while driving. The appellant again, however, did not give evidence of what he claimed had happened, he being the only witness. In the event the appellant was convicted and appealed. The central issue was whether the proceedings should have been stayed because of the premature destruction of the car. Could the defendant receive a fair trial despite the wrongful deprivation of the opportunity to test the findings of the prosecution as to there being no evidence of mechanical fault?

5.33 When considering the law on abuse Neil LJ analysed it as follows:

> 'The jurisdiction to stay can be exercised in many different circumstances. Nevertheless two main strands can be detected in the authorities:
>
> (1) cases where the court concludes that the defendant cannot receive a fair trial;
> (2) cases where the court concludes that it would be unfair for the defendant to be tried.'

5.34 Neil LJ considered *Gajree* which the defence argued was analogous to this case. Without asserting that *Gajree* was of no use to his consideration, Neil LJ emphasised that, 'each case has to be considered on its own facts'. Having stated this, he concluded that the judge was correct to reject the abuse application. According to Neil LJ there was no evidence to support the defence hypothesis as to the cause of the accident and that the trial was fair: 'There had been no evidence of problems of steering the car in the past, no marks on the road that the brakes had been applied, and the prosecution witnesses were of the opinion that the position of the car did not accord with the defence hypothesis of a steering-wheel lock.' At the end of his judgment Neil LJ said: 'It is to be hoped that procedures have been put in place to ensure that cars are not scrapped before express permission has been given by the police and that permission will never be given where serious criminal charges are to be brought which may involve the possibility of some mechanical defect in a car.'

5.35 Are the decisions in *Gajree* and *Beckford* reconcilable?

5.36 In the light of the clear similarities between the cases of *Gajree* and *Beckford*, at first it is difficult to comprehend the Court's finding in the *Beckford* case that no unfairness resulted. On the face of it, is this not yet another clear case where the defence were wrongly deprived of the opportunity to either put forward a defence or discredit the Crown's case? The difference and the distinguishing feature between these two cases is that in *Gajree* it was accepted that there had been in existence evidence which was relevant to the defence, ie the carpet. Similarly in *Birmingham*. In both these cases the defence had positively asserted that such evidence, if obtainable, would have assisted their cases. But in *Beckford* the relevance of the scrapped car arose only because of a defence expert advancing a hypothesis at the trial. No positive assertion of mechanical failure could be made because the defendant, who could have provided such evidence, had nonetheless chosen not to provide a version of events specifically. He had declined to answer any questions on arrest and interview detailing exactly how the steering-wheel had locked.

5.37 It is submitted that the Court of Appeal (and probably the trial judge) took great cognisance of the fact that the defendant himself had chosen not to give an explanation and not to allow this to be tested by cross-examination. Almost certainly to the Court, such a decision had all the hallmarks of a defence being concocted as a result of the discovery of the failure of the police to preserve the car. In such a circumstance, despite the obvious failure by the police and its obvious prejudicial affect, the Court was determined to ensure that the defendant did not unfairly profit from this. It is also to be borne in mind that the burden of proving an abuse lies on the defendant and in the final analysis, the court was not satisfied that this burden had been satisfied by the mere fact of the premature destruction of the car and the advancing of a hypothesis by the defence expert at the trial.

5.38 The paradox of the situation in *Beckford* is, of course, that in satisfying the burden on him the appellant's job was made more difficult because of the loss of evidence. One might well share the view of an author who commented:

> 'The Court [in Beckford's case] declined to draw the inference proposed by the Appellant, because he produced little or no evidence in support of it. But was that not precisely what he was telling the Courts at the trial and on appeal – that he could produce little or no evidence because he had been deprived of it by police inaction.'

1 See J Cr L 1995 p 59.

R v Northard

5.39 In *R v Northard*[1] the Court of Appeal allowed an appeal based on another video destruction abuse submission. A jeweller's employee was robbed, of a bag containing a quantity of cash, while en route to the bank in a town's shopping centre. The prosecution case was that the appellant had been the 'getaway driver' of a motor car into which the robber had fled. One prosecution witness had an opportunity to observe the driver of the car for some three minutes or so at close range, and took a note of the registration number, at about 11.30 a m. The owner of the vehicle was traced and gave evidence between 10 and 11 a m on the same day the appellant borrowed his car. That same evening the car was found abandoned, some three miles away from the scene of the robbery. When the owner looked at it, he found a flat battery, burned wiring and a missing radio. Further, police officers at trial conceded that the state of the car was consistent with it having been stolen. At 2.15 p m that day, some hours after the robbery, the appellant visited the town's police station and reported that the car he had borrowed was stolen. He was duly arrested.

1 Transcript 95/1475/3 (19 February 1996, unreported).

5.40 In police interviews he repeated that he had borrowed the car, and had spent the material time shopping in the town centre (noting the particular shops he had been in or looked in), before visiting a public house between noon and 12.30 p m, which visit several witnesses confirmed at trial in statements which were read. Further, in interview he agreed to stand on an identification parade, gave a detailed account of his movements, and challenged the police to verify his movements by viewing shop video films. At a later stage, he withdrew the offer to stand on an ID parade, but nevertheless invited officers to show photographs to the witnesses who claimed to have seen the robbers.

5.41 On appeal, the appellant argued the failed abuse submissions in the lower court, which consisted of numerous complaints into the police and/or prosecution investigation or conduct of the case. It was claimed that the defence had been led to believe that the police would make every effort to trace and preserve any available video evidence that might have supported the alibi. In reality, the police did obtain and view the videotape evidence but neither the police nor the CPS disclosed its existence to the defence. The officer in the case stated that having viewed the videos of the shopping centre, which showed large crowds of shoppers, it had not been possible to identify any individuals. Twenty-eight days after the incident the videos had been re-used and the recordings lost. A second defence complaint was that the investigating officer failed to adequately instruct other officers to check the appellant's alibi, by visiting two particular shops.

5.42 Additionally, there were further alleged failures to check security videos, arrange ID parades and failures to conduct expert examination of the vehicle in question.

5.43 Auld LJ held that the trial judge should either have stayed the prosecution as an abuse, or withdrawn it from the jury. The Court was concerned by a number of deficiencies and unsatisfactory features and identified 'an accumulation of lost opportunities to the defence to vouch for the alibi, if a true one'. The failure of the prosecution to disclose the existence of the video, until it was too late, was held to deprive the defence of the opportunity to check the video for themselves, to see if it supported the defence account. Auld LJ wisely noted that the appellant and his solicitor may have examined the video with *'keener eyes'* than the police officer. The police were further found to have failed to act on the appellant's initial offer to stand on an ID parade in respect of the only witness who apparently had had a good opportunity to observe the robbers. As Auld LJ noted, 'her evidence would have damned or exonerated the appellant.'

R v Reid

5.44 In *R v Reid*[1] Owen J considered some of the above authorities in the context of yet another video destruction case. Reid had faced robbery and assault charges arising out of an incident in a chemist's shop. The dispute at trial was as to whether the appellant had been acting by way of self-defence. While both complainants had knife wounds (from the appellant's knife), the appellant had suffered acid burns, and the simple issue was who had started to use force first. A police officer testified that there had been a recording of the interior of the shop (from an internal security video) but that it had not been preserved. The officer stated that he watched it and nothing on it appeared relevant. By the time of trial the recording, for reasons that are not clear, had been destroyed. The defence apparently requested, and were granted, a voir dire before the jury were empanelled, for evidence to be heard. In such a hearing the judge accepted the officer's account that having scanned the video nothing of relevance arose.

1 (10 March 1997, unreported).

5.45 In dismissing the appeal, Owen J sought to distinguish the facts in Reid's case from those of *Birmingham* and *Northard.* The Court of Appeal found itself unable to conclude, either that the video had been relevant, or that the circumstances in which it had disappeared were so unfair as to make the conviction unsafe. It is submitted that the case might, of course, have been decided differently if the cameras been trained on a more relevant part of the premises, or in circumstances where the officer had made concessions as to relevance of the video.

5.46 Taking the opportunity available to him in *Reid* Owen J clearly enunciated the existence of the abuse of process jurisdiction in circumstances where there has been a failure to preserve relevant material in criminal proceedings:

> 'There is now a clear duty to preserve material which might be relevant, and nothing in this judgment is meant in any way to cast a doubt on that duty. However, clearly there must be a judgment of some kind by the investigating officer. He must decide whether material may be relevant, and if he does not preserve material which may be relevant, then for sure in the future he may be required to justify his decision, and he may find that, if the breach of his duty is sufficiently serious, that somebody who is in fact a guilty man has to go free because there has been an abuse of process ... The position is that if there has been a failure to preserve relevant material then it may be found that to proceed with a prosecution in those circumstances would be an abuse of process.'

5.47 It is interesting to note that Owen J's judgment in *Reid* was delivered a few weeks before police officers acquired a statutory duty, pursuant to para 5 of the CPIA code of practice, to retain material which may be relevant to a police investigation. The wording of the judgment may not, in these circumstances, have been entirely coincidental.

R v McNamara

5.48 The final authority which is reviewed on this topic is *R v McNamara.*[1] In this case police officers had searched the family home and allegedly found quantities of drugs. As the search continued, an officer recorded items of interest and the appellant's comments, some of which amounted to admissions to possession of cannabis. The same were recorded in the proforma Book 101, being the search record. The appellant later denied making the admissions and, by the time of trial, the Book 101 had been lost, apparently due to 'poor exhibit management'. The defence argued at trial, and on appeal, that the loss of the Book 101 rendered the proceedings an abuse of process. A variety of authorities were relied on, principally *Birmingham.*

1 [1998] CrimLR 278.

5.49 The Court of Appeal unsurprisingly rejected the appellant's argument that the *Birmingham* situation was analogous. First, the Court noted that unlike *Birmingham*, the Book 101 was not deliberately destroyed by any officer. Second, the loss of the exhibit would only be of detriment to the Crown and finally, unlike the video film example, the Book 101 was not an item of original evidence.

5.50 *McNamara* is a good example of the courts being concerned to ensure that unfair advantage is not taken of a police lapse. As in the cases on delay, the mere fact of a police lapse is not sufficient to found an abuse application, the defence must establish the prejudice which has arisen in consequence.

THE CRIMINAL PROCEDURE AND INVESTIGATIONS ACT 1996 CODE OF PRACTICE

5.51 This code of practice was promulgated pursuant to s 23(1) of the Criminal Procedure and Investigations Act 1996 ('CPIA'). It applies in respect of all criminal investigations conducted by police officers which began on or after 1 April 1997. One highly significant aspect of the code is that for the first time the way in which police or other investigators conduct a criminal investigation generally is governed by a public code of practice. In comparison, the PACE code of practice which is concerned only with a narrow area of police operation, mainly the treatment and questioning of suspects post-arrest, this Code is directed at all police conduct pre- and post-arrest and is designed to impose clear standards of fairness and accountability. As any breach of the code may found a successful s 78 or abuse application, its contents are highly important to any defence practitioner.

5.52 In general terms, the code of practice sets down detailed regulations in respect of:

(1) the presentation of material by an 'investigator';
(2) the revelation of such material by the investigator to the prosecutor.

5.53 Within the context of this chapter, it is necessary to examine the relevant provisions of the code. Such provisions directed to the retention and preservation of relevant material which comes into the possession of investigators during their investigation.

5.54 The following are relevant extracts taken from the code:

> '*General Responsibilities*
>
> 3.3 The officer in charge of an investigation may delegate tasks to another investigator or to civilians employed by the police force, but he remains responsible for ensuring that these have been carried out and for accounting for any general policies followed in the investigation. In particular, it is an essential part of his duties to ensure that all material which may be relevant to an investigation is retained, and either made available to the disclosure officer or (in exceptional circumstances) revealed directly to the prosecutor.
> 3.4 In conducting an investigation, the investigator should pursue all reasonable lines of inquiry, whether these point towards or away from the suspect. What is reasonable in each case will depend on the particular circumstances.
> 3.5 If the officer in charge of an investigation believes that other persons may be in possession of material that may be relevant to the investigation, and if this has not been obtained under paragraph 3.4 above, he should ask the disclosure officer to inform them of the existence of the investigation and to invite them to retain the material in case they receive a request for its disclosure. The disclosure officer should inform the prosecutor that they may have such material.'
>
> *Recording of Information*
>
> 4.1 If material which may be relevant to the investigation consists of information which is not recorded in any form, the officer in charge of an investigation must ensure that it is recorded in a durable or retrievable form (whether in writing, on video or audio tape, or on computer disk).
> 4.2 Where it is not practicable to retain the initial record of information because it forms part of a larger record which is to be destroyed, its contents should be transferred as a true record to a durable and more easily-stored form before that happens.
> 4.3 Negative information is often relevant to an investigation. If it may be relevant it must be recorded. An example might be a number of people present in a particular place at a particular time who state that they saw nothing unusual.

Retention of material

(a) Duty to retain material

5.1 The investigator must retain material obtained in a criminal investigation which may be relevant to the investigation. This includes not only material coming into the possession of the investigator (such as documents seized in the course of searching premises) but also material generated by him (such as interview records). Material may be photographed or retained in the form of a copy rather than the original, if the original is perishable, or was supplied to the investigator rather than generated by him and is to be returned to its owner.
5.3 If the officer in charge of an investigation becomes aware as a result of developments in the case that material previously examined but not retained (because it was not thought to be relevant) may now be relevant to the investigation, he should, wherever practicable, take steps to obtain it or ensure that it is retained for further inspection or for production in court if required.
5.4 The duty to retain material includes in particular the duty to retain material falling into the following categories, where it may be relevant to the investigation:

- crime reports (including crime report forms, relevant parts of incident report books or police officers' notebooks);
- custody records;
- records which are derived from tapes of telephone messages (for example, 999 calls) containing descriptions of an alleged offence or offender;
- final versions of witness statements (and draft versions where their content differs from the final version), including any exhibits mentioned (unless these have been returned to their owner on the understanding that they will be produced in court if required);
- interview records (written records, or audio or video tapes, of interviews with actual or potential witnesses or suspects);
- communications between the police and experts such as forensic scientists, reports of work carried out by experts, and schedules of scientific material prepared by the expert for the investigator, for the purpose of criminal proceedings;
- any material casting doubt on the reliability of a confession;
- any material casting doubt on the reliability of a witness;
- any other material which may fall within the test for primary prosecution disclosure in the Act.'

Relevant material

5.55 In its definition in para (2.1) the code defines material as 'material of any kind, including information and objects, which is obtained in the course of a criminal investigation and which may be relevant to the investigation.' In an equally broad definition of relevance it states 'material may be relevant to an investigation if it appears to an investigator or to the officer in charge of an investigation, or to the disclosure officer, that it has some bearing on any offence under investigation or any person being investigated, or on the surrounding circumstances of the case, unless it is incapable of having any impact on the case.' It is submitted that the definition of relevance is effectively the same as the *Keane* disclosure test.

Significance of para 3.4

5.56 The above extracts from the code demonstrate the various obligations and responsibilities imposed on all criminal investigators. Perhaps the most significant and wide-ranging obligation cast on criminal investigators is para 3.4. This paragraph requires investigators not simply to act fairly but also imposes a positive obligation to investigate all relevant lines of defence in the manner required. It is submitted that never before has an explicit legal obligation been imposed on a criminal investigator to act in the manner stipulated. Previously in our adversarial system of criminal justice, it was a respectable argument for a prosecutor to make that it was the duty of the accused and his legal team to investigate any matter which was inconsistent with the prosecution's case. If the defence failed to do so and the prosecution were not on notice of any defect or undermining factor so far as their case was concerned, then responsibility for pursuing an exculpatory line of enquiry rested squarely on the defence. Such an argument in the light of para 3.4 is, it is submitted, no longer tenable.

5.57 The significance of para 3.4 can further be emphasised by taking into account that it was presumably inserted into the code as a quid pro quo for the curtailment under CPIA of the defence's common law rights to prosecution disclosure. If the object of the statutory disclosure regime created by CPIA was to place the prosecution squarely in a management role in so far as decision making concerning disclosure was concerned then this paragraph, acting as a counterweight, created a clear responsibility to act fairly and impartially while exercising that role.

5.58 Of course it all depends by what is meant by 'reasonable'. For example, if during interview a suspect has answered questions and put forward a particular defence or referred to a particular witness, how far are the investigators obliged to go in an effort to seek to verify or refute such references? An officer's candid admission that he failed to follow up a particular line of defence which was disclosed at a time when it could have been followed up, could well found a successful abuse application. But conversely, the officer may be able to convince the court that investigating the defendant's version may not in the circumstances have been reasonably required.

Duty of retention

5.59 In so far as the duty to retain material set out in para 5.4 is concerned, the code provides a non-exhaustive list of examples of what should be retained, but this is also coupled with a very wide definition of relevance and unused material in para 2.1 (see para 5.54). It is certainly an object of the code to ensure that a criminal investigator retains material which could have 'some bearing on any offence under investigation ... ' Accordingly, the police in *Beckford* for example, who allowed the car to be scrapped would, it is submitted, be squarely in breach of this paragraph. It is therefore arguable that had the defence in *Beckford* been able to rely on this explicit breach of the code then their abuse argument would have been reinforced by this and the case would have been decided differently.

5.60 The significance of this duty of retention enshrined in the code is that a breach of this provision alone can successfully found an abuse or s 78 application. There is nothing in the code which states that a mere breach is insufficient. For it to constitute a proper basis for an abuse submission in addition there must be evidence of prejudice. This common law obligation of proving prejudice, illustrated for example in *McNamara*, is arguably removed and it may be easier for the defence to mount applications. Moreover, in relation to the common law principle that the burden of establishing an abuse submission always lies on the defence, the code sits uncomfortably with this. If a breach is established then surely it must be for the prosecution to justify or excuse this and to negate a presumption that a breach has caused prejudice. It will be interesting to see how the case law develops on these points.

Conclusion

5.61 It is submitted that the provisions of the code provide a much greater opportunity for the making of abuse applications at a defendant's trial. The same point arises in relation to s 78 applications where part of the prosecution's evidence is sought to be excluded. Bearing in mind that the code only became operative from 1 April 1997 case law regarding its provisions generally is in its infancy. At the time of writing there are only two relevant authorities to consider. It is too early to tell whether the code, especially para 3.4, will turn out to be a Pandora's box for the prosecution.

CASE LAW CONCERNED WITH PREJUDICE TO THE DEFENCE ARISING UNDER THE CODE

5.62 At the time of writing there are only two authorities to consider.

R v DPP, ex p Lee

5.63 In *R v DPP, ex p Lee*[1] the fairness of the prosecution's refusal to make disclosure pre-committal to the defence was considered by the Divisional Court. The prosecution contended that the code of practice does not require disclosure of unused material until post-committal when it would be regulated by the provisions of the code and CPIA. The defence contended that their case would be prejudiced if no disclosure was made until a subsequent stage in the proceedings, ie post-committal, because it would delay defence preparation generally and hinder the making of a successful contested bail application.

1 [1999] 2 All ER 737.

5.64 Faced with compelling arguments from both sides, Kennedy LJ held that the prosecution did have a residual common law obligation to make pre-committal disclosure. Kennedy LJ provided examples of circumstances where such an obligation would arise. Two relevant examples were first, where the disclosure of unused material could reasonably be expected to assist in making an application for bail and second, where such material could assist an application made in the magistrates' court for a stay based on abuse. While Kennedy LJ was concerned to prevent the notion arising that 'full-blown' common law disclosure is required pre-committal, he was also anxious to ensure that the defence were not unfairly prejudiced by the provisions of the CPIA.

5.65 *Ex p Lee* is therefore authority for the proposition that there is a common law duty of disclosure from the prosecution to make disclosure of material which would assist defence preparation at the earliest possible opportunity in the proceedings. Accordingly, a failure to abide by this duty may subsequently found an application for a stay. It is submitted that while in this regard the decision in, *ex p Lee* is undoubtedly correct, it is entirely at odds with the disclosure regime created by CPIA which specifically postponed in indictable proceedings issues of disclosure until the committal stage had passed. Moreover, via its fundamental carrot-and-stick approach, rewarding defendants who made defence statements with secondary prosecution disclosure and penalising with inferences of guilt those who do not, CPIA certainly envisages that disclosure of unused material appertaining to a possible abuse application would only occur once a defence statement had been served. *Ex p Lee* has the potential to upset this delicate but fundamental approach to prosecution disclosure created by CPIA.

DPP v Metten

5.66 In *DPP v Metten*[1] the defence alleged a breach of para 3.4 of the code in a failure by the police to make any effort to ascertain the identities of potential witnesses to a public order incident for which the defendant was being prosecuted. It is submitted that on the facts of this case, there appeared a clear breach of para 3.4, the officers having singularly failed at the only possible moment to speak to those who may have assisted or undermined the prosecution's case. Buxton LJ sitting in the Divisional Court was, it is submitted, nonetheless determined to ensure that despite a clear breach of this paragraph, the defence did not profit from it. While the terms of his judgment are beyond the scope of this chapter, Buxton LJ adopted a highly technical approach to the wording of the code of practice holding that there was no breach because the police had not conducted any criminal investigation. As the editor of Criminal Law Week observes concerning Buxton LJ's judgment, 'the decision does indeed drive a coach and four through the legislation'.[2]

1 Criminal Law Week Issue 13.
2 Criminal Law Week Issue 13 para 5.

6. Investigative impropriety

6.1 This chapter explores the development of the law on abuse of process as it relates to investigatory impropriety. The term 'investigatory impropriety' is intended to encompass illegal or oppressive behaviour by investigators and the recently coined expression 'executive lawlessness'. While perhaps it matters little which choice of phraseology is preferred, underlying this head of abuse is an attachment to the basic legal principles of fairness and the rule of the law. In *R v Horseferry Magistrates' Court, ex p Bennett*[1] Lord Griffiths succinctly expressed the issue as follows:

> 'in the present case there is no suggestion that the appellant cannot have a fair trial ... if the Court is to have the power to interfere with the prosecution in the present circumstances it must be because the judiciary except a responsibility for the maintenance for the rule of law that embraces a willingness to oversee executive action and to refuse countenance behaviour that threatens either basic human rights or the rule of law' (page 61).

1 [1994] AC 42.

6.2 In *R v Latif* Lord Steyn expressed the issue in a similar vein:

> 'in this case the issue is whether, despite the fact that a fair trial was possible, the judge ought to have stayed the criminal proceedings on broader considerations of the integrity of the criminal justice system ... the speeches in *Bennett* conclusively established that proceedings may be stayed in the exercise of the judge's discretion but only where a fair trial is impossible but also where it would be contrary to the public interest in the integrity of the criminal justice system that a trial should take place' (page 101).

6.3 The decision of the House of Lords in *ex p Bennett* can be understood as an extension of the doctrine of abuse of process to include investigatory impropriety. Previously abuse of process had been concerned with the jurisdiction of a court to stay criminal proceedings against a defendant on the grounds that he, for whatever reason, could not receive a fair trial. The celebrated judgment and exposition of the law on abuse by Sir Roger Ormrod in *R v Derby Crown Court, ex p Brookes*[1] exemplifies this. Sir Roger Ormrod confined the power of a court to stop a prosecution to two sets of circumstances:

> 'either (a) the prosecution have manipulated or misused the process of the court so as to deprive the defendant of a protection provided by the law or to take unfair advantage of a technicality, or (b) on balance of probability a defendant has been, or will be, prejudiced in the preparation or conduct of his defence by delay on the part of the prosecution ...' (page 168).

Based on that judicial statement, which has been repeated and approved in subsequent abuse cases, it is axiomatic that a person charged with having committed an offence should receive a fair trial and if he cannot be tried fairly for that offence, he should not be tried at all.

1 (1985) 80 Cr App Rep 164.

6.4 In *ex p Bennett* the House had to consider whether the concept of abuse of process should be extended a stage further. Despite the absence of any suggestion of unfairness or oppression to the defendant in the trial process itself, the issue was whether a court should stay proceedings on the ground of some antecedent executive activity. Alternatively, should the courts be willing to stay a prosecution as a means of overseeing or controlling abuses of executive power which lead up to otherwise properly instituted and perfectly regular, even fair, criminal proceedings? The answer of the House of Lords in, *ex p Bennett* to these questions was an emphatic yes: the doctrine of abuse of process should be widened to allow a court to inquire into the executive acts of law enforcement agencies occurring before the process of the court has been evoked, even if this has no bearing whatever on the fairness of the trial.

6.5 The cases to be considered in this chapter can conveniently be divided into the following categories:

(1) those concerned with an allegation of illegal extradition, where it is alleged that the defendant's appearance before the court is a

result of breach of international law on the part of the prosecution, specifically a breach of extradition procedures of the country from where the accused was brought. Such cases are therefore always concerned with alleged executive lawlessness at an international level;

(2) those cases concerned with the use by investigators of tactics, such as trickery or deception, as a means of inducing the defendant to either incriminate himself or to take an act prejudicial to their own interests. An example of this being where investigators for the purpose of apprehending the defendant, lure him into the jurisdiction of the court by means of deception;

(3) those cases where the investigators, invariably an undercover officer, have acted unlawfully or illegally. For example where to maintain his cover, an undercover officer has engaged in the planning and/or commission of an offence.

Before considering these three groups of cases it is important to set this subject in context.

Covert policing and abuse of process

6.6 Covert policing methods, normally the use of informers and/or undercover police officers, raise profound issues as regards the fairness of trials. In English law there is no rule that evidence obtained by the use of trickery and deception, even by provocation and entrapment be automatically excluded. Nonetheless abuse of process and s 78 of PACE is based on the principle of fairness and the protection of the rights of the defendant. Bearing in mind the extension of the doctrine of abuse by the House of Lords in, *ex p Bennett* it is necessary to appreciate that courts have a responsibility to protect the overall integrity of the criminal justice system. This must, therefore, inevitably mean that in setting standards of fairness, a court in a particular case must consider whether to condone particular investigatory methods or instead condemn them by resort to its common law power to stay the proceedings or exclude the evidence under s 78.

6.7 It is clear that issues raised as the result of covert policing methods are at present the most controversial, in regard to the law concerned with abuse of process. There are, it is submitted, basically three reasons for this which are helpful to consider. First, covert policing is on the increase. In its report 'Under Surveillance'[1] justice stated:

'modern policing no longer relies solely or mainly on detection, confession in the hope that witnesses will come forward. Increasingly, police, Customs and other law enforcement agencies in the UK and other countries are turning to proactive, intelligence-led policing methods. Essentially this means using covert investigative methods to target known or suspected criminals rather than waiting to investigate a crime which has happened. Informers and undercover officers, together with increasingly sophisticated aural and visual surveillance devices, provide both intelligence on potential crimes and evidence to prosecute those who are committed.'

1 Justice report (1998).

6.8 Proactive policing, especially as regards the investigation and detection of serious crime has transformed the nature of modern policing. Second, this development has in turn raised increasing concerns regarding the lack of adequate safeguards or remedies against abuse or misuse of power by investigators and the executive generally. Largely in response to adverse rulings by the European Court of Human Rights, there have been piecemeal reforms designed to increase the element of legal oversight or accountability in relation to particular investigatory methods. The two most significant statutes which created specific mechanisms for independent scrutiny are the Interception of Communications Act 1985 and Part III of the Police Act 1997. Nonetheless, it is important to recognise that even under current arrangements there are, for example, no discrete mechanisms designed to ensure fairness and accountability in relation to the use of informants and the activities of undercover officers.[1] From an abuse perspective, when such methods may have been adopted in a particular case and the defendant alleges impropriety in consequence, there is a legal vacuum. In such a case the only body who can provide scrutiny, an effective remedy and ensure fairness is the court of trial. Increasingly therefore, confronting this absence of executive accountability, coupled with an increase in covert policing methods giving rise to concern, a criminal court albeit at long range is having to grapple with such issues via its abuse jurisdiction and to set standards of fairness.

1 There is only Home Office Guidance circulated in 1969 and unpublished ACPO Guidelines.

6.9 Third, the impact of the European Convention on Human Rights post its implementation by the Human Rights Act will undoubtedly be profound.[1] Issues concerned with the exclusion of evidence and proactive policing methods will need to be examined afresh against a context of individual rights guaranteed under the Convention, which may place restrictions on the efforts of the police to prevent and detect crime. Articles 6 and 8 protections will in particular, force courts to consider fair trial and privacy rights whenever a breach of either or both of these articles is complained of. Also, the European Court has held that interference by a public authority with a person's right to privacy by Art 8 must be in accordance with law. Inevitably therefore, limits must be imposed on the use of investigative techniques such as covert surveillance and the use of agent provocateurs.

1 Implementation date is October 2000.

6.10 Since the decision in *Malone,* the direction of international conventions concerned with the investigation and detection of crime has been to honour this principle of legality. See for example Art 11 of the UN Convention against Illicit Traffic in Narcotic Drugs and Psychtropic Substances 1988 (the Vienna Convention) and Art 4 of the Council of Europe Convention on the Proceeds of Crime 1990. Both these articles are concerned with undercover policing or, as the Council of Europe Convention terms it, 'special investigative techniques'. They both recommend legal oversight in relation to undercover policing methods but notably the UK has not responded and implemented such oversight. While this non-response is not unlawful under English law, neither convention having been given the status of primary legislation, this nonetheless is relevant to abuse of process. The absence of a clear legal framework in this regard may be judged to be in breach of Art 8 of the European Convention which after implementation of the Human Rights Act will constitute binding legislation.

6.11 It is submitted that if Malone was able to convince the Court that the then telephone tapping regime had an insufficient clear legal basis, then it follows that the legal vacuum described in para 6.10 will be open to a direct challenge under Art 8.[1] For this reason, from an abuse perspective it is likely that Art 8 will be of greater significance than Art 6. It remains to be seen whether, before the date of implementation of the Human Rights Act, the Home Office will have created and promulgated a code of practice and/or oversight arrangements in relation to undercover policing in order that challenges based on lack of legality as interpreted by the European Court, can be rebuffed. Such a development, however, to be fully effective in this respect will need also to govern the activities of MI5 and MI6 if, in a particular case, such agencies have assisted the police investigation.

1 The Court came to a similar conclusionin *Malone and Halford v United Kingdom* (1997) 24 EHRR 523.

6.12 The forthcoming intertwining and probable eventual fusion of the English common law concerned with abuse of process and Convention rights as enshrined by the Human Rights Act will perhaps be one of the most significant and interesting developments in the field of criminal law in the next decade. Moreover, at least initially, this may be concentrated on issues raised by alleged investigative impropriety.

Illegal extradition

The issues raised

6.13 Do the courts have a jurisdiction to examine the circumstances by which a defendant is brought into the United Kingdom for the purposes of trial? If there has been impropriety, does the court have discretion to stay the proceedings as an abuse? If there is a discretion, should it be always exercised in favour of the defendant albeit that he is on trial for a serious offence? (It is hardly likely that if the offence alleged was not serious, the prosecution would have bothered to seek the return of a defendant to the UK.)

Bennett

6.14 The cornerstone of present law is the House of Lords case of *R v Horseferry Magistrates' Court, ex p Bennett.* That case was concerned with the deportation of B from South Africa to England. Ostensibly he was to be deported by the South African police to New Zealand, B being a New Zealand citizen. However, despite the obvious geographical factors, it was decided to fly him home via England. He was placed on a flight to Heathrow, handcuffed to the seat, and on arrival there was immediately arrested by the police. He never flew on to New Zealand which it was claimed, was his intended ultimate destination. In *Bennett* the House was not concerned to ascertain the truth or whether there had really been collusion between the South African and English police in relation to a decision not to institute proper extradition procedures. Instead only to consider, as a matter of principle, whether English courts had any jurisdiction to inquire into such matters.

6.15 The Divisional Court had held that even if there was evidence of collusion between the two police forces in kidnapping B and securing his enforced illegal removal to England from South Africa, criminal courts had no jurisdiction to inquire into the circumstances by which he came to be within the jurisdiction. Accordingly, it dismissed his application for review. Relying on previous authorities, the Divisional Court had held that the role of the judge is confined to the forensic process, to see that the accused has a fair trial and that the process of the court is not manipulated to his disadvantage so that the trial itself is unfair. It held that the wider issues of the rule of law and the behaviour of those charged with its enforcement, be they police or prosecution authority, are not the concern of the judiciary unless such issues impinge directly on the trial process. In support of this view the court relied on the House of Lords case of *R v Sang*[1] where Lords Diplock and Scarman emphasised that it is no part of the judge's function to exercise disciplinary powers over the police or the prosecution. Lord Diplock said, '... the function of the judge at a criminal trial as respect to the admission of evidence is to ensure that the accused has a fair trial according to law. It is no part of a judge's function to exercise disciplinary powers over the police or prosecution as respect into the way in which evidence is to be used at the trial is obtained by them' (page 290).

1 (1979) 69 Cr App Rep 282.

6.16 However, in a 4-1 majority the House in *Bennett* held that in a situation of illegal extradition the courts did have a power to stay proceedings for abuse.

6.17 In his judgment Lord Griffiths perceived the issues posed before the House in this case as follows:

> 'In the present case there is no suggestion that the appellant cannot have a fair trial, nor could it be suggested that it would be unfair to try him if he had been returned to this country through extradition procedures. If the court is to have the power to interfere with the prosecution in the present circumstances it must be because the judiciary except a responsibility for the maintenance of the rule of law that embraces an willingness to oversee executive action and to refuse to countenance behaviour that threatens either basic human rights or the rule of law' (page 150).

6.18 Having clearly set out the significance of the issues to be confronted, Lord Griffiths was in no doubt that the courts should widen their abuse jurisdiction:

> 'I have no doubt that the judiciary should accept this responsibility in the field of criminal law ... If it comes to the attention of the court that there has been a serious abuse of power it should, in my view, express its disapproval by refusing to act on it' (page 150).

6.19 In conclusion Lord Griffiths said:

> 'In my view your Lordships should now declare that where process of law is available to return an accused to this country through extradition procedures our courts will refuse to try him if he has been forcibly brought within our jurisdiction in disregard of those procedures by a process to which our own police, prosecuting or other executive authorities have been a knowing party' (page 151).

6.20 Lord Bridge said:

> 'When it is shown that the law enforcement agency responsible for bringing a prosecution has only been able to do so by participating in violations of international law and laws of another state in order to secure the presence of the accused within the territorial jurisdiction of the court, I think that respect for the rule of law demands that the court take cognisance of that circumstance to hold that the Court may turn a blind eye to executive lawlessness beyond the frontiers of its own jurisdiction is, to my mind, an insular and unacceptable view. Having then taken cognisance of the lawlessness it would again appear to me to be a wholly inadequate response for the Court to hold that the only remedy lies in the civil proceedings at the suit of the defendant or a disciplinary or criminal proceedings against the individual officers of the law enforcement agency who were concerned in the illegal action taken. Since the prosecution could never have been brought if the defendant had not been illegally abducted, the whole proceeding is tainted' (page 155).

6.21 Lord Lowry said:

> 'I consider that a court has a discretion to stay any criminal proceedings on the ground that to try at those proceedings would amount to an abuse of its own process; either (1) because it would be impossible (usually by reason of delay) to give the accused a fair trial or (ii) because it offends the courts sense of justice and propriety to be asked to try the accused in these circumstances of a particular case ... The court, in order to protect its own process from being degraded and misused must have the power to stay proceedings which have come before it and have only been possible be acts which offends the court's conscience as being contrary to the rule of law. Those acts by providing a morally unacceptable foundation for the exercise of jurisdiction over the suspect taint the proposed trial and, if tolerated would mean that the court's process has been abused' (page 162).

6.22 In answer to the counter-suggestion that the seriousness of an offence alleged against a defendant means that there is an overriding public interest in trying him no matter under what circumstances he was brought before a court, Lord Lowry was unpersuaded. He said:

> 'It maybe that the guilty accused finding himself in the circumstances predicated is not deserving of much sympathy, but the principle involved goes beyond the scope of such a pragmatic observation and even beyond the rights of those victims who are or maybe innocent. It affects the proper administration of justice according to the rule of law and with respect to international law' (page 163).

6.23 Lord Lowry in his speech was also concerned to deal with two other but connected issues; first, whether via its abuse jurisdiction the court should exercise disciplinary powers over the police and second, whether by its preparedness to penalise unworthy conduct on the part of investigators, the House was encouraging a flood of abuse applications. In common with Lords Diplock and Scarman in *Sang* Lords Lowry and Bridge both emphasised that the abuse jurisdiction was not a disciplinary one. Lord Lowry said 'the discretion to stay is not a disciplinary of jurisdiction and ought not to be exercised in order to express the court's disapproval of official conduct ... The court ought not to stay the proceedings merely "pour encourager les autres"' (page 161). In answer to the 'floodgates' argument Lord Lowry held, 'if proceedings are stayed when wrongful conduct is proved, the result will not only be a sign of judicial disapproval but will discourage similar conduct in future and thus would tend to maintain the purity of a source of justice'. No 'floodgates' argument applies because the executive can stop the flood at source by refraining from impropriety' (page 163).

6.24 Lord Oliver dissented. Lord Oliver could see no justification for a criminal court involving itself in questions of a defendant's apprehension and detention if such issues have no bearing on the fairness of the trial.

6.25 In relation to issues of unfairness, *Bennett* therefore established that courts have a wider supervisory jurisdiction; to protect persons from being prosecuted in circumstances where it would be seriously unjust to do so. However, the judgments of Lords Griffiths, Bridge and Lowry make plain that the House in *Bennett* was concerned with a particular instance of illegality and abuse of power, namely breach of extradition procedures. The presence of that fact was crucial, as Lord Griffiths said: 'If extradition is not available various considerations will arise on which I express no opinion' (page 151). Moreover, for a court to stay criminal proceedings as an abuse under *Bennett*, it must be satisfied that there was collusion between the foreign and English authorities to avoid the defendant being extradited. In the absence of such evidence, the burden being on the defence, an application for a stay could not succeed.

6.26 A reading of the speeches of the majority of the House of Lords in *Bennett* reveals a clear determination that courts should not countenance 'executive lawlessness' (per Lord Bridge). To fail to do so would result in a 'degradation of the courts criminal process' and be an 'affront to the public conscience'. When, therefore, a court is confronted by executive lawlessness it is entitled to stay the trial for abuse of process.

Post *Bennett* authorities

6.27 While the attitude of the House in *Bennett* to executive lawlessness is unambiguous the speeches do not clarify whether a rule or merely a principle was being pronounced. Did the House in *Bennett* support an absolutist or mandatory stance whereby any prosecution based on illegal extradition should always be stayed or alternatively should a court in such a situation exercise a discretion in deciding whether or not such lawlessness should result in a stay? The only speech which dealt with this subject directly was that of Lord Lowry who said, '... it is not jurisdiction which is in issue but the exercise of a discretion to stay proceedings, whilst speaking of "unworthy conduct", I would not expect a court to stay the proceedings of every trial which has been preceded by a venial irregularity. If it be objected that my preferred solution replaces certainty by uncertainty, the latter quality is inseparable from judicial discretion' (page 163).

Latif

6.28 In *Latif* and *Shahzad*[1] the House, three years on from its decision in *Bennett,* took the opportunity to reconsider its stance. The sole speech in that case was delivered by Lord Steyn who held that in *Bennett* the House had concluded that in a proven situation of executive lawlessness, the trial judge had a discretion to decide whether there had been an abuse of process. Lord Steyn thereby in *Latif* made plain that executive lawlessness should not automatically result in a stay; the court had to exercise a more flexible and pragmatic case-by-case approach. (The judgment of Lord Steyn in *Latif* is fully considered in paras 6.43 to 6.50.)

1 (1996) 2 Cr App Rep 92.

R v Swindon Magistrates' Court, ex p Nangle[1]

6.29 Nangle, who was arrested in Scotland at Glasgow airport having been deported from Canada, contended that the UK authorities had improperly procured his presence in the UK by means other than extradition which in his submission, was the only way of properly procuring his presence in the UK. He contended that what had happened was disguised extradition which the House in *Bennett* had condemned as an abuse. For their part the authorities denied this, there was no taint of impropriety and what had happened was not disguised extradition but simply undisguised deportation.

1 [1998] 4 All ER 210.

6.30 Nangle had originally arrived in Canada in 1989 where he was convicted of 48 offences and received a term of six years imprisonment. During his imprisonment a deportation order was duly made and served on him. During his imprisonment via Interpol the London Police made their Canadian counterparts aware of their wish to arrest Nangle should he be found at any stage in the UK. At the end of his sentence Nangle was informed that he was to be deported to Ireland where he had been granted citizenship. He would be flown on a flight from Toronto to Glasgow, with an onward transfer to Dublin. However, when the flight arrived in Glasgow, Nangle was arrested and so he never arrived in Ireland. The CPS/police, in answer to Nangle's allegation of collusion, denied that they in any way sought to influence the Canadian authorities and in particular denied that they had asked that a route of travel be taken which would allow Nangle to pass through the UK. The Canadians agreed with this version stating that at the time of Nangle's removal there were no direct flights to Ireland from Canada and flying him via Glasgow was the most expedient route.

6.31 In his judgment Lord Bingham CJ had the advantage of not simply relying on the House's judgment in *Bennett* but also in the subsequent *Bennett* case, *Bennett v H M Advocate.*[1] Interestingly, the Scottish High Court had held after hearing all the evidence, as a matter of fact that there had not been any collusion between the UK and the South African authorities and that there had not been any flouting of extradition procedures. Having considered these authorities Bingham CJ perceived the test for the court to be as follows:

> 'The question in each of these cases is whether it appears that the police or the prosecuting authorities have acted illegally or procured or connived at unlawful procedures or violated international law or the

domestic law of foreign states or abused their powers in a way that should lead this court to stay the proceedings against the applicant' (page 222).

1 (1995) SLT 510.

6.32 Bingham CJ held that on the facts there was no abuse: 'It is not suggested ... that the flight via Glasgow was in anyway contrived or sinister or other than an ordinary route to chose in order to reach that destination. There is nothing whatever to suggest that the British authorities influenced the Canadian authorities to deport or procure the choice of route. Again, they did not resist it and probably welcomed the outcome. But again, there is no reason why they should have resisted that decision and no reason why they should not welcomed it. There was in my judgment no illegality, no violation of international law, no violation of the domestic law of Canada, and no abuse of power' (page 223).

Mullen

6.33 In *R v Mullen*[1] in contrast to *Nangle*, the Court found that there had been collusion and illegal behaviour on the part of the authorities. Shortly before his arrest for terrorist offences, Mullen fled from the UK to Zimbabwe. While there, during the early part of 1989, the British and Zimbabwean authorities agreed a process whereby Mullen would be arrested and deported to England from Zimbabwe in a manner which would prevent him from exercising legal right available to him under Zimbabwean law which could have frustrated this plan.

1 [1999] 3 Archbold News.

6.34 Before considering the judgment of the Court of Appeal it is important to appreciate that Mullen accepted that he had received a fair trial and was properly convicted of extremely serious offences. Furthermore, with the law on abuse as it stood in 1990, the year of his trial, it is unlikely that had the circumstances concerning his deportation from Zimbabwe been disclosed by the prosecution then a stay would have been granted or that the Court of Appeal would have intervened.

6.35 At the hearing of Mullen's appeal the Crown's argument was principally that, having conceded the fact of improper collusion between the two authorities, the grounds for his deportation under Zimbabwean law were so convincing that even if the proper extradition procedures had been followed, his removal back to England, would have inevitably been the same. Discretion should not therefore, despite the abuse, be exercised in the appellant's favour.

6.36 In deciding whether or not to hold that there had been an abuse, Rose LJ set out the factors considered by the Court of Appeal in reaching its decision. The first factor was the seriousness of the offence, 'As a primary consideration, it is necessary for the Courts to take into account the gravity of the offence in question'. Next, on whether Mullen constituted a threat to peace and security in Zimbabwe, it was held that he did not. Next, 'It is necessary to consider the nature of the conduct of those involved in the deportation on behalf of the British Government'. Rose LJ then went through the material facts in order to conclude that the British authorities had, 'initiated and subsequently assisted in and procured the deportation in the appellant by unlawful means, in circumstances in which there were specific extradition facilities between this country and Zimbabwe. In so acting they were not only encouraging unlawful conduct in Zimbabwe but they were also acting in breach of Public International Law.'

6.37 Having reached this conclusion Rose LJ then considered the various and competing public interests involved, the serious nature of the offences committed by Mullen versus the need to discourage wrongful official conduct on the part of those who are responsible for criminal prosecution. Rose LJ concluded that in Mullen's case, 'The discretionary balance comes down decisively against the prosecution of this offence'. In arriving at this conclusion Rose LJ purported to apply the balancing exercise described by Steyn LJ in *Latif*. Rose LJ said: 'In arriving at this conclusion we strongly emphasise that nothing in this judgment should be taken to suggest that there may not be cases, such as *Latif* in which the seriousness of the crime is so great relative to the nature of the abuse of process that it would be a proper exercise of judicial discretion to permit a prosecution to proceed ... notwithstanding an abuse of process in relation to the defendant's presence within the jurisdiction. In each case it is a matter of discretionary balance, to be approached with regard to a particular conduct complained of and a particular offence charged.'

6.38 Interestingly in his judgment Rose LJ sought to distinguish what he regarded as '*Bennett*-type abuse' from other types of abuse. *Bennett*-type abuse is different from other abuse types because according to Rose LJ: 'It arises not from the relationship between the prosecution and the defendant but from the relationship between the prosecution and the Court.' It is submitted that the purpose of isolating illegal extradition from other improper acts was because, in effect, Rose LJ wished to establish a rule and not simply a presumption that in such a situation the prosecution should always be stayed. Whether this submission as to Rose LJ's intentions is correct, bearing in mind the highly unsympathetic facts appertaining about Mullen's activities and that he also received a fair trial, the fact that the Court still held an abuse must mean the de facto emergence of a rule that where a court finds that there has been a *Bennett*-type abuse, ie illegal extradition, the proceedings will almost always be stayed.

Investigative resort to trickery and deception

6.39 In *Latif* the prosecution accepted that in the course of the undercover operation there was resort to the tactics of trickery and deception. At Latif's trial the defendant submitted that the use of such tactics was oppressive and accordingly the trial should be stayed as an abuse. The trial judge disagreed, his reasoning was as follows:

> 'Although no court will readily approve of trickery and deception being used, there are some circumstances in which one has to recognise living in the real world, that this is the only way in which some people are every going to be brought to trial, otherwise the courts will never get to try this sort of offence against people who are seriously involved in it.'

The judge continued:

> 'To my mind there is nothing of substance here which is unfair to the defendant in admitting this evidence ... he was not deprived of any rights which he had or sought to avail himself. It is not evident to me that any legislation or rules of practice designed to protect people from authority, has been infringed. Nor is it evident to me that the defendant is in anyway handicapped from conducting his defence, whatever that maybe, to this charge.'

Accordingly the judge refused the abuse application and in the event Latif was convicted.

6.40 Before considering how the House of Lords in *Latif* perceived the use of trickery and deception by investigators in an abuse context, it is convenient firstly to consider the earlier judgment of the Privy Counsel in *Somchai Liangsiriprasert v Government of the United States of America.*[1]

1 [1990] 2 All ER 866.

6.41 In that case an operation was undertaken by the Drug Enforcement Administration of the United States (DEA) to lure the defendant, a suspected major exporter of heroin based in Thailand, from Thailand to Hong Kong in order that his extradition could then be sought to stand trial in the United States. At that time drug offences were not extraditable crimes in the extradition treaty between the USA and Thailand. An undercover US official, acting as a willing buyer of heroin, agreed to purchase heroin from the defendant for sale in New York. The deceptions continued and ultimately as planned by the DEA, the defendant agreed to travel to Hong Kong to collect his share of the proceeds. On his arrival in Hong Kong, the defendant was arrested and his extradition to the USA then sought. Ultimately the defendant while detained in Hong Kong appealed to the Privy Counsel. He contended that his detention was unlawful because it was an abuse for a government agency to entice a person to a jurisdiction from which extradition was then available. Furthermore such official conduct was oppressive. Lord Griffiths however, peremptorily rejected this submission:

> 'As to the suggestion that it would be oppressive or an abuse of process, the short answer is that international crime has to be fought by international cooperation between law enforcement agencies. It is notoriously difficult to apprehend those at the centre of the drug trade; it is only their couriers who are usually caught. If the courts were to regard the penetration of a drug dealing organisation by the agents of a law enforcement agency and a plan to tempt the criminals into a jurisdiction from which they could be extradited as an abuse of process it would indeed be a red-letter day for the drug barons' (page 872).

6.42 Lord Griffiths thus expressly approved, not just condoned, the use of such undercover techniques for the purpose of bringing major criminals to justice. Deception and trickery alone could never constitute in the court's eyes, an affront to public conscience, oppression or an abuse of process. A similar approach was taken by the House of Lords in *Re Schmidt*[1] where the conduct by which the defendant was tricked into coming to the UK from Ireland was condoned rather than deplored. The House overruled the Divisional Court which had held that the use of trickery in that case was so unsavoury, deciding that it did amount to an abuse.

1 [1995] 1 AC 339.

Latif

6.43 The facts in *Latif* were briefly as follows: in Pakistan a paid informant of the DEA was tasked to make contact with local suppliers for heroin. The informant duly made contact with the defendants who expressed a willingness to export heroin to the UK. The informant offered to facilitate this. Subsequently, a plan for the export of heroin to the UK was agreed, the arrangement being that the defendants would deliver the heroin to the informant who would then arrange for it to be brought to the UK. Once here the defendants would subsequently travel to the UK for the purpose of collecting the heroin and arranging for its distribution. This arrangement went according to plan, along with the acquiescence of the Pakistani authorities. The defendants came to England and after meeting the informant in London were promptly arrested.

6.44 The trial judge rejected the abuse of process application holding that the defendants were not incited or entrapped by the informant and there was no breach of extradition laws. The judgment of the trial judge has already been quoted in para 6.2.

6.45 Before the House of Lords, the defendants submitted abuse of process based on the following grounds; first, the resort to deception in relation to the luring of the defendants to England was oppressive. Second, the customs officers and the informant had encouraged the defendants to commit the offence. Third, the customs officers who were responsible for the bringing of the heroin to England had themselves committed the same criminal offence of which the defendants were convicted. The defendants contended that overall the substantial evidence of executive lawlessness constituted the kind of abuse which the House in *Bennett* had refused to countenance.

6.46 The defendants recognising the force of Lord Griffiths' remarks in *Liangsiriprasert* abandoned their allegation of oppression. In dealing with their second and third grounds, Lord Steyn was concerned to outline the legal framework in which the issue of abuse should be considered in such circumstances:

> It is now necessary to consider the legal framework in which the issue of abuse of process must be considered ... If the court always refuses to stay such proceedings, the perception will be that the court condones criminal conduct and malpractice by law enforcement agencies. That would undermine pubic confidence in the criminal justice system and bring it into disrepute. On the other hand, if the court were always to

stay proceedings in such cases, it would incur the reproach that it is failing to protect the public from serious crime. The weakness of both extreme positions leaves only one principled solution. The court has a discretion; it has to perform a balancing exercise. If the court concludes that a fair trial is not possible, it will stay the proceedings. That is not what the present case is concerned with. It is plain that a fair trial was possible and that such a trial took place. In this case the issue is whether, despite the fact that a fair trial was possible, the judge ought to have stayed the criminal proceedings on broader considerations of the integrity of the criminal justice system. The law is settled. Weighing countervail considerations of policy and justice, it is for the Judge in the exercise of his discretion to decide whether there has been an abuse of process, which amounts to an affront to the public conscience and requires the criminal proceedings to be stayed' (pages 100-101).

6.47 After referring to the speeches in *Bennett* Lord Steyn explained the challenge faced by the courts in exercising discretion in such circumstances:

> 'It is possible to say that in a case such as the present the judge must weigh in the balance the public interest in ensuring those that are charged with grave crimes should be tried and the competing public interest is not conveying the impression that the court will adopt the approach that the end justifies any means' (page 101).

Having set out this framework in these very general terms Lord Steyn was, however, reluctant to elaborate and provide any guidance as to how a trial judge should conduct the balancing exercise. Lord Steyn markedly shied away from providing any general guidance as to why abuse discretion should be exercised, 'general guidance as to how the discretion should be exercised in particular circumstances would rarely be useful ...' This unwillingness on the part of Lord Steyn is analogous with the approach of the Court of Appeal in relation to s 78 of PACE discretion, for example in *R v Samuel*[1] the Court said, 'it is undesirable to attempt any general guidance as to the way in which a judge's discretion under s 78 or his inherent powers should be exercised. Circumstances vary infinitely' (page 934). In relation for example as to whether a breach of the PACE code of practice should mean that the evidence obtained by virtue of the breach should be excluded, the answer appears to be negative and a breach of the code is only one factor to be borne in mind.

1 [1988] Q 615.

6.48 Having set out the proper approach for the court to follow,

Lord Steyn held that the trial judge had performed the balancing exercise correctly and had rightly rejected the abuse submission.

6.49 *Latif* is thus clear authority that a resort to trickery and deception by investigators for the purpose of incriminating and arresting those engaged in criminal activity will be condoned by the courts. The use of ruses amounting to trickery and deception is, therefore, unlikely to form the basis of a successful defence application to stay proceedings. This principle, it is submitted, is wholly consistent with the approach of the courts in similar circumstances when applications are made pursuant to s 78 of PACE to exclude evidence obtained by undercover officers as a result of a trick. In *R v Christou and Wright*[1] undercover police officers set up a shop purporting to be conducting the business of buying and selling jewellery. The purpose of the shop was to recover stolen property and obtain evidence against those who had either stolen or dishonestly handled it. At the defendants' trial the admissibility of the undercover evidence was challenged. Lord Taylor CJ sitting in the Court of Appeal rejected this submission holding that the admission of the evidence was not unfair or contrary to public policy. In Lord Taylor's view, 'the trick was not applied to the appellance; they voluntarily applied themselves to the trick. It is not every trick producing evidence against an accused which results in unfairness' (page 269).

1 (1992) 95 Cr App Rep 264.

6.50 A trial judge following Lord Steyn's speech in *Latif* has to conduct a balancing exercise between two competing public interests. First, the imperative for the courts as part of the criminal justice system based fundamentally on the rule of law to preserve their moral integrity by disassociating themselves from investigative impropriety. The fair administration of justice cannot be sacrificed for the sake of expedience. Second, those who are charged and convicted of the serious crimes should not escape justice because such a situation would undermine public confidence in the criminal justice system. As Lord Steyn put it: 'If a court were always to stay proceedings in such cases, it would incur the reproach that it was failing to protect the public from serious crime' (page 101).

The impact of the Convention

6.51 Inevitably, most forms of covert surveillance necessitate an interference with a person's right to privacy protected by Art 8. This does not, however, mean that such activities are prohibited as the prevention of crime and the protection of the rights of others are legitimate grounds for interfering with Art 8 rights. In a series of cases before the Court several requirements have been created which may justify a state's resort to covert techniques, including the use of trickery and deception. These requirements are:

(1) The activity in question must be 'prescribed by law' (see paras 6.11 to 6.12).
(2) The activity in question must be necessary and proportionate, ie that trickery and deception was necessary to achieve the required objective, the prevention or detection of serious crime. It must be appreciated that an undercover officer in nurturing the relationship with the suspect will probably gain access to the suspect's home and private life. Such an intrusion into a person's privacy or interference with their Art 8 rights must be justified.
(3) There are in place adequate methods of accountability over the authorisation and use of police information-gathering activities.
(4) There must be remedies for those whose privacy has been wrongly invaded.

See especially *Huvig v France*,[1] and *Kopp v Switzerland*.[2]

1 (1990) 12 EHRR 528.
2 (1998) 27 EHRR 91.

Deprivation of Legal Rights

6.51a One situation, not considered by Lord Steyn in *Latif*, was where a defendant is lured by investigators into this country for the purposes of arrest and charge, the consequence of this being that he is thereby denied legal rights and privileges which would have been available to him in the foreign jurisdiction had the investigators instead sought his extradition.

6.52 The legal rights and privileges denied to the defendant may be significant. For example, if the authorities had instead decided to follow the extradition route the defendant might having strong community ties in his country of residence, have been granted bail by the foreign court pending an application for extradition. If the defendant is denied bail in England because of the seriousness of the alleged offence and because of the lack of community ties, then one can see how the actions of the prosecution have put the defendant at a legal disadvantage. Second, pursuant to the law on extradition of the foreign jurisdiction the defendant may have had certain legal advantages which are now denied; for example the right to insist within a specified time limit that the prosecution present a prima facie case, the right to cross examine witnesses and the right to make an abuse of process submission. Other rights and privileges which may have been afforded to the defendant in the country from which he was lured may spring to mind, for example the right to be present during searching of premises which was only denied because of the defendant's incarceration in England.

6.53 The authors are unaware of an English authority concerned in an abuse context with a situation of trickery and deception where, as a direct consequence, the defendant has been deprived of foreign legal rights and privileges. Will the courts soon find that such an instance of prosecution manipulation amounts to misuse of process or even mala fides? Bearing in mind the increase in both undercover policing and international investigation of serious crime, this issue is bound to arise in a case in the form of an abuse application.

Incitement or entrapment by undercover officers

6.54 A proper consideration of the law relating to entrapment, incitement or the use of agent provocateurs is beyond the scope of this chapter. Accordingly, it shall only briefly be considered here and only as it relates to abuse of process.

6.55 The starting point of the law concerned with this subject is the decision of House of Lords in *R v Sang*[1] where the House made clear that there is no substantive defence of entrapment or agent provocateur in English criminal law. Further, that a trial judge has no discretion to exclude otherwise admissible evidence, 'on the ground that it was obtained by improper or unfair means' (Lord Diplock page 291). In *Smurthwaite and Gill*[2] Lord Taylor CJ held that this rule in *Sang* was unaffected by the implementation of s 78 of PACE. However, he held that, 'the fact that the evidence has been obtained by entrapment, or by agent provocateur, or by a trick does not of itself require the judge to exclude it. If, however, he considers that in all the circumstances the obtaining of the evidence in that way would have an adverse effect on the fairness of the trial then he will exclude it' (page 440).

1 (1979) 69 Cr App Rep 282.
2 (1994) 98 Cr App Rep 437.

6.56 Lord Taylor concluded that one of the factors that a judge may take into account when deciding to whether omit or exclude the evidence of an undercover officer was whether that officer was acting as an agent provocateur, 'in the sense that he was enticing the defendant to commit an offence he would not otherwise have committed' (page 440). In effect therefore, Lord Taylor provided a basis for courts to decide whether the evidence should be excluded or proceedings stayed.

6.57 In *Latif* the House was not directly concerned with entrapment. Lord Steyn held that the informant and customs officers had not encouraged the defendant to commit the offence: 'The highest that the argument for Shahzad can be put is that Honi gave him the opportunity to commit or to attempt to commit the crime of importing heroin into the UK if he was so minded. And he was so minded' (page 99).

6.58 It is submitted that while the rule enunciated by the House in *Sang* concerning entrapment not being a substantive defence is still extant, it is nonetheless increasingly being undermined in an abuse context by courts who, in the exercise of their discretion, are deciding to exclude evidence or stay proceedings based on such a method. The use of entrapment is increasingly regarded by courts as an example of oppressive behaviour or investigative impropriety that should not be tolerated or countenanced.

6.59 Undoubtedly the recent judgment of the European Court in *Teixeira de Castro v Portugal*[18] will have a decisive effect on English jurisprudence concerning entrapment. In *Teixeira* the Court held that the applicant had been incited by undercover police officers to commit an offence of drug trafficking for which he was later convicted. The applicant complained that as a result of this incitement he had not received a fair trial in breach of Art 6 of the Convention. The Government of Portugal disagreed contending that all the officers had done was to expose a latent predisposition on the part of the applicant to commit the offences. The Court held, on the facts, that the applicant had been incited: 'The court concludes that the two police officers' actions went beyond those of undercover agents because they instigated the offence and there is nothing to suggest that without their intervention it would have been committed. That intervention and its use in the impugned criminal proceedings meant that, right from the outset, the applicant was definitively deprived of a fair trial. Consequently there has been a violation of Art 6(1)' (para

39 page 541). Earlier in its judgment the Court had expressed a general view as to the tactic of entrapment:

> 'The use of undercover agents must be restricted and safeguards put in place even in cases concerning the fight against drug trafficking. While the rise in organised crime undoubtedly requires that appropriate measures be taken, the right to a fair administration of justice nevertheless holds such a prominent place that it cannot be sacrificed for the sake of expedience ... the public interest cannot justify the use of evidence obtained as a result of police incitement" (para 36 page 540).

1 (1998) 4 BHRC 533.

6.60 It is submitted that the European Court was unambiguous in its condemnation of the use of entrapment as a means of obtaining evidence against an accused and bringing him to trial. Significantly, the court held that such a pre-trial tactic or technique was so offensive that it infringed a person's right to a fair trial guaranteed by Art 6. As *Teixeira* will be binding authority on the English courts from October 2000 when the Human Rights Act 1998 is fully implemented, it is clear that English courts will be required to stay proceedings or exclude evidence obtained by these means. The effect of *Teixeira* is to remove this issue from the realm of judicial discretion or balancing act and instead replace it with a clear mandatory rule that there can be no judicial tolerance of evidence obtained by such means.

6.61 The verdict of the trial jury in *R v (Lord) Hardwicke and Thwaites*[1] in September 1999 deserves a passing mention in this context. On the evidence, the defendants were entrapped by News of the World journalists into supplying drugs. The jury was directed that entrapment was no defence and were, in effect, told to convict the defendant. While it duly obeyed with guilty verdicts, it added a rider stating that it would have acquitted had the fact of entrapment been taken into account. It seems therefore that at least this jury felt the principle in *Sang* considered in para 6.15 was inconsistent with justice. The appeal against conviction of these defendants will perhaps pose an interesting opportunity for the appellate courts to reconsider the rule that entrapment cannot be a substantive defence.

1 Southwark Crown Court (22 September 1999, unreported).

Illegal or unlawful conduct: mala fides

6.62 Mala fides can encompass malicious prosecution or a prosecution tainted by illegal or unlawful conduct. In an abuse context, the courts have only considered complaints of illegal or unlawful conduct and so the possibility of malicious prosecution is not considered further here.

The impact of the Convention

6.63 In relation to the terms 'illegal' or 'unlawful' conduct, the courts have generally interpreted them synonymously. The approach has been that while logically there may be a difference of meaning between the two terms this is a matter of semantic if not pedantic interest only. However, this view may be in difficulty when the impact of Convention law is fully appreciated. Bearing in mind that when the Human Rights Act is implemented and Convention law becomes binding legal authority it will be unlawful under s 6 of the Act for a court to act inconsistently with it and it follows that a breach by the authorities of any article of the Convention is thereby per se unlawful. However, it may not be illegal because neither the Convention nor the Human Rights Act states that a breach of an article constitutes of itself an illegal act. As a result therefore criminal courts whether in an abuse or in a Human Rights Act context, will be called on to consider investigative conduct which may be unlawful but not illegal. The conduct would only be illegal if it constituted a crime persuant to pre-existing English criminal law. Section 6 of the Act simply declares, 'it is unlawful for a public authority to act in a way which is incompatible with Convention rights'. It will be interesting to see whether this distinction, as a consequence of the incorporation of the Convention into English law, becomes significant. Will courts in an abuse context treat unlawful conduct less seriously than illegal conduct?

6.64 While the speeches of the House of Lords in this case have been considered earlier in this chapter (in paras 6.13 to 6.38), what was said in *ex p Bennett* is also of crucial relevance to the issues considered. The abuses of power referred to in Bennett and the response of courts must be borne in mind, as it was the clear intention of the House that any illegality or improper conduct should never be ignored.

Covert policing

6.64a Covert policing often involves the use of undercover police officers pretending to join conspiracies in order to gain information about the plans of the criminals but having no intention of taking any part in the planned crime. As the crime of conspiracy requires an agreement between two or more persons to commit an unlawful act with the intention of carrying it out, an undercover officer who has no intention of committing the crime lacks the necessary mens rea to be a conspirator. Accordingly, so long as the undercover officer does not intend to participate in the intended crime, his involvement in the alleged conspiracy will not constitute illegal or unlawful conduct. The issue can also arise in practice in relation to money laundering, where officers become covertly involved as launderers or couriers. This can be legal because of the mens rea requirement in s 49(2) of the Drugs Trafficking Act 1994.

6.65 The courts in England are reluctant to acquiesce with the conduct of investigators which of itself is illegal or unlawful. Policing in England is based on the premise that police officers are simply citizens in uniform, subject like anyone else to the criminal law. As opposed to the situation governing the security services, for example, there is no principle in English law that police officers acting as some kind of militia, enjoy extra rights and legal powers for their protection. Accordingly it is conceivable that police officers, wittingly or unwittingly, may commit criminal offences in the course of their duty. For their part, the criminal courts have preserved this constitutional position. This is demonstrated by the scathing judgment of Lord Goddard CJ in *Brannan v Peek.*[1] Lord Goddard said:

> 'The court observes with concern and with strong disapproval that the police authority ... apparently thought it right in this case to send a police officer into a public house for the purpose of committing an offence ... I hope that the day is far distant when it will become common practice in this country for police officers, who are sent into premises for the purpose of detecting crime, to be told to commit an offence themselves for the purpose of getting evidence against another person ... I think, this conviction must be set aside' (page 72).

1 [1948] 1 KB 68.

6.66 As well as such conduct being regarded as unsavoury by courts, it is submitted that the courts have also recognised that in a parliamentary democracy, unless the legislature intends that the executive can validly authorise investigators to commit acts which in all other circumstances would constitute criminal offences then it is dangerous, if not unconstitutional, for courts to condone executive illegality even if it is for benign purposes and said to be in the public interest.

6.67 In *Yip Chiu-Cheung v R*[1] the Privy Counsel considered a case where, on the facts, the undercover officer had committed an offence under Hong Kong anti-drugs trafficking law. Giving judgment on behalf of the Board Lord Griffiths clearly regarded with a distaste a submission that the undercover officer had not committed a criminal offence. He said:

> 'Neither the police, nor customs, nor any other member of the executive have any power to alter the terms of the Ordinance frustrating the export of heroin and the fact that they may turn a blind eye when the heroin is exported does not prevent it from being a criminal offence.'

1 (1994) 99 Cr App Rep 406.

6.68 Lord Griffiths quoted with approval the ruling of the High Court of Australia in *A v Hayden (No 2)*.[1] There it declared emphatically that there was no place in Australian criminal law for a general defence of superior orders or of Crown or executive authority. Gibbs CJ said:

> 'It is fundamental to our legal system that the executive has no power to authorise a breach of the law and that it is no excuse for an offender to say that he acted under the orders of a superior officer' (page 540).

Having quoted this passage, Lord Griffiths observed:

> 'This statement of the law applies with the same force in England and Hong Kong as it does in Australia' (page 410).

1 [1984] 156 CrimLR 532.

R v Schlesinger[1]

6.69 This case is an example of investigative impropriety and mala fides which the Court of Appeal described as 'disgraceful'. In 1985 the appellants were convicted of illegally exporting arms to Iraq. Before their trial the defence became aware of various embassy officials in London who were prepared to state that the arms had not in fact gone to Iraq. However, before witness statements could be taken, the officials announced they could no longer assist, their permission to do so from their embassies having been withdrawn. In the event the defendants pleaded guilty.

1 [1995] CrimLR 137.

6.70 In 1993 the Scott Inquiry discovered why this volte-face had occurred. The Foreign Office at the behest of Customs (the prosecutorial agency) had urged the embassies not to allow their officials to assist the defence. When this information was published the defendants appealed against their convictions.

6.71 The Court of Appeal readily quashed the convictions. It held that the prosecution had first, improperly interfered with the course of justice and second, had concealed this from the defence and trial judge. In holding abuse, the Court held that a defendant does not receive a fair trial if he is prevented by the prosecution from calling witnesses who are believed will be helpful to the defence.

Latif

6.72 The issue of unlawful conduct arose in a domestic context in *Latif* the facts of which have already been recounted in para 6.43. One of the grounds of the appellant's abuse application was that the customs officer, who had brought the heroin to England had himself committed the offence for which the appellants were convicted. After argument, the prosecution conceded this point but denied that this gave rise to a finding of abuse. Lord Steyn agreed with this view, 'the conduct of the customs officer was not so unworthy or shameful that it was an affront to the public conscience to allow the prosecution to proceed. Realistically, any criminal behaviour of the customs officer was venial compared to that of *Shazhad*' (page 101). In coming to their conclusion that the behaviour of the officer was merely 'venial' Lord Steyn took account of the following factors;

(1) *That the crime was already in existence* – The appellants' had already planned to be concerned in the importation of the heroin into England before the customs officer became involved and were therefore already guilty of conspiracy to import heroin into England. Lord Steyn rejected the appellants assertion that they had been incited.

(2) *Motive* – Lord Steyn accepted that the officer was acting under the authority of his superiors and was motivated by a courageous desire in his attempt to break a drugs ring and ensure the punishment of those involved.

(3) *Comparative involvement in the crime* – Lord Steyn compared the degree of criminality of the customs officer ('venial') and that of the appellants who were major drug smugglers.

6.73 It is submitted that on the facts before him, Lord Steyn was determined to ensure that those who were guilty, on abundant evidence, of major crime were not going to escape justice because of some peripheral unlawful conduct by the customs officer. While one can readily appreciate this reasoning in *Latif* it surely must, as a matter of public policy, be important that illegal or unlawful acts are not routinely condoned by the courts. The sentiments of Gibbs CJ, in para 6.68, should be treated as a powerful warning against any temptation on the part of the executive and judiciary that first, the end can justify the means and second, that the executive has the power to waive or negate Parliaments' intentions as set out in statute. It must be the responsibility of the executive, particularly of those who supervise and engage in undercover operations, to ensure that the line between legality and illegality is never crossed or blurred.

Post-Latif

6.74 Following *Latif*,[1] an example of 'venial' but nonetheless unlawful conduct by investigators is *Khan*.[2] In this case, a former Thai diplomat brought with him to Heathrow from Thailand a quantity of heroin in his diplomatic bag. On arrival, the bag was searched and the drugs discovered.[3] At his trial an abuse submission was made on the ground that this search was unlawful as, it was claimed, it was in breach of the Vienna Convention. At the time of the search the defendant was entitled to diplomatic immunity and there was no lawful authority, until this was waived, to search his bag. The trial judge was not attracted to this argument and dismissed the application.

1 [1997] CrimLR 508.
2 [1997] CrimLR 508.
3 Subsequently the Thai Embassy in London waived his immunity.

6.75 The subject of mala fides arising out of illegal unlawful conduct by investigators had recently become high profile as a result of two successful abuse applications made during 1999 at Bristol Crown Court. Both prosecutions were brought by HM Customs where the defendants were alleged to be major drug traffickers. However, those prosecutions were stayed arising out of discoveries concerning illegal and unlawful conduct. These cases can conveniently be considered separately.

R v Carrington[1]

6.76 The defendants were charged with drug trafficking. The prosecution's case rested on the discovery of a cargo of cannabis resin in a boat which was bound for the UK. At the time of the seizure of the boat and discovery of the cannabis, the boat was in international waters off Portugal. By reason of international maritime law, before the boat could be lawfully intercepted and boarded by agents of HM Customs (in this case British Special Forces) the consent was required of the Attorney General of Malta. This was because the boat had begun its voyage from there and such consent was required in order to make the interception lawful. This would remain the legal position until the boat entered the territorial waters of another state. However, for some reason customs did not wish to track the boat until it entered the territorial waters of the United Kingdom and then board it but wished to do so on the high seas.

1 Judgment of Foley HHJ (February 1999, unreported).

6.77 When the consent of the Maltese Attorney General was sought, it transpired that he was informed by customs that the location of the boat was 'off the coast of the United Kingdom'.[1] Having made this false representation, consent from the Maltese was forthcoming. At the trial the defence submitted that the prosecution intended to mislead the Maltese and this constituted mala fides which in turn constituted an abuse. At the voir dire to investigate the matter, Maltese witnesses confirmed that they would not have given consent if they were aware of the true position of the boat. The trial judge held that the behaviour of customs was shameful; 'this case has revealed a culture, a climate, of carelessness and recklessness for disregard for the rules of procedures, convention of Maltese law, British law and International law ... this court cannot abdicate its judicial responsibility. It gives me no pleasure, the case for a stay is overwhelming, there was mala fides here' (page 1051 of transcript).

1 It appears that when the request was made, the boat was in fact 900 miles from Britain off the coast of Portugal.

R v Doran[1]

6.78 The facts of this case are complex and therefore difficult to summarise. There is also a history of trial, appeal and retrial. It transpired at the retrial that both the judge in the first trial and the defence had been deliberately misled by customs concerning two factual issues; first whether consent had been obtained from the management of various hotels to the bugging of hotel rooms by customs officers. Contrary to what was claimed it was established that such consent had not been obtained. Second, that customs' own internal authorisation procedures which the investigating officers should have obeyed before placing the defendants under surveillance had in fact been ignored. Moreover, to conceal this fact the officers had allegedly created a trail of false paperwork. The trial judge, Turner J held: 'By abuse of executive authority, the prosecution, viewed as a single entity, have, by means which are at least arguably unlawful, deprived the defence of its strategic ability to mount the challenge to the integrity of the prosecution case ...' In assessing the seriousness of the officers conduct Turner J held that, 'the conduct which I have already discussed in some detail cannot fairly be dismissed as "venial" or as mere "regrettable error" as the prosecution have invited me to accept ... it is wholly inaccurate to describe what has happened as "regrettable error." What has happened has had a significant impact on the ability of the defendants properly to defend themselves and to that extent, as a matter of probability, they have been seriously prejudiced in the conduct of their defence'. In those circumstances Turner J held that the prosecution were guilty of abuse and that the conduct of the officers struck at the rule of law.

1 Bristol Crown Court (6 July 1999, unreported).

R Gokal

6.79 Finally, the case of *R v Gokal*[1] can also be mentioned in this context. In that case the defendant was arrested at Frankfurt airport in July 1994, en route from Pakistan, where he lived to New York where he was due to meet American prosecutors, them already having granted him immunity from prosecution there. His arrest was occasioned by the intervention of the Serious Fraud Office who had issued a warrant for his arrest in London as a precursor to asking the German police to arrest the defendant pending his extradition to England. On the defendant's extradition to England and at the beginning of his trial, he argued in favour of a stay on the grounds that the Serious Fraud Office (SFO) had colluded with the US authorities to deceive the defendant into believing that he had free passage, whereas all along his arrest in Germany and extradition to England was intended. Alternatively, the SFO had deceived the US authorities. The SFO denied both allegations, they claimed that the US authorities had inadvertently tipped-off the SFO of the defendant's movement which led to them independently decide to seek his arrest and extradition. The judge, on the evidence put before him, was not persuaded as there being any collusion or deception by the SFO on the American authorities and accordingly held that the principle in *Bennett* did not apply.

1 Central Criminal Court (May 1997, unreported).

Burden of proof of establishing illegal or unlawful conduct on the defence

6.80 It should be remembered that if the defence argues abuse arising out of such conduct, it carries the burden of establishing that it occurred. In *R v MacDonald*[1] the defendants alleged an abuse, claiming that during the course of their investigation, police officers had stolen £32,000. Defence counsel submitted that the fact that this money could not be accounted for questioned the honesty and credibility of the police witnesses, with the effect that the defendant could not have a fair trial. In the exercise of his discretion, the trial judge rejected this submission holding that, first, the defence had not proved their allegation and second, suspicion concerning the missing money did not render a fair trial impossible. The Court of Appeal subsequently upheld this ruling, the judge had correctly conducted the balancing act required of him by *Latif* weighing the countervailing considerations of prosecuting criminals charged with serious offences and discouraging abuse of power.

1 [1998] CrimLR 808.

6.81 In *Bray and Others (No 2)*[1] the Court of Appeal dealt with an interlocutory appeal made by the prosecution against a ruling of the trial judge during a preparatory hearing. During that hearing the judge had excluded pursuant to s 78 of PACE evidence which the police had obtained from their counterparts in Holland. It transpired during the hearing that this evidence had not been obtained pursuant to the proper procedures and that in the view of the trial judge, it had been obtained via a cynical and prolonged breach of undertakings. However, the Court of Appeal granted the prosecution's appeal holding that the quality of the evidence was unaffected by the Dutch illegality.

1 31 July 1998 para E41, Archbold's Criminal Appeal Office Index (second cumulative supplement.)

6.82 This case is surprising principally because it appears that the defence did not mount an abuse application which would pursuant to *Bennett* have obliged the court to focus on the means by which the evidence was obtained irrespective of its quality. Second, *Bray* appears to suggest that when it comes to the issue of prosecution illegality two separate legal tests are to be applied depending upon whether an abuse or a s 78 application is made. If s 78 then the defence must not only show illegality but also prejudice but if only abuse, then simply show illegality. Whether the creation of such the dichotomy is attractive is, however, doubtful.

7. Prosecution manipulation or misuse of process

7.1 In *R v Derby Crown Court, ex p Brooks*[1] Sir Roger Ormrod defined the jurisdiction of abuse of process as follows:

> 'The power to stop a prosecution arises only when it is an abuse of the process of the court. It may be an abuse of process if either (a) [the prosecution have manipulated or misused the process of the court so as to deprive the defendant of a protection provided by the law or to take unfair advantage of a technicality], or (b) on the balance of probability the defendant has been or will be, prejudiced in the preparation or conduct of his defence by delay on the part of the prosecution ...' (page 169) [Emphasis added].

1 (1985) 80 Cr App Rep 164.

7.2 There are an infinite number of situations in which an allegation of prosecutorial manipulation or misuse of the process of the court can be made. This chapter considers only a number of miscellaneous instances of where the abuse jurisdiction has been invoked. It is emphasised that the situations considered below are but mere examples of this head of abuse and the situations in which this can arise cannot be fully predicted. Fairness is obviously a concept whose parameters cannot be fixed or discerned.

Proof of prejudice not required

7.3 A characteristic of the law on abuse concerned with manipulation on misuse of process is that the court does not require any evidence of actual prejudice caused to the defendant. Manipulation or misuse, if established, tends to be regarded so gravely that the courts will stay the proceedings without further consideration. This approach differs from that in relation to delay where there is an insistence by the courts of the need to establish prejudice even when there has been massive delays.[1]

1 See Chapter 1.

Circumvention of statutory time limits

7.4 The cases under this heading can be conveniently divided into two parts; first, those concerned with s 127(1) of the Magistrates' Court Act 1980 which states that summonses must be issued within six months of the commission of the alleged offence and second, those concerned with alleged circumvention of custody time limits.

Section 127 Magistrates' Court Act 1980

7.5 The leading case is *R v Brentford Justices, ex p Wong*.[1] Here the defendant was summonsed for driving without due care and attention. The summons was applied for and issued two days before the expiry of the six-month time limit. The defence solicitor whose suspicions were aroused by the timing of this manoeuvre made inquiries. Ultimately the prosecution disclosed that the information (the pre-requisite for the issuance of the summons) was laid in order that more time be obtained pending a decision as to whether the defendant should be prosecuted with this offence or not. The prosecution admitted therefore that the information was laid before any decision had been made in relation to prosecution. The magistrates held that they had no jurisdiction to consider an abuse application based on an allegation of misuse of process and the case went to the Divisional Court. The Court held that it would be an abuse for the prosecutor to lay on information when he has not reached a decision to prosecute. This judgment in this case is considered in paras 1.12 to 1.14.

1 [1981] 1 All ER 884.

Custody Time Limits

7.6 Two cases under this heading can be considered:

R v Great Yarmouth Magistrates, ex p Thomas[1]

7.7 The applicants were remanded in custody charged with a drugs offence. The custody time limit had expired and the prosecutor's application for an extension was refused. The applicants were then released but at the behest of the prosecutor, they were immediately rearrested and charged with a connected but separate drugs offence.

Unsurprisingly the defence alleged abuse, that the prosecutor had dishonestly contrived to manipulate the prosecution process so as to bring the applicants back within the custody time limit regulations in order that they may be deprived of their right to bail. In the Divisional Court, Watkins LJ was unwilling to inquire into the truth of what had happened merely holding that if the defence case here was made out, this would be an abuse. Intriguingly, Watkins LJ did not hold that the bringing of additional charges to prevent the release on bail of a defendant of itself amounted to mala fides or dishonesty. It is submitted that for reasons which are not apparent, Watkins LJ strove to find some rationale for not stigmatising the conduct of the prosecutor in this case with the badge of mala fides.

1 [1992] CrimLR 116.

R v Wolverhampton Magistrates' Court and Stafford Crown Court, ex p Uppal[1]

7.8 The applicants were originally charged with rape. The magistrates refused to extend the custody time limit in respect of this charge which was about to expire. The day after this refusal an additional charge of false imprisonment was laid which attracted its own custody time limit. The Divisional Court held that it would be an abuse if the fresh charge had been preferred simply for the purpose of avoiding a custody time limit but in this case it was satisfied on the evidence that this was not the prosecutor's motive. Based on the evidence, the prosecutor was entitled to bring the additional charge and the Court accepted the prosecutor's explanation that this was to enable the trial court to see the full picture. In this case all the Divisional Court were prepared to do was to suggest that in future where the evidence was clear from the beginning, all possible charges should be laid at that stage.

1 [1995] CrimLR 223.

Prosecutor's improper motive

7.9 Such allegations normally arise in relation to the bringing of private prosecutions where the defendant alleges that the underlying motive of the prosecutor is either revenge, obsession or some wholly collateral motive to cause embarrassment to the defendant. The attitude of the Divisional Court to such allegations is a permissive one, generally permitting the bringing of private prosecutions unless there is very clear evidence of improper motive. There are perhaps three reasons explaining this reluctance to intervene; first, the Court does not wish to bear the burden of inquiring into the detail of the facts of a case including the alleged underlying motive of the prosecutor. Second, the Court knows that where there is a flagrant abuse then the Crown Prosecution Service has the statutory power to take over and discontinue the proceedings. Third, it appears that the policy of the courts is generally to facilitate the bringing of private prosecutions. This has perhaps been encouraged by a recent Law Commission report supporting this.[1]

1 Report No 255, Consents to Prosecution [1998].

7.10 The following cases can be considered.

R v Bow Street Metropolitan Stipendiary Magistrates, ex p South Coast Shipping[1]

7.11 The defendant alleged that the bringing of this private prosecution was an abuse because it was being used as a means of drawing publicity to the Marchioness shipping disaster and as a means of creating political pressure in favour of a public inquiry. The prosecution was alleged to be a mere device to achieve a collateral purpose. The Divisional Court held that even if this attribution of motive to the prosecutor was true, the prosecution would not be an abuse unless this was the prosecutor's sole or dominant motive. That the prosecutor has an ulterior motive other than to bring criminals to justice is not therefore necessarily fatal or open to objection on the grounds of abuse or oppression.

1 [1993] CrimLR 221.

R v Durham Magistrates, ex p Davies[1]

7.12 A similar approach was also taken in this case. Here, the private prosecutor was alleged to be obsessed with achieving the successful prosecution of the defendant. Accordingly his motives were improper, they tainted the prosecution and it should be stayed as an abuse. The Divisional Court disagreed holding that the motivation of a prosecutor was irrelevant to consideration of the abuse claim. It is submitted that the decision in this case is consistent with the cautionary words expressed by Lord Salmon in *DPP v Humphrys*:[2] 'I respectfully agree that a judge has not and should not appear to have any responsibility for the institution of prosecutions; nor has he any power to refuse to allow the prosecution to proceed merely because he considers that, as a matter of policy, it ought not to have been brought. It is only if the prosecution amounts to an abuse of the process of the Court and is oppressive or frivolous that the judge has the power to intervene' (page 46). Lord Edmund-Davies said: 'Judges should pause long before staying proceedings which on their face are perfectly regular' (page 55).

1 (1993) Times, 25 May 1993.
2 [1977] AC 1.

R v Gloucester Crown Court, ex p Jackman[1]

7.13 There was another private prosecution, where the criminal prosecution and a civil claim were being run in tandem by the same person against the same defendant. The solicitors acting for the prosecutor/claimant offered to settle both proceedings with the defendant provided that the defendant paid compensation to the prosecutor/claimant. When settlement negotiations broke down, the defendant asserted that the prosecution was oppressive because it was being used as a means of pressuring the defendant to accept settlement terms in relation to the civil proceedings. The Court held that the evidence to support this claim was insufficient although it expressed its disapproval of the proposed terms of settlement which included an offer to discontinue the prosecution.

1 [1993] COD 100. See also *R v Horseferry Magistrates' Court, ex p Stephenson* [1989] COD 470.

R v Milton Keynes Magistrates, ex p Roberts[1]

7.14 This was a prosecution brought by the Trading Standards Department of Buckinghamshire County Council for breach of the Trade Descriptions Act 1968. It was alleged that the defendant was dealing in counterfeit parts for Ford cars. The defendant alleged abuse on the ground that the prosecutor was a mere puppet of the Ford motor company who had provided the resources for the investigation. The prosecutor had not allegedly exercised independent judgment and Ford were the real prosecutors. The Divisional Court held that the Trading Standards Department had exercised independent judgment. A stay would only be imposed, 'if a prosecutor did indeed make himself the creature of a private interest in exercising his powers, then that conduct would at least be prima facie abusive'. Furthermore a prosecution would only be stopped if to allow it to continue would be 'tantamount to endorsing behaviour which undermines or degrades the rule of law' or 'is an affront to justice'.

1 [1995] CrimLR 224.

Removal of right to a particular type of trial

R v Rotherham Justices, ex p Brough[1]

7.15 The defendant was alleged to have committed the offence when aged 16. Pursuant to s 24 of the Magistrates' Court Act 1980 if, when the issue of mode of trial was dealt with by the magistrate, the defendant was under 17, then the case could only be remitted to the magistrates for trial. However, the charge was indictable only if the defendant was aged 17. In the event, the return date of the applicant's summons was fixed for the day after his 17th birthday. His suspicious defence solicitor inquired with both the Court and the CPS why this should be so and after initial denials from the CPS, ascertained that the timing of the defendant's hearing was not a matter of chance but because the CPS felt that the case should only dealt with by the Crown Court. The applicant alleged misuse of process. The Divisional Court held that manipulation of the date in this way by the CPS was an unacceptable way of advancing the interests of justice. However, the Court declined to attribute any element of misconduct or mala fides to anyone within the CPS. The Court held that this was not a case where there was 'some element of bad faith or sharp practice or oppressive or overreaching behaviour or, to use a colloquialism some form of dirty trick'. Furthermore, the Court held that the defendant was not prejudiced.

1 [1991] CrimLR 522.

R v Redbridge Justices and Fox, ex p Whitehouse[1]

7.16 The defendant was charged with an either way offence and expressed a preference for summary trial. This was opposed by the prosecution who wished for a Crown Court trial. Subsequently, an additional more serious charge was laid making the case indictable only. The defendant alleged that this additional charge was motivated by a desire to deprive the defendant of his right to elect for summary trial. The Divisional Court held that such a motive by a prosecutor was permissible provided that the additional more serious charge was justified on the evidence.

1 [1992] COD 234.

R v Martin[1]

7.17 The appellant was charged with murder and convicted. The conviction was awarded by a court-martial which had been convened in Germany. What was exceptional about this case was that the appellant had been brought from England, where he was eligible to trial by jury, to stand trial by a court-martial in Germany. The reason for this was because when the alleged murder occurred, the appellant was subject to military law. The appellant argued that the court-martial procedure was unfair principally for two reasons; first, the trial of a young civilian by court-martial was inherently unfair and oppressive. Second, the decision to try the appellant by court-martial in Germany rather than allow him to be tried in England constituted an abuse.

1 [1998] 1 All ER 193.

7.18 The House of Lords dismissed this appeal. It construed the relevant provisions of the Army Act 1955 to hold that Parliament had approved trial by court-martial as an appropriate mode of trial for young civilians in certain circumstances. Furthermore, the decision not to allow a trial in England on the grounds of forum conveniens was not inherently unfair or an abuse.

Breach of duty to make disclosure

7.19 Since April 1977 the prosecution's duty of disclosure of unused material has been governed by Part I of the Criminal Procedure and Investigations Act 1996 and also the code of practice promulgated under Part II of that Act. These provisions, however, only concern disclosure of unused material, not evidence.

7.20 Prior to the enactment of the CPIA's disclosure provisions, the position was governed by common law. In cases, breach of such common law duties by the prosecution was judged to constitute an abuse.[1] However, bearing in mind the new statutory regime it would not be helpful to consider such authorities here. Furthermore, bearing in mind the relatively recent change to the statutory regime there have not as yet been reported cases dealing with breach of the various statutory duties on the prosecution to make disclosure of unused material. It must surely be clear that breach of such a duty could properly found in abuse application.

1 See D Corker, *Disclosure in Criminal Proceedings*, Sweet & Maxwell.

7.21 In *R v Stratford Justices, ex p Imbert*[1] the Divisional Court considered whether, in a summary only case, a refusal of the CPS to furnish the defence in advance of the trial the statements of prosecution witnesses was unfair. The Divisional Court rejected this contention and followed the decision in *R v Kingston-on-Hull Justices, ex p McCann* where it was held that in summary trials there was no requirement for advance disclosure of witness statements. In *Imbert* the Court, however, did state that in all but the most exceptional cases, disclosure ought to be given following a reasonable defence request.

1 (1999) 2 Cr App Rep 276.
2 (1991) 155 JP 569.

7.22 Buxton LJ in this case took the opportunity available to him to consider whether this decision of the court would need to be reviewed once the European Convention was fully implemented. Buxton LJ considered the relevant principles of Convention jurisprudence and the relevant authorities especially *Foucher v France.*[1] He concluded that Art 6 did not require the granting of an entitlement to defendants of an absolute right to pre-trial disclosure in all cases.[2]

1 (1997) 25 EHRR 234.
2 See considerations of *DPP v Metten* considered in para

7.23 An interesting and original submission was made by the defence in *R v Jackson.*[1] The appellant was subject to a retrial, the jury in the first trial having failed to agree on a number of counts in the indictment. During the first trial the trial judge had ordered disclosure of a specific document which could not then be found and so no disclosure of it occurred. However, in the interim period between the first and second trials this document was discovered and disclosed. At the commencement of the retrial the defence submitted that this document was highly material. If it had been available and had been relied on by the defence at the original trial the first jury might have acquitted. Accordingly, the second trial should be stayed as an abuse. The trial judge and the Court ruled against this submission. The Court of Appeal held that it occasionally happened that new evidence was discovered and disclosed between two trials which could then assist either party. That fact alone however did not render the verdict of a jury in the second trial unsafe.

1 [1998] CrimLR 835.

Prosecution overcharging

7.24 This allegation was made in *Hui Chi-Ming v R.*[1] The defendant was alleged to have been an accomplice to murder and was tried for this offence. Prior to his trial, the alleged killer had been acquitted of murder. The prosecution had also offered a plea bargain; the murder count would be dropped in return for a plea of guilty to manslaughter. This was rejected but ultimately the defendant was convicted of murder. He submitted that his trial for murder was an abuse. Bearing in mind the previous acquittal of the alleged principal for murder it was unfair for this trial to proceed. Furthermore, the prosecution should only have charged manslaughter. The Privy Counsel held that there was no evidence of deliberate overcharging by the prosecution and that on the evidence, the prosecution were entitled to bring a charge of murder despite the earlier acquittal of the alleged principal offender. In Lord Lowry's view there is nothing which could credibly be described as an abuse of process, 'that is, something so unfair and wrong that the courts should not allow a prosecutor to proceed with what is in all respects a regular proceeding. There can be no suggestion that the appellant was the victim of a plea bargaining situation ... there was no sign of fraud or deceit as between the Crown and the appellant' (page 251).

1 (1991) 94 Cr App Rep 236.

Trial in absence of a co-accused

7.25 In *R v Forsyth*[1] the defendant was charged with handling stolen goods. Her prosecution arose out of allegations concerning the fugitive Asil Nadir. Her prosecution was exceptional in the sense that, following the absconding of Nadir, the prosecution (Serious Fraud Office) had conceded that the trial of the second defendant should not proceed because in Nadir's absence, it could not be fair to that defendant. However, in relation to Forsyth the SFO pressed ahead despite accepting that she was a peripheral defendant on the fringe of an immense fraud allegedly committed by Nadir and the second defendant. Beldam LJ held that the decision of the SFO to prosecute Forsyth in the circumstances, 'seems a strange decision' but nonetheless, 'the decision to do so is the prerogative of the SFO and does not in our judgement itself amount to an abuse of process. It is not for us to say whether such a choice accords with ordinary notions of even handedness, or is likely to enhance the public perception of the fairness of a prosecuting authority' (page 311).

1 (1997) 2 Cr App Rep 299.

Repeated committal proceedings

7.26 In *R v Manchester City Stipendiary Magistrate, ex p Snelson*[1] Lord Widgery CJ held that a criminal prosecution could be restarted against a defendant by way of fresh committal proceedings or voluntary bill of indictment even where the original proceedings against the defendant at committal had been dismissed. Lord Widgery, however, considered the danger which his judgment might create as vexatious repeated committal proceedings for the same offence against the same defendant. He said: '... the only aspect of the whole case which has troubled me is the feeling that if the prosecution are right in their argument there seems to me to be a risk that a defendant might be prejudiced by repeated committal proceedings all failing, resulting in a committal being repeated time after time ... I am satisfied that this particular difficulty is overcome ... by saying that this Court has a discretionary power to see that the use of repeated committal proceedings is not allowed to become vexatious or an abuse of the process of the Court' (page 232).

1 (1977) 66 Cr App Rep 44.

7.27 This issue arose in *R v Horsham Justices, ex p Reeves*[1] where Lord Ackner held that the repeated committal in that case was an abuse. He said, 'should the prosecution be entitled as they see it, to treat the first committal proceedings for all practicable purposes as a dummy run and, having concluded that they over-complicated them, for virtually the same proceedings but in a form which they should have been brought if proper thought had been given by the prosecution to them in the first place? In my judgment, to allow such a course in the particular circumstances of this case would be vexatious to the applicant, and for that reason it would, in my judgment, be an abuse' (page 234). Lord Ackner held that the second set of proceedings although simplified and shortened compared to the first were vexatious on abuse.

1 [1981] CrimLR 566.

7.28 However, in *R v Grays Justices, ex p Graham*[1] the Divisional Court held that the proceedings were not vexatious, the defendant having been discharged in the original proceedings on the grounds of delay.

1 (1982) 75 Cr App Rep 229.

The rule in *Hunter*

7.29 In *Hunter v Chief Constable of the West Midlands*[1] the Birmingham Six, following their conviction for terrorist offences, initiated a civil action against the police for assault. Their statement of claim alleged that during their interviews with individual police officers in which they made alleged confessions, they were beaten and sustained physical injuries. At their criminal trial, the circumstances under which their confessions were obtained was a central issue. A major plank of each of the defendants' cases was the assertion that the confessions were untrue, unreliable and were coerced. The jury however must have disbelieved this because they convicted all six. At the hearing of this civil action, the defendant police officers contended that the initiation of the civil action was an abuse of process as in effect the action sought to refute or throw into doubt, the finding of both the trial judge and the jury at the criminal trial that the Birmingham Six had not been assaulted by the police. In holding that this action constituted an abuse of process Lord Diplock articulated a rule which has subsequently become to be known as 'The rule in Hunter':

> 'The abuse of process which the instant case exemplifies is the initiation of proceedings in a court of justice for the purpose of mounting a collateral attack on a final decision against the intending plaintiff which has been made by another court of competent jurisdiction in previous proceedings in which the intending plaintiff had a full opportunity of contesting the decision in the court by which it was made' (page 541).

1 [1982] AC 529.

7.30 The rule in *Hunter* was exclusively applied in a criminal context in *R v Belmarsh Magistrates Court, ex p Watts*.[1] The facts of this case have already been recounted in Chapter 6 and are not repeated here. One of the matters to be decided in, *ex p Watts* was whether the rule in *Hunter* extended to criminal rather than simply civil proceedings. In his judgment Buxton LJ held that the rule in *Hunter* did apply to criminal proceedings. However, he was careful to restrict its application to where the second proceedings, 'must in fact and in effect, and not merely in intention, be a challenge to the finding in the first proceedings'. In other words if the second proceedings were successful, this would contradict the judgment in the earlier proceedings. Buxton LJ also relied on the judgment of Bingham MR in *Smith v Linskills*:[2]

> 'The main considerations of public policy which underlie the existing rule are, as we understand, threefold; (i) the affront to any coherent system of justice which must necessarily arise if there subsist two final but inconsistent decisions of courts of competent jurisdiction ...(ii) the virtual impossibility of fairly retrying at a later date the issue which was before the court on the earlier occasion ...(iii) the importance of finality in litigation' (page 773).

1 [1999] 2 Cr App Rep 188.
2 [1996] 1 WLR 763.

7.31 Turning to the merits of the case before him Buxton LJ held that the intention of the prosecutor was to undermine his earlier conviction. However, he should have followed the route of appeal rather than initiate collateral criminal proceedings for the same purpose.

7.32 As to the jurisdiction of the Divisional Court to rule that the rule in *Hunter* applied to exclusively criminal proceedings, Búxton LJ cited Lord Lowry in *Bennett*[1] that it should offend the Courts' sense of justice and propriety to be asked to try the accused in the circumstances of this case (page 74). Buxton LJ held that this prosecution fell within that category and could therefore be stayed. This, it is submitted, is a novel application to domestic proceedings of *Bennett* which hitherto had been regarded as applying only with regard to international executive lawlessness.

1 [1994] AC 42.

Abuse of process in extradition proceedings

7.33 In *R v Governor of Pentonville Prison, ex p Sinclair*[1] the question considered by the House of Lords was: 'Has the magistrates in extradition proceedings jurisdiction to consider whether such proceedings may be an abuse of process of the court?' The House held that a magistrate has no such jurisdiction. This decision was applied and followed in *R v Governor of Pentonville Prison, ex p Alves*.[2]

1 [1991] 2 AC 64.
2 [1993] AC 284.

7.34 Post the decision of the House of Lords in, *ex p Bennett* the question arose of whether the High Court had a jurisdiction to inquire into the circumstances in which a person was brought into the United Kingdom to face extradition proceedings. In *R v Secretary of State for the Home Department, ex p Schmidt*[1] the House of Lords held that the *Bennett* principle had no application to extradition from the United Kingdom. In other words, the courts had not power to refuse extradition on the grounds that a surrender would be unjust or oppressive. The House of Lords had made plain that matters of this kind are for the exclusive consideration of the Secretary of State.

1 [1995] 1 AC 339.

Failure to conduct a fair interview

7.35 Interviews under caution are governed by Code C of the PACE codes of practice. Most abuse or s 78 applications relating to interviews are in connection with some allegation of unfairness or oppression which was said to have occurred during the defendants interview. However, recently the courts have recognised that an abuse can arise where the police/investigators failed to interview the defendant at all or failed to interview him fairly.

7.36 In *Trustham*[1] the accused stood trial for drug-money laundering. Following his arrest he was never interviewed but simply charged. The trial judge held that this had prejudiced the defendant in the following way: 'A defendant who does not give evidence having answered questions in interview is nevertheless entitled to have that explanation considered by the jury.' The trial judge also found that the defendant was further prejudiced as follows: 'To deprive a suspect of the right to give an explanation at the earliest opportunity, despite him having been cautioned, that anything he did say would be written down and may be given in evidence, must be a breach of a person's human rights and is clearly an abuse.'

1 Southwark Crown Court, (27 November 1997, unreported).

7.37 In the circumstances of *Trustham*, the trial judge held that the defendant had a right to be interviewed and had a right during such interview to provide an explanation as to his state of mind. Depriving the defendant of an interview deprived him from setting out at the earliest opportunity his defence/innocence which the judge held was unfair because this meant that at his subsequent trial, the defendant could not point to what he said immediately after his arrest.

8. Procedural considerations

INTRODUCTION

8.1 In this chapter it is proposed to analyse the various options open to practitioners seeking to make abuse of process applications, from the magistrates' court level up to the Court of Appeal. Procedural opportunities will be considered as much as the constraints on the same, the object being to answer the various issues of when, where and how such applications may be made. In addition, the aim is to assist the defence practitioner with practical advice on how best to present an abuse submission.

8.2 The starting point naturally is to satisfy oneself that a proper argument exists on the merits, and that the case meets the stringent criterion required. While this may sound self-evident the Courts continue to sound out regular warnings to practitioners as to the need for self-restraint before embarking. Indeed, since the *A-G's Reference (No 1 of 1990)*[1] the courts have, in the face of an ever burgeoning body of abuse case law, sought to encourage practitioners to exercise greater self-restraint, in the light of a history of what some courts clearly consider to be a significant number of palpably unmeritorious applications.

1 [1992] QB 630.

8.3 Lord Bingham CJ, *Environment Agency v Stanford*[1] stated that the Courts have repeatedly emphasised how the jurisdiction to stay proceedings as an abuse of process ought to be exercised with the greatest caution. His Lordship commented that the lower courts were too often invited to stay proceedings in inappropriate circumstances, for example, where a prosecution was merely ill advised or unwise, issues which in his view, were largely relevant in relation to mitigation.

1 Judgment delivered QBD, No CO/462 97 [1998] COD 373.

8.4 It is however, submitted that whatever the 'floodgates' position may be, in terms of the great volume of cases, the likelihood is that the Courts will be as unsuccessful as King Canute in holding back the tide of applications. In the light of the ever-expanding nature of the doctrine, the judiciary will expect that, at the very least, the parties use the correct procedures.

8.5 Finally, any observer of recent judicial policy in the criminal courts will notice an increased willingness to use wasted costs orders as a means of punishing unmeritorious defence applications and to deter others. Practitioners should bear this possibility closely in mind.

THE MAGISTRATES' COURT: JURISDICTION TO RULE ON ABUSE APPLICATIONS

The legal context

8.6 Magistrates' courts may encounter defence applications to stay the proceedings on the grounds of abuse in two sets of circumstances. First, in relation to a summary trial to be heard before them and second, in relation to when they act as examining justices in the context of committal proceedings. In practice, as summary proceedings rarely give rise to abuse of process issues and they are, in any event, never concerned with serious crime, it is in the context of committal that the issue arises of whether magistrates should have the power to halt a prosecution: in effect, to stigmatise it as an abuse of process at this preliminary stage and prior to any member of the judiciary being able to decide the issue.

8.7 Bearing in mind that the law concerning abuse of process is exclusively derived from the common law and that magistrates are inferior tribunals wholly subject to the supervisory jurisdiction of the High Court, the issue of whether magistrates should enjoy a jurisdiction to rule on abuse applications is ultimately a policy issue to be decided by the High Court. As abuse applications frequently involve complex matrices of fact and law, usually accompanied by defence complaints of prosecution impropriety in the context of serious allegations of criminality against the defendant, it is understandable that the High Court has, in various cases which have come before it, wanted to consider carefully the wisdom of allowing magistrates jurisdiction in this area.

The general position

8.8 In *R v Derby Crown Court, ex p Brookes* Sir Roger Ormrod said: 'The discretionary power of a magistrates' court to stop a prosecution has only recently been recognised by this Court, and this development of the law is in a phase of rapid growth. It has no statutory basis ...' Sir Roger Ormrod then referred to various authorities and held that a magistrates' court did have this discretionary power. Sir Roger Ormrod observed, 'the ultimate objective of this discretionary power is to ensure that there should be a fair trial according to law, which involves fairness both to the defendant and the prosecution'. Another useful statement of general principal in this regard is the statement of general principle laid down by Mann LJ in *R v Telford Justices, ex p Badhan.*[3] In that case Mann LJ affirmed that magistrates did enjoy an abuse jurisdiction; 'We ... can see no reason why examining justices (even one examining magistrate; see the Act of 1980, s 4(1)) should not be able to decide that an initiation of the process of committal is an abuse of that process. A question of abuse is one which is within the ability of justices to decide, and it is one they admittedly have power to determine on summary trial.'

1 (1991) 93 Cr App Rep 171.

The creation of a split jurisdiction in, *ex p Bennett*

8.9 In *R v Horseferry Road Magistrates' Court ex p Bennett*[1] the House of Lords followed the principle of the *Telford Justices* case holding that magistrates enjoy a power to stay proceedings on the grounds of abuse in relation to both summary trials and committal proceedings. However, bearing in mind that in *Bennett* the House of Lords had significantly pushed outwards the boundaries of the abuse jurisdiction generally, the question naturally arose as to whether it was wise to vest in magistrates, in common with the judiciary, a full jurisdiction over abuse matters. In the context of the facts in *Bennett* which are recounted elsewhere in this book,[2] it was understandable that various speeches in that case were concerned in part with whether magistrates really were a competent tribunal to determine complex matters concerned with alleged international lawlessness by the executive and breach of extradition procedures neither of these matters strictly having an impact on the fairness of the trial. It was one thing for the House as it did in *Bennett,* to widen the circumstances in which a Crown Court could stay proceedings and another to provide the same ambit of discretion to legally unqualified persons sitting as part-time magistrates in context of a committal.

1 [1994] AC 42.
2 See paras 6.14 to 6.26.

8.10 The result of such concerns in *Bennett* led to the creation of a split jurisdiction in relation to abuse matters. Whereas the judiciary would enjoy a full jurisdiction, magistrates would not and their jurisdiction would be made more narrow. In *Bennett* Lord Griffiths held that magistrates' jurisdiction in this context 'should be strictly confined to matters directly affecting the fairness of the trial of the particular accused' at p 127 of Lord Griffiths's judgment.[1] Examples of matters falling within this category were according to Lord Griffiths those concerning delay or the unfair manipulation of court procedures.

1 (1994) 98 Cr App R.

8.11 According to Lord Griffiths, a line could be drawn between this and a special exclusive category of abuse concerned with upholding the rule of law which he held should be confined to the jurisdiction of the High Court. Accordingly, when an allegation of abuse akin to that made in *Bennett* arose then magistrates were not competent to decide the matter. The remedy in this situation was for magistrates to exercise their discretion to allow an adjournment of the proceedings before them in order to enable the defence to then immediately make an application to the Divisional Court which would be empowered to rule.

Problems arising from the split jurisdiction

8.12 Before considering the relevant authorities subsequent to *Bennett* it should be appreciated that the creation of this split jurisdiction in the context of abuse and the powers of magistrates creates two practical difficulties. First, is it really possible in practice to draw a line between what Lord Griffiths said were 'matters directly affecting the fairness of the trial of the particular accused' and avowedly more policy-type issues concerned with upholding the rule of law? On what side of the line, for example, does an allegation of prosecution mala fides or oppressive conduct fall? Second, by creating a system whereby in the context of committal proceedings, abuse applications concerned with the rule of law category are to be remitted for consideration to the Divisional Court, a problem is thereby created in relation to the powers of a trial judge sitting in the Crown Court. If a complaint of abuse is referred to the Divisional Court and rejected following which the accused is committed for trial to the Crown Court, what is a trial judge to do when he becomes seised of the case and the defence then makes a similar abuse application? In the context of a prior adverse ruling by magistrates, there is no difficulty in principle as a Crown Court judge can examine the issues afresh and reach a different conclusion? His discretion is unfettered in this respect. The problem however, arises when the Divisional Court composed of a Lord Justice of Appeal and a High Court judge has ruled against the defendant and the trial judge is then in effect being asked to reconsider the matter.

8.13 To this problem there appears only one principled solution, that the trial judge abide by the ruling of the Divisional Court even though generally speaking the Divisional Court as a court of review is less equipped to give careful consideration to the complex issues of fact and law which generally surround abuse applications than a trial judge before whom, for example, live evidence can be called and be cross-examined. But in a less clear-cut situation, what is a trial judge to do when the defence submit that there have been supervening matters between the ruling of the Divisional Court and the application before him which had they occurred or been known about at the time of the Divisional Court application, could have led that court to have reached an opposite conclusion. If such supervening matters really have arisen, can a trial judge de facto or de jure confine consideration of abuse to only these events posing the theoretical question of what would the Divisional Court have done if it had been aware of such events?

8.14 Bearing in mind that the decision in *ex p Bennett* is relatively recent and that international lawlessness or *Bennett*-type abuse applications are rare, the problems in paras 8.12 and 8.13 do not appear in practice to have caused real difficulty. However, from time to time the Divisional Court is called on to clarify whether a magistrates' court should have jurisdiction to entertain a particular abuse application. For example, in *R v Belmarsh Magistrates' Court, ex p Watts*[1] the defendant made an abuse application at committal on the grounds that the prosecution fell foul of the *Hunter*[2] rule. This rule is discussed fully in Chapter 7. In *ex p Watts* the magistrate found that he did not as a matter of law have jurisdiction to entertain this application. In the Divisional Court Buxton LJ disagreed: 'We are indeed satisfied that the magistrate was wrong to think that he lacked jurisdiction to act on a finding of abuse of process on Hunter grounds.' The judgment in *ex p Watts* is more fully considered subsequently in this chapter.

1 [1999] 2 Cr App Rep 188.
2 *Hunter v Chief Constable of West Midlands Police* [1982] AC 529.

Post *Bennett* authorities – widening of magistrates' jurisdiction

8.15 Post *Bennett* the next relevant authority is the judgment of Lord Bingham CJ in *R v Staines Magistrates' Court, ex p Westfallen*. In his judgment Lord Bingham considered the 'narrow category' of *Bennett*-type abuse and concluded that Lord Griffiths was there 'plainly concerned with a flouting of the rule of law and abuse of power by police and prosecuting authorities'.

8.16 By the time of the judgment of Rose LJ sitting in the Court of Appeal in *R v Mullen* the area of abuse jurisdiction beyond that of magistrates had become characterised or described as a useful shorthand as '*Bennett*-type abuse'. In *Mullen* Rose LJ described *Bennett*-type abuse as follows: 'it seems to us that *Bennett*-type abuse, where it would be offensive to justice and propriety to try the defendant at all, is different both from the type of abuse which renders a fair trial impossible and from all other cases where an exercise of judicial discretion is called for. It arises not from the relationship between the prosecution and the defendant but from the relationship between the prosecution and the court. It arises from the courts' need to exercise control over executive involvement in the whole prosecution process, not limited to the trial itself'. The import of this definition was an attempt to clarify the dividing line between the abuse categories available to magistrates and those which are not. Respecting the dichotomy created by the House in *Bennett*, Rose LJ was perhaps seeking to helpfully explain the parameters in a more clear and useful way.

8.17 The final authority to consider is *R v Belmarsh Magistrates' Court, ex p Watts*.[1] The facts of the case were briefly as follows: Watts an HM Customs and Excise officer had been an important prosecution witness in a trial leading to the conviction for drugs trafficking offences of the defendant. Subsequently and presumably as a reaction to later confiscation proceedings initiated against him, the defendant launched a private prosecution of Ms Watts alleging false defamatory libel and misfeasance. Following issuance of the summonses Watts contended that they were an abuse of process and the (private) prosecution should be stayed. The particular abuse alleged was that the defendant was in fact seeking to reopen the safety of his conviction and was therefore in breach of the rule established by the House of Lords in *Hunter v Chief Constable of the West Midlands Police*.[2]

1 See para 8.14.
2 [1982] AC 529.

8.18 While the magistrate held that the defendant's summonses did amount to a violation of the rule in *Hunter* he also held that because of the dichotomy of jurisdiction created in *Bennett* this meant that he had no jurisdiction to stay the proceedings as an abuse this being a matter exclusively for the Divisional Court. Accordingly, the magistrate declined to stay the proceedings and Ms Watts then appealed to the Divisional Court in part contending that the magistrate was wrong in law to hold that he lacked the power to stay the proceedings. The ruling of the Court was given by Buxton LJ. Buxton LJ concluded 'that *Bennett*-type abuse was a narrow category of a very peculiar nature. *Bennett*-type abuse was not concerned with any particular unfairness suffered by the defendant in the context of his trial but whether the courts should stigmatise international lawlessness by the prosecution or executive'. Buxton LJ held that in all circumstances in alleged abuse short of *Bennett*-type abuse magistrates did enjoy a jurisdiction. On the facts of the case before him, Buxton LJ held that the magistrate did have jurisdiction to inquire into allegations concerning the bona fides of the prosecution and whether the prosecution had been commenced oppressively or unfairly. This would include an allegation of abuse arising out of a purported breach of the rule in *Hunter* and accordingly, the magistrate had wrongly decided that he lacked the jurisdiction to deal with that complaint. Having established this point of principle, Buxton LJ held that the defendant summonses were an abuse and stayed the proceedings.

Significance of *ex p Watts*

8.19 In addition to seeking to clarify the dividing line between *Bennett*-type abuse and all other types of abuse with only the former being beyond the jurisdiction of magistrates, Buxton LJ's clear policy was to seek as far as possible to allow magistrates a discretion to determine abuse applications. Moreover, the Divisional Court does not wish to find itself regularly embroiled in abuse applications arising out of magistrates declining jurisdiction believing that they are unable to rule on an application. Magistrates should therefore accept, except in extreme and hopefully very rare circumstances, the role of dealing with abuse applications while respecting the split jurisdiction created in *Bennett*.

8.20 While holding that magistrates did enjoy a wide jurisdiction in this context Buxton LJ also made two further pronouncements. First, that where there was uncertainty as to which side of the dividing line an abuse application fell, then magistrates should remit the matter to the Divisional Court adjourning the proceedings in the meantime. Second, in relation to cases which clearly did not fall into the *Bennett*-type abuse category Buxton LJ made clear that magistrates who still felt themselves unsuited to determining a particularly difficult or convoluted abuse application always possessed the discretion to decline jurisdiction and in effect tell the defendant to refer his complaint to the Divisional Court instead. The Court will act as a sort of safety-net or last resort for troubled magistrates, for as Buxton LJ stated: 'It will however, always be open to magistrates in cases that do not fall within the narrow *Bennett* category to decline jurisdiction, and require the matter to be pursued in the Divisional Court, whether because of the complexity or novelty of the point, or because of the length of investigation that is required. Any such decision by a magistrate, being one taken within the limits of his judgment, will be unlikely to be overturned in this court.'

8.21 One largely pragmatic advantage of allowing magistrates jurisdiction here is the obvious saving of time and legal cost gained by staying a case at the earliest opportunity. If there is an abuse which should result in the proceedings being halted then there is advantage to all concerned in magistrates being able to do so. From a defendant's perspective, it is probably also correct in principle that he should be able to complain about the proceedings being brought at the earliest opportunity.

Conclusions

8.22 On the basis of all the authorities listed above it is submitted that magistrates have jurisdiction to consider abuse applications in almost all circumstances. These circumstances can be categorised as follows:

(1) abuse complaints directed at the propriety or fairness of the trial process or procedure;

(2) abuse complaints concerning mala fides of the prosecution, investigations of the bona fides of the prosecution, or investigations into whether the prosecution had been instituted oppressively or unfairly;
(3) in cases of delay;
(4) in cases of alleged unfair manipulation of court procedures.

8.23 Further examples of instances where jurisdiction would exist, given the above headings, are non-availability of evidence type abuses, non-disclosure abuses and double jeopardy species of abuse. Finally, it is contended that a magistrate does not have jurisdiction in these particular areas:

(1) instances of abuse of process under the narrow category of *ex p Bennett*;
(2) deliberate abuse of extradition procedures;
(3) illegality and abuse of power by police, prosecution authorities or government officials pursuant to ulterior motives or wrongful purposes in violation of international law and for fundamental human rights.

Likely future developments

8.24 Owing to changes in the law concerning proceedings generally, it is likely that in the near future this subject of the ambit of their jurisdiction to consider abuse applications will begin to decline in importance. This is because of the planned virtual abolition of committal proceedings as a whole in relation to indictable only offences. Section 51 of the Crime and Disorder Act 1998 envisages that indictable only cases will be fast-tracked into the Crown Court after only one hearing in the magistrates' court. The mechanism of transfer trial pioneered in serious fraud cases is to be applied more universally and to replace the mechanism of committal. Under the transfer regime envisaged by s 51, abuse applications will only fall to be considered in the Crown Court by the trial judge. Moreover, the intended rapidity of proceedings for such defendants, charged with serious offences, is likely to curtail opportunities for abuse applications.

Summary trials

8.25 The timing of the making of any such application obviously depends on a variety of factors most important of which is usually the timing of service by the prosecution of its evidence on the defence. Absent a prosecution duty to act with expedition when the defendant is in custody so as to respect custody time limits and a magistrates' overall jurisdiction concerned with case management and delay, there is no timetable for the service of evidence. Furthermore, as practitioners will be aware, the peculiar feature remains in our law that there is no obligation on the prosecution in relation to summary only matters to serve any evidence at all, although curiously there is an obligation to serve unused material.

8.26 There have been several recent authorities concerned with alleged abuse arising from non-disclosure by the prosecution of unused material and evidence prior to committal. The two important cases are *R v Stratford Magistrates, ex p Imbert*[1] and *R v DPP, ex p Lee.*[2] Both these authorities are considered in Chapter 5 supra.

1 See 8 February 1999, QBD No CO/0557/98 [1999] 2 Cr App Rep 276.
2 [1999] 2 All ER 737.

8.27 An application to stay proceedings is obviously a preliminary issue which should be raised either pre-trial or at the outset of the trial. Self-evidently as a successful abuse application may bring an end to the entire proceedings (although this is not necessarily so, for a successful abuse application may only relate to a stay of part of the prosecution's case) it ought to be heard at the earliest opportunity. In *R v Aldershot Youth Court, ex p A*[1] the Divisional Court held that by its nature an application to stay proceedings as an abuse is a plea in bar and as with a plea of autrefois acquit or convict, the plea was to be taken and determined before the accused pleaded to the indictment/charge.

1 (1997) 3 Archbold News 2, QBD No Co/1911/96.

Committal proceedings

8.28 With regard to committal proceedings, it is obviously sensible that the abuse application be made and determined before the committal itself commences. A successful application in this circumstance means that the committal stage may never be reached. In *R v Worcester Magistrates' Court, ex p Leavesley*[1] the question arose of whether magistrates who hear and adjudicate on an abuse application were in effect acting as examining justices in a committal hearing. In *ex p Leavesley* the magistrates rejected the defence's abuse application and then adjourned the proceedings. Following the adjournment, a fresh (stipendiary) magistrate was appointed to hear the committal but the defence objected to this substitution. The Divisional Court held that a committal did not commence until either the prosecution opened its case, or called witnesses or took some other step which was pertinent to committal. An abuse application was not pertinent to committal and so a different constitution of magistrates could hear the abuse application on the one hand and the committal on the other.

1 *R v Worcester Magistrates' Court, ex p Leavesley (1993) Times, 14 January*; *R v Worcester Magistrates' Court, ex p Bell* (1992) 157 JP 921.

8.29 From a magistrates' court perspective it is usually preferable, bearing in mind the frequent significant factual overlap between the making of an abuse application and the submission of no case to answer, for the same magistrates whenever possible to hear an abuse application and deal with committal. If not, then a problem may arise where the defence having made one unsuccessful abuse application then proceed at the later committal hearing to make another arguing that there has been a significant change of circumstances. As a magistrates' court is not a court of record it would perhaps be difficult to resist such a representation and so refuse to hear the renewed application.

8.30 However, from a defence perspective it is usually preferable for the abuse application and the committal hearing to be heard separately. If the two hearings are disconnected then it follows that there is no reason why abuse applications cannot proceed any other application or hearing in a magistrates' court, for example plea before venue and mode of trial. There may be positive advantages to making an abuse application prior to these hearings, for example when the defendant will plead guilty if the abuse application fails. If the application is made before a plea before venue then his/her mitigation is fully preserved.

Transfer for trial cases

8.31 Reference has already been made to the likely significant effect, when implemented, of s 51 of the Crime and Disorder Act 1998. The transfer system envisaged by that section is largely a replica of the transfer system in relation to serious or complex fraud cases contained in the Criminal Justice Act 1987 and sexual and violent offences concerning children contained in the Criminal Justice Act 1988. The issue is whether, under such a regime, magistrates possess the jurisdiction to determine abuse applications if they are made before the transfer takes place? It is submitted that there is no clear authority on this subject but bearing in mind that under all the relevant statutes, a notice of transfer served by a prosecutor in effect extinguishes the jurisdiction of magistrates over the relevant proceedings, save for matters concerning bail and Legal Aid, it would appear that if this notice is served on the court before any abuse application is begun, the magistrates would be prevented from hearing and determining it. Certainly the underlying aim of all of the relevant statutes is to allow a Crown Court judge to be seised of an indictable case as soon as possible and it would therefore seem anomalous and contrary to the transfer scheme if despite this, magistrates could embark on a complex abuse application.

In the Crown Court can the defence repeat its abuse application previously rejected by magistrates?

8.32 This issue was in part considered by the Divisional Court in, *ex p Hole*[1] and *ex p Malpas*.[2] The Divisional Court held that the defence is not prevented or debarred from advancing the same or indeed even a different abuse application in the Crown Court when one had previously been made before magistrates. The Crown Court can consider the application de novo and in effect therefore the defence is allowed a second attempt. In practice the defence rarely take advantage of these two chances preferring for tactical reasons 'to keep the power dry' for the Crown Court judge; for example, by virtue of a wish to preserve the weapon of surprise or to minimise the possibility of the prosecution serving notices of further evidence to cure any exposed deficiency in its case.

1 *R v Cardiff Magistrates' Court, ex p Hole* [1997] COD 84.
2 *R v Barry Magistrates' Court, ex p Malpas* [1998] COD 90.

CASE STATED AND JUDICIAL REVIEW IN THE MAGISTRATES' COURT

8.33 Case stated is a remedy of ancient origin. It developed at a time when there was no Court of Appeal in criminal cases. It was a facility whereby the opinion of the High Court could be taken on a difficult area of law by a quarter session. In the Crown Court the procedure is now governed by s 28(1) of the Supreme Court

Act 1981. No appeal lies by way of case stated on an interlocutory matter from the Crown Court. In *Loade v DPP*[1] the court decided that 'any order, judgment or decision' in s 28(1) meant the final decision.

1 [1989] 3 WLR 1281.

Appeal by way of case stated

8.33a Appeals by way of case stated are relatively uncommon in the context of abuse of process. Indeed, authorities on the subject are few, which is unsurprising given the limitations inherent in such an avenue of appeal. Case stated is a procedure whereby the High Court is able to review the decisions of inferior courts in relation to points of law. Unlike judicial review, case stated is not generally concerned with how a decision was reached, but only as to its legal merit. If an appeal was therefore to be based for instance on an alleged breach of natural justice by magistrates, the general rule suggests that judicial review is the appropriate option.

8.34 This right of appeal, under s 3 of the Magistrates' Courts Act 1980, states that an aggrieved person may question a magistrate on the ground that:

(1) he is acting in excess of the jurisdiction; or
(2) he is wrong in law.

Availability of case stated

8.35 In *Atkinson v USA*,[1] a case concerned with extradition proceedings, Lord Reid opined that there was no power to state a case unless there had first been some final adjudication (see page 234). It is, however, submitted that s 111(1) of the Magistrates' Court Act 1980 does provide for the possibility of the availability of this remedy. In *Environment Agency v Stanford* it was held that in summary proceedings a decision against the prosecution on grounds of abuse is final and is therefore capable of being the subject of case stated. Stanford, however, did not deal with the situation where a decision adverse to the Crown in committal proceedings can similarly be so subject.

1 [1971] AC 197.

8.35a The procedure is applicable where there are no factual disputes, for the Divisional Court is bound by the findings of fact as stated by the magistrates' court (except where it is contended there was no evidence on which one could have arrived at a particular finding of fact). The aggrieved party may question 'the conviction, order, determination or other proceeding of the court' and the remedy is available to both prosecution and defence. The majority of appeals by way of case stated are based on attempts to overturn either a summary conviction or a summary acquittal. Indeed, it is only available where there has been a final determination in the proceedings, such as a conviction, sentence, acquittal, or (as in abuse case) an order to stay proceedings.[1] Given this restriction, where a magistrates' court has ruled against the defence at a pre-trial review or preliminary hearing, it has no jurisdiction to state what is, in essence, an 'interlocutory' case throughout the hearing.[2]

1 See *DPP v Karl Metten* (22 January 1999, unreported); and *Environment Agency v Standford* [1998] COD 373.
2 See *Streames v Copping* [1985] 149 JP 305; which was followed in *R v Greater Manchester Justices, ex p Aldi GmbH & Co KG* (1994) 159 JP 717.

8.36 It is submitted that as the prosecution very rarely accept all the factual assertions made by the defence in abuse applications, so the case stated route is inappropriate and the judicial review route is almost always to be preferred. On a purely tactical point, however, if it is felt that the case stated is available the question then arises of whether the route should be pursued in respect of the magistrates' ruling. Alternatively, should the matter be left for the judgment of the trial judge?

8.36a There seems, in principle, only two advantages why the case stated route might be preferred. First, if the magistrate has not provided any reasoning when rejecting an abuse submission or holding it, this remedy can be used to expose the underlying reasoning. Second, the case stated procedure does not require leave from any superior court prior to the hearing.

JUDICIAL REVIEW

Applications for judicial review

8.37 An application to the Divisional Court for judicial review may be made by either the defence or the prosecution, in respect of any ruling or decision of the magistrates' court. Judicial review, which is designed to be expeditious, is not an appeal from a decision, but rather a review of the manner in which it was made.[1]

1 See *Chief Constable of North Wales Police v Evans* [1982] 1 WLR 1155; the procedure for Judicial Review is governed by ss 29-31 of the Supreme Court Act 1981, and Order 53 of the Rules and the Supreme Court 1965, as amended; note the Revised Ord 53 and the new CPR Practice Directions.

8.38 In the context of abuse of process applications, the case law suggests that the two most sought after prerogative orders are prohibition[1] and certiorari.[2] The order of prohibition would have the effect, in essence, of having the proceedings stayed, for such an order would prevent magistrates from starting or continuing with a hearing. The object of the order is to prevent magistrates from acting in a manner which is either inconsistent with or in excess of their jurisdiction. In practice this may be used, for example, to challenge a decision to commence or continue with a summary trial or committal proceedings, the abuse of process arguments having been rejected, possibly at an earlier preliminary hearing. The order of certiorari, by way of contrast, would have the effect of quashing the magistrates' decision to permit the proceedings to continue. Less common remedies in the abuse context would be found in mandamus and in declarations. In the case of *Hindle*[3] one finds an example of a case where an order of mandamus was sought to oblige the magistrate to exercise the abuse of process discretion to stay proceedings.

1 See *R v Brentford Justices, ex p Wong* (1980) 73 Cr App Rep 67; *R v Horsham Justices, ex p Reeves* (1980) 75 Cr App Rep 236n; *R v Derby Magistrates' Court, ex p Brooks* (1984) 80 Cr App Rep 164; *R v Willesdon Justices, ex p Clemmings* (1987) 87 Cr App Rep 280; *R v Telford Justices, ex p Badham* [1991] 2 WLR 866.
2 See *R v Guildford Magistrates' Court, ex p Healy* [1983] 1 WLR 108; *R v Liverpool Stipendary Magistrate, ex p Ellison* [1990] RTR 220n; *R v Rotherham Justices, ex p Brough* [1991] CrimLR 522; *R v Croydon Justices, ex p Dean* (1993) 98 Cr App Rep 76.
3 See *R v Newcastle-upon-Tyne Justices, ex p Hindle* [1984] 1 All ER 770.

8.39 Where magistrates have ruled that it is permissible for proceedings to continue, there have also been instances of defendants seeking declarations that such decisions were unlawful.[1]

8.40 The prosecution, on the other hand, also have an interest in the remedies available through judicial review. Such interest would normally lie in the orders of mandamus and certiorari, in the reverse abuse circumstances. For while they may seek mandamus to oblige a magistrate to allow proceedings to continue,[1] equally they may seek an order of certiorari to quash a magistrate's decision to stay proceedings.[2]

1 See *R v Colwyn Justices, ex p DPP* (1988) 154 JP 989; *R v Bow Street Stripendiary Magistrate, ex p DPP and Cherry* (1989) 91 Cr App Rep 283; *R v Bow Street Metropolitan Stipendiary Magistrate, ex p DPP* (1992) 95 Cr App Rep 9.
2 See *ex p DPP and Cherry*; and *R v Bow Street MSM, ex p DPP.*

The grounds for judicial review

8.41 The grounds on which the Divisional Court may grant relief fall broadly into the following three categories, namely;

(1) *Illegality* – where the magistrates' court has exceeded or abused its powers, or made an error in law;
(2) Procedural impropriety – where the Court has acted in breach of the rules of natural justice;
(3) Irrationality – where the Court has reached a decision, which no reasonable tribunal, properly directed and on the evidence, could have reached.

8.42 Defendants seeking a review of a failed abuse application in the magistrates' court will be seeking to argue that the magistrates acted irrationally or were *Wednesbury*[1] unreasonable. In other words, on the merits of the application put forward by the defence, the application ought to have succeeded.

1 *Associated Provincial Picture House Ltd v Wednesbury Corpn* [1948] 1 KB 223.

Approach of the Divisional Court

8.43 On numerous occasions the Divisional Court has shown itself to be unwilling to become a de facto Court of Appeal in relation to failed abuse applications made in the magistrates court. The overall policy of the Divisional Court in relation to judicial review proceedings arising out of criminal proceedings was set out by Bingham CJ in *R v DPP, ex p Kebilene.*[1]

> 'Where the grant of leave to move judicial review would delay or obstruct the conduct of criminal proceedings which ought, in the public interest, to be resolved with all appropriate expedition, the court will always scrutinise the application with the greatest care, both to satisfy itself that there are sound reasons for making the application and satisfy itself

that there are no discretionary grounds (such as delay or the availability of alternative remedies or vexatious conduct by the applicant) which should lead it to refuse leave. The court would be very slow to intervene where the applicant's complaint is one that can be met by appropriate orders or directions in the criminal proceedings ...' (page 867).

1 [1999] 3 WLR 175.

8.44 Commenting on this principle, Lord Steyn in *ex p Kebeline* said:

'There is a common law principle ... which provides a strong presumption against the Divisional Court entertaining a judicial review application where the complaint can be raised within the criminal trial and appeal process.'

8.45 It is submitted that the root of this principle can be traced to the judgment of Lord Mustill in *Neill v North Antrim Magistrates' Court.*[1]

'it is, however, one thing to hold that it is for the magistrates to rule on admissibility, if invited to do so, so that a decision on the issue must in principle be reviewable, and quite another to say that the grant of relief should follow as a matter of course. I wholly share the sentiments of those who, over the years, have exclaimed in dismay at the vision of the streams of applications by persons committed for trial seeking to put off the evil day by drawing attention to supposed errors in the application at the committal stage of the high technical rules of criminal evidence. It is only in the case of a really substantial error leading to a demonstrable injustice that the Judge in the Divisional Court should contemplate the granting of leave to move' (page 131) [Emphasis added].

1 (1992) 97 Cr App Rep 121.

8.46 The principle expressed in this case was reaffirmed by the House of Lords in *R v Bedwellty Justices, ex p Williams.*[1]

1 [1997] AC 225.

8.47 With regard to applications for judicial review based on an alleged abuse of process application which has failed before the magistrates, two recent authorities make the position plain. First, the judgment of *Brook LJ in R v Liverpool City Justices, ex p Price.*[1]

'It still did not seem sufficiently well-known that it is only in a very exceptional case that the High Court will exercise its supervisory jurisdiction to intervene and quash a decision by justices in the exercise of their discretion not to stay criminal proceedings for abuse of process. The test was not whether the court agreed with the decision which the

> Magistrates reached, but whether their decision was so plainly irrational and untenable that no reasonable bench of justices, properly directed, could have reached it'.[2]

1 *R v Liverpool City Justices, ex p Price* (1998) 162 JP 766 and at [1998] COD 453 at 455.
2 See also *R v Willesden Magistrates' Court, ex p Clemmings* (1997) 87 Cr App Rep 280; *R v Barry Magistrates' Court, ex p Malpas* [1998] COD 90; *R v Canterbury and St Augustine Justices, ex p Turner* (1983) 147 JP 193.

8.48 The Divisional Court is, therefore, expressing the view that the burden of proof on the defence is high and necessarily higher than the burden which it will face in the Crown Court where, if a Crown Court judge disagrees with a magistrate's decision, he can overrule it.

8.49 In *R v Bow Street Magistrates' Court, ex p Finch and Bossino*[1] an application was made for judicial review of the committal, in part because of the magistrates' rejection of abuse submission, where Auld LJ held:

> 'the courts have made plain that stays by any court on the ground of abuse of process should only be granted in the most exceptional circumstances and where a defendant is able to demonstrate that he has suffered serious prejudice. This is particularly so in committal proceedings before magistrates where the final airing of the evidence and decision at trial are yet to come' (page 9).[2]

1 (9 June 1999, unreported).
2 (Here a complaint of covert non-disclosure by the prosecution at committal of edited parts of tapes was relied on. Auld LJ held that the Court of trial would be best placed to determine the propriety and effect of this alleged non-disclosure.)

Procedural tactics in summary cases

8.50 An accused in summary proceedings who has made a failed abuse application before magistrates faces a choice of avenues. He can seek judicial review of the refusal in the Divisional Court or instead exercise the right for a re-trial in the Crown Court. The existence of an accused having this choice was doubted in *R v Peterborough Magistrates' Court, ex p Dowler*[1] which questioned whether an accused should have a right to apply for judicial review when there was a subsisting right of appeal to the Crown Court. However, in *R v Hereford Magistrates' Court, ex p Rowlands*,[2] *Dowler* in this regard was doubted and the existence of a choice affirmed. However, bearing in mind the present largely unwelcoming attitude of the Divisional Court as considered above, in most cases and unless the accused feels very confident as to the strength of his abuse claim, it would seem that the accused should opt for the Crown Court over the Divisional Court.

1 [1996] 2 Cr App Rep 561.
2 [1998} QB 110.

8.51 There are also other disadvantages which appertain to the Divisional Court practice which favour the Crown Court. Judicial review is not a suitable forum for a re-examination of facts found by justices and a detailed reassessment of how such findings should determine the final determination. The Divisional Court by its nature has a need for expedition in its hearings and it will not be sympathetic to being asked to reconsider complex facts especially when it is probably known that there is a judge in the Crown Court available with greater ability and time to consider such matters. The authors have experienced judges sitting in the Divisional Court stating that while it would seem that the applicant has an arguable abuse case on the merits, it is the trial judge who will be best suited to determining this and accordingly so have refused leave to move for judicial review.

8.52 It should also be appreciated that before a Crown Court judge, the accused has the potential to request a voir dire and therefore the calling of live evidence, a facility unavailable in the Divisional Court which is purely based on statement of truth or affidavit evidence. Perhaps finally it can rarely be in the defendant's interest to embark on a judicial review application which is unlikely to succeed and thereon renew it in the Crown Court. An adverse finding in the Divisional Court, even if it is only at the 'permission'[1] stage, with admittedly there being no detailed consideration of the facts, is still nonetheless unlikely to seem appealing to a Crown Court judge.

1 'Permission' being the new term for 'Leave', per the recent CPR practice directions.

8.53 However, if the judicial review is to be pursued then applications must promptly be made in both courts. Bearing in mind the superiority of the Divisional Court over the Crown Court it would appear necessary that, when lodging an appeal with the Crown Court, that court be asked to adjourn the hearing of that appeal until the outcome of the judicial review application. In relation to this application, it should be made clear that an appeal has been lodged with the Crown Court but it has been asked to be adjourned.

THE CROWN COURT

Appeals to the Crown Court

8.54 A defendant who has been convicted, after summary proceedings before the justices, may appeal to the Crown Court against his conviction.[1] The appeal is by way of rehearing and, consequently, there would be nothing to prevent the defence practitioner from raising the same abuse of process argument as adopted in the lower court, or indeed in amending the same, or trying a new approach altogether. Likewise there is no obligation on the prosecution to put their case forward, on the same basis or in the same manner, as was the case before the justices.[2]

1 See MCA, 1980, ss 108-110, rr 6-11 Crown Court Rules 1982, and s 79(3) Supreme Court Act 1981.
2 See *Hingley-Finch v DPP* (1998) 1 Archbold News 2 (DC).

8.55 If either or both of the parties seek to call evidence, in support of an abuse of process application, it is contended that they must first, if a short voir dire is to be held at the outset of the appeal, seek the court's leave so to do (as with any other such application before a Crown Court judge). It will be within the judge's discretion as to what evidence may be allowed or not, whether or not it was called in the lower court, the criteria for such discretion presumably being one of relevance.[1]

1 Procedure on abuse applications in the Crown Court generally is considered later.

8.56 As is the case with any appeal against conviction, the practitioner will no doubt want to advise the appellant that the appeal will put the sentence at large together with a possible liability as to costs, in the event of an adverse finding or conviction. No grounds of appeal need actually be provided (so long as the notice states that the appeal is against conviction, as opposed to sentence) within the 21 days of sentence. Nevertheless the better practice is to briefly state the basis of the appeal, in general terms, putting both the court and prosecution on notice.

Abuse of process applications in the Crown Court

8.57 Once a case has been committed or transferred for trial in the Crown Court, the first occasion on which it would be appropriate to raise the question of an abuse of process application is normally at a

Plea and Directions Hearing (PDH) (or a Preparatory Hearing if a transfer case).[1] At a PDH the defence would be expected to inform the court as to 'any point of law anticipated' in addition to a list of other obligations which both parties have in relation to general matters of case management and preparation. A similar situation applies to the preparatory hearings regime whether they be for serious or complex cases under Part III of the Criminal Procedure and Investigations Act 1996 or serious or complex fraud cases under the Criminal Justice Act 1987.

1 See the *Practice Direction: Crown Court (Plea and Directions Hearings)* [1995] 1 WLR 1318.

8.58 In relation to pre-trial hearings, which are now governed by s 39 of the CPIA, the special feature that rulings made in such hearings have, pursuant to s 40 of that Act, is that they are binding until the determination of all the proceedings. The commencement of s 40 (subsections 3-5) is as follows:

> '(3) Subject to subsection (4), a ruling made under this section has binding effect from the time it is made until the case against the accused or, if there is more than one, against each of them is disposed of; and the case against an accused is disposed of if –
>
> (a) he is acquitted or convicted, or
> (b) the prosecutor decides not to proceed with the case against him
>
> (4) A judge may discharge or vary (or further vary) a ruling made under this section of it appears to him that it is in the interests of justice to do so; and a judge may act under this subsection -
>
> (a) on an application by a party to the case, or
> (b) of the judge's own motion.
>
> (5) No application may be made under subsection (4) unless there has been a material change of circumstances since the ruling was made or if a previous application has been made, since the application (or last application) was made.'

8.59 It is submitted that the effect of this more formalised regime is that while a trial judge always has the discretion to review a pre-trial ruling made by him it means that the defence, if they wish to renew a previously unsuccessful abuse application, will have to establish pursuant to Subsection (5) a material change of circumstances. This may not be easy and so it is submitted that an abuse application should not be mounted until the optimum moment when all material evidence has been gathered and arguments refined.

Challenging adverse rulings of the Crown Court

8.60 Whether the Divisional Court has power to entertain an application for judicial review arising out of a ruling made a Crown Court judge is a matter, not of common law principle, but of statutory construction. Section 29(3) of the Supreme Court Act 1981 provides:

> 'In relation to the jurisdiction of the Crown Court, other than its jurisdiction in matters relating to trial on indictment, the High Court shall have all such jurisdiction to make orders of mandamus, prohibition or certiorari as the High Court possesses in relation to the jurisdiction of an inferior court [in matters relating to trial on indictment]' [emphasis added].

8.61 Section 29(3) therefore prevents a decision made by the Crown Court from being challenged by an application for judicial review if it was deemed to be relating to a matter relating to trial on indictment. The same rule is applicable to appeals by way of case stated from the Crown Court.[1]

1 Section 28 Supreme Court Act 1981.

8.62 The rationale for s 29(3) was explained by Lord Bridge in *Re Smalley*[1] as follows:

> 'it is not difficult to discern a sensible legislative purpose in excluding appeal or judicial review of any decision affecting the conduct of a trial on indictment, whether given in the course of the trial or by way of pre-trial directions. In any such case to allow an appellate or review process might ... seriously delay the trial. If it is the prosecutor who is aggrieved by such a decision, it is no way surprising that he has no remedy, since prosecutors have never enjoyed rights of appeal or review when unsuccessful in trials on indictment. If, on the other hand, the defendant is so aggreived, he will have his remedy by way of appeal against conviction ...' (pages 642-643).

1 See *Re Smalley* [1985] AC 622.

8.63 This explanation was approved by Lord Slynn (speaking for a unanimous House) in *Re Ashton*).[1] In *Ashton* the trial judge had refused an application to stay the trial for grounds of abuse and judicial review of this refusal was sought.

1 See *Re Ashton* [1994] AC 9.

8.64 In relation to a future application for judicial review in relation to a Crown Court judge refusing to hold a prosecution to be an abuse of process by reason of an alleged breach of the European Convention, the House of Lords held in *R v DPP, ex p Kebilene* that s 29(3) would likewise prohibit such an application.[1]

1 See for example the judgment of Lord Steyn page 9 of transcript (Times, 2 November 1999).

Preparatory hearings and interlocutory appeals

8.65 The preparatory hearing regime introduced by the Criminal Justice Act 1987 was a central part of the new scheme for serious fraud trials. One of the radical concepts introduced by the Act was that of interlocutory appeals allowing the parties to appeal to the Court of Appeal pre-trial any ruling on a point of law which could effect the outcome of a trial. Section 9(11) of the Act granted this right of interlocutory appeal in respect of such rulings made during a preparatory hearing. One of the earliest interlocutory appeals under this new scheme was *Re Gunawardena*.[1] In *Gunawardena* the defence sought to appeal pursuant to s 9(11) the trial judge's decision to reject an application to stay the indictment on the grounds of abuse. The defence contended that the trial judge had heard the abuse application in a preparatory hearing and therefore the interlocutory appeal route was available.

1 (1990) 91 Cr App Rep 55.

8.66 The Court of Appeal took a different view, holding that while admittedly the abuse application had fallen under the aegis of a preparatory hearing in that case, the issue of abuse was nonetheless more akin to part of an 'informal pre-trial review'. The abuse application as construed by the Court of Appeal, did not fall within s 7(1) of the Act (dealing with the purposes of a preparatory hearing) and therefore could not be the subject of an interlocutory appeal. Although an abuse application was an argument of law objectively-speaking the Court held, it did not relate to any of the purposes under s 7(1). Preparatory hearing issues were very narrow and fundamentally only concerned with case management.

8.67 While *Gunawardena* is the only direct authority for the serious fraud regime under the 1987 Act, it is submitted that the Court of Appeal will follow it in respect of any other regime which allows an interlocutory appeal in any circumstances. Ironically the result is therefore that under the transfer for trial system the defendant has less protection than hitherto under the committal system because at least under the latter, he had been able to seek judicial review of an adverse ruling by the magistrates.

Decisions which do not relate to trial on indictment

8.68 Appeal by way of case stated or judicial review are both possible options open to an applicant seeking to question a Crown Court decision in a matter not relating to trial on indictment.[1] A Crown Court decision to allow or dismiss an appeal from a magistrates' court would clearly fall within that category and thus allow the unsuccessful party a further appeal, from the Crown Court to the Divisional Court, by case stated. This also applies to an aggrieved prosecutor who had a summary conviction overturned, or else, to a defendant who was convicted for the second time, on appeal to the Crown Court. An appellant contemplating an appeal by case stated, on the basis of some form of abuse of process submission, must have regard to the fact that an appeal would only lie on the ground that the Crown Court decision was either wrong in law or in excess of jurisdiction. The principles which govern the granting of relief by way of judicial review of a Crown Court decision, are broadly the same as those discussed supra in relation to judicial review of magistrates' courts decisions.[2]

1 See ss 28 and 29(3) Supreme Court Act 1981.
2 See also, in relation to the powers of the High Court; *R v Chelmsford Crown Court, ex p Chief Constable of Essex Police* (1994) 99 Cr App Rep 59, DC: and *R v Leeds Crown Court, ex p Barlow* [1989] RTR 246, DC.

APPEALS TO THE COURT OF APPEAL AGAINST ADVERSE RULINGS ON ABUSE OF PROCESS

8.69 As a result of the amendment of s 2 of the Criminal Appeal Act 1968[1] the single criterion for interference by the Court of Appeal with a conviction reached by a jury is now its unsafety. The amended s 2(1) is as follows:

'Subject to the provisions of this Act, the Court of Appeal –
(a) shall allow an appeal against conviction if they think that the conviction is unsafe; and
(b) shall dismiss such an appeal in any other case.'

1 By virtue of the Criminal Appeal Act 1995.

8.70 The Court's jurisdiction is entirely statutory and it depends on interpretation of the word 'unsafe'. What does 'unsafe' mean? In the absence of any statutory definition, this crucial word has been the subject of debate by lawyers, academics and judges alike. Sir John Smith, in his prescient 1995 article, predicted that the powers of the Court of Appeal to allow an appeal against conviction were in danger of being severely curtailed (albeit that was never the intention of the Royal Commission, the Home Office or Parliament) on the basis of the simple rules of statutory construction.[1] As it was to transpire, the deletion by the 1995 Act of the second limb criteria; 'or unsatisfactory', 'wrong decision of any question of law' and 'material irregularity' found in the 1968 Act was to cause significant difficulties in the years to come for practitioners seeking to argue abuse of process as a ground of appeal. This was largely because the Court of Appeal in some cases drew an restrictive and narrow definition of 'unsafe' which appeared to rule out certain forms of abuse of process as a route to appeal.

1 See Sir John Smith 'The Criminal Appeal Act 1995' Crim LR 920, his commentary at 1997 CLR 48 and Professor JR Spencer 'When is a Conviction 'Unsafe' Archbold News, 16 June 1998, Issue 5.

8.71 Against a background of uncertainty and ambiguity in the case-law, the lowest point for abuse of process as a ground of appeal, was the decision of *R v Chalkley and Jeffries*[1] which defined 'unsafe' in a most narrow fashion. Recently, however, the pendulum appears to have swung strongly back in favour of a broader interpretation of 'unsafe' as in the case of *R v Mullen*[2] where the Court of Appeal acknowledged the various circumstances in which abuse of process submissions could lead to successful appeals against conviction.

1 (1998) 2 Cr App Rep 79.
2 [1999] 3 WLR 777, CA.

8.72 Before turning to an analysis of the recent case law on the subject, it is proposed to start by briefly looking at the pre-1995 Act practice of the Court of Appeal (which is still of relevance in the light of *Mullen*).

Pre-1995 Act practice

8.73 In the 1984 decision of *Heston-Francois*,[1] the Court of Appeal acknowledged abuse of process as a ground of appeal. Lord Justice Watkins stated that: 'Where there has been oppressive conduct savouring of abuse of process, it seems clear that the Court of Appeal ... may quash a conviction on the ground that it is 'unsatisfactory' or 'unsafe.' He added that the Court of Appeal was well placed to decide whether or not a particular accused suffered any actual prejudice in the course of a trial. In 1992, the Court reaffirmed this doctrine as a ground of appeal in the *A-G's Reference (No 1 of 1990)*.[2]

1 *R v Heston-Francois* (1984) 78 Cr App Rep 209.
2 *A-G's Reference* (1992) 95 Cr App Rep 296.

8.74 One of the other popular catch phrases of the Court of Appeal pre-1995 was the 'lurking doubt' approach formulated by Widgery LJ in *Cooper*.[1] This was an alternative approach to considering a conviction as being unsafe or unsatisfactory. However, in *Farrow*[2] the Court denigrated the continued use of this phrase arguing that unsafety was a simpler, briefer and therefore a superior concept.

1 *R v Cooper* [1969] 1 QB 267, 53 Cr App Rep 82.
2 See *R v F* [1999] CrimLR.

8.75 The other significant issue which concerned the role of the Court was its jurisdiction to hold a conviction unsafe or unsatisfactory when the defendant has unequivocally pleaded guilty. As a plea of guilty is said to be the best evidence of a defendant's guilt, how then could the Court seek to upset this? In suitable circumstances this paradox did not trouble the Court. For example, in two cases concerned with the cause celebre of the Arms to Iraq affair, *Schlesinger* and *Blackledge*, the appellants had pleaded guilty. The investigation by Sir Richard Scott however, revealed that prior to the respective trials, important evidence which undermined the prosecution's case had not been disclosed and accordingly when the defendants decided to plead guilty they had done so without knowledge of this abuse by the prosecution. In *Schlesinger* and *Blackledge* the Court was in no doubt that the appellant's convictions were unsafe and unsatisfactory. Prosecution machinations had deprived the appellants of their right to a fair trial, they had pleaded guilty on a false basis and therefore their convictions could be overturned.

Post-1995 Act but pre-Mullen case law

8.76 A better understanding of the *Mullen* decision will no doubt be reached by a brief review of the earlier authorities, which place it in a proper context. In *Graham*[1] the Court of Appeal held that the amended version of s 2(1) pursuant to the 1995 Act, was intended to focus attention on one question only, namely whether the court considered the conviction unsafe. Where the Court was satisfied, despite any misdirection or irregularity in the conduct of the trial or any fresh evidence, that the conviction was nonetheless safe the appeal would be dismissed. So arguably if the Court felt that the trial judge should have granted an abuse application and stayed the proceedings on the evidence before him but nonetheless the trial was fair then according to this logic, the conviction could still nonetheless be safe.

1 [1997] 1 Cr App Rep 302.

8.77 In *Chalkley* the appellant had pleaded guilty following an adverse s 78 ruling as to the admissibility of certain highly damaging evidence. It was contended that if the ruling of the trial judge was wrong in law then this should lead to the quashing of his conviction. The Court found this argument legally erroneous. An irregularity in the trial procedure including an error of law by the judge, which might prior to amendment by the 1995 Act have rendered a conviction unsatisfactory, is not of itself a ground for quashing a conviction. Now it is only a ground if it leads on to the conclusion that the conviction is for some reason unsafe. The Court of Appeal held that, when considering an appeal against conviction the previous tests of 'unsatisfactoriness' and 'material irregularity' were no longer at the disposal of the Court, save as aids in determining the safety of a conviction. Accordingly, the Court held that it had no power to allow an appeal against conviction which was not considered unsafe, albeit that in some regard the conviction was unsatisfactory.

8.78 In relation to a plea of guilty the Court held that a conviction here would only be unsafe where the affect of an incorrect ruling of law on admitted facts was to leave an accused with no legal escape from a verdict of guilty on those facts. A conviction, however, would not normally be unsafe, per Auld LJ, where an accused was influenced to change his plea to guilty having recognised that, as a result of a ruling to admit damming evidence against him, a defence was hopeless. 'The Court has no power under the substituted s 2(1) to allow an appeal if it does not think the conviction unsafe but is dissatisfied in some way with what went on at the trial.' The Court did not consider the scenario as to whether a conviction may be held to be unsafe where there has been an abuse of process. In other words, can a conviction be regarded as unsafe where the appellant has had a fair trial but it was for some reason unfair to try him? Better in such a circumstance that the accused was never tried at all but the accused was and had a fair trial and was properly convicted. Is such a conviction 'safe'? The approach of the Court in *Chalkley* was that even if the Court held there was an abuse, the conviction could still be safe.

8.79 In *Martin* the House considered obiter the same issue and there was a difference of opinion. Lord Hope in an abuse context, adopted a broader interpretation of 'unsafe':

> 'I do not think it can be doubted that the Appeal Court ... have power to declare a conviction to be unsafe and to quash a conviction if they find that the course of proceedings leading to what would otherwise have been a fair trial has been such as to threaten either basic human rights or the rule of law.'

8.80 Lord Lloyd, however, felt that it would not be sufficient for the appellant to establish that the proceedings constituted an abuse of process for the conviction to be quashed.

8.81 Two other cases were decided by the Court soon after *Chalkley* and *Martin*. In *Simpson* the Court pondered whether it could ever quash a conviction as unsafe arising out of a prosecution abuse if no abuse application had ever been made at the trial. In *McDonald* Auld LJ took the opportunity to withdraw from the position which he had adopted in *Chalkley*. Considering what should happen in a *Bennett* type abuse situation Auld LJ said:

> 'It may be that a conviction in a trial which should never have taken place is to be regarded as unsafe for that reason. It may be that, despite the statutory basis of the court's jurisdiction, it also has some inherent or ancillary jurisdictional basis for intervening to mark abuse of process by quashing a conviction when it considers that the court below should have stayed the proceeding. Or it may be that the recent amendment to the 1968 act has removed the supervisory role of this court over abuse of criminal process where the affront to justice, however, outrageous, has not so prejudiced a defendant in his trial as to render his conviction unsafe. All that is for decision by another court in an appropriate case.'

8.82 The *Mullen* decision neatly fits the description of that 'appropriate case.' It is proposed, finally therefore, to turn to the *Mullen* case itself.

The decision in *Mullen*

8.83 Until the recent Court of Appeal decision in *Mullen*[1] the state of the case law in relation to post-amendment appeals on abuse of process, was highly unsatisfactory. The pre-*Mullen* case law was frequently in a state of ambiguity and uncertainty where certain decisions are submitted to have been decided on an overly restrictive interpretation of the word 'unsafe', the *Chalkley* case being a prime example. It is submitted that the *Mullen* decision is a landmark case, of fundamental importance to the question of abuse of process in the context of appeals to the Court of Appeal.

1 [1999] 3 WLR 777, CA.

8.84 In the judgment of the Vice President, Rose LJ, considerable attention was given to the proper meaning of the amendment to the Criminal Appeal Act, and the correct interpretation of the word 'unsafe'. Rose LJ held that:

> '... for a conviction to be safe it must be lawful; and if it results from a trial which should never have taken place it can hardly be regarded as "safe". Indeed the Oxford dictionary gives the legal meaning of "unsafe" as "likely to constitute a miscarriage of justice". Sir John Smith's article to which we have referred does not deal with "unsafe" in relation to abuse, though his commentary on *Simpson* ... raises directly pertinent questions. But, for the reasons which we have given, we agree with his 1995 conclusion that "unsafe" bears a broad meaning and one which is apt to embrace abuse of process of the *Bennett* or any other kind.'

8.85 While Rose LJ stressed, elsewhere in the judgment, that there may be certain circumstances where a finding of abuse of process by the Court of Appeal may not necessarily lead to the quashing of a conviction on appeal, nevertheless this judgment clearly opens up many avenues for arguing abuse of process as a ground of appeal. It is of considerable significance that Rose LJ ended the above passage with reference, not only to the *Bennett*-type abuse (ie where it would be unfair for a defendant to be tried, for example, by reason of procedural unfairness by the prosecution) situation, but also to abuse of 'any other kind'. This must presumably include the first main limb of abuse of process (using the two limb *Beckford* test), where the circumstances are such that it is not possible for a defendant to receive a fair trial.

8.86 A number of points of principle and procedure emerge from this important judgment. First, the Court of Appeal re-affirmed that it has a supervisory discretion to oversee appeals on the ground of abuse of process. Second, that it will entertain appeals which cover all species of abuse of process, that is, consider appeals on the basis that the trial was unfair or that it was unfair to try the accused because of some abuse. Third, that not all findings of abuse of process by the Court will necessarily lead to a conviction being quashed or a re-trial avoided. Rose LJ explained that in this circumstance the Court would not exercise its power to quash convictions automatically: 'In each case it is a matter of discretionary balance, to be approached with regard to the particular conduct complained of and the particular offence charged.' Furthermore he added:

> 'In arriving at this conclusion we strongly emphasise that nothing in this judgment should be taken to suggest that there may not be cases, such as *Latif*, in which the seriousness of the crime is so great relative to the nature of the abuse of process that it would be a proper exercise of judicial discretion to permit a prosecution to proceed or to allow a conviction to stand notwithstanding an abuse of process of this kind.'

8.87 The *Latif* case[1] which Rose LJ referred to in the above passage involved strong public policy considerations in relation to the fight against organised crime, in the context of a serious drugs case (where customs officers arranged for the appellant to be lured from Pakistan to the United Kingdom by trickery and deception and also committed criminal offences). The 'discretionary balance' mentioned by Rose LJ was in *Latif* described by Lord Steyn in the following terms:

> 'If the court always refuses to stay such proceedings, the perception will be that the court condones criminal conduct and malpractice by law enforcement agencies. That would undermine public confidence in the criminal justice system and bring it into disrepute. On the other hand, if the court were always to stay proceedings in such cases, it would incur the reproach that it is failing to protect the public from serious crime. The weakness of both extreme positions leaves only one principled solution. The court has a discretion; it has to perform a balancing exercise.'

1 *R v Latif, R v Shahzad* [1996] 1 All ER 353 HL.

8.88 Weighing up the public policy considerations involved, the House held that the officer's conduct was not so unworthy or shameful that it was an affront to the public conscience to allow the prosecution to proceed. Lord Steyn observed; 'realistically any criminal behaviour of the customs officer was venial compared to that of *Shahzad*' who was said to have been an organiser in the heroin trade.[1]

1 See WG Roser 'Entrapment: Have the Courts Found a Solution to this Fundamental Dilemma to the Criminal Justice System? [1993] 67 ALJ 722 and Andrew L-T Choo Halting criminal prosecutions: The abuse of process doctrine revisited [1995] Crim LR 864 as referred to in *Latif*.

8.89 It is submitted that *R v Mullen* should be regarded as the authoritative decision on appeals to the Court of Appeal. The judgment of Rose LJ both answers the questions posed by *Chalkley* and rids us of the ambiguities it created.[1] Indeed, not only has *Mullen* given effect, to a large extent, to the intention of the Home Office, the Royal Commission and Parliament (in conferring a broad meaning to 'unsafe') it has also rejuvenated the pre-amendment case law and resurrected, after their temporary demise at the hands of *Chalkley*, the decisions of *Bloomfield, Mahdi* and *Blackledge*. The test of whether a conviction is safe no longer simply depends on whether the Court is satisfied that the appellant is guilty on the evidence. The Court now has a discretion to consider issues such as procedural unfairness by the prosecution, for example, non-disclosure, material irregularities and abuse.

1 Note Professor Smith's commentary on *Mullen* at [1999] CrimLR 562.

8.90 We shall have to wait for the development of the case law to see how, in practice, the Court of Appeal applies its discretion to quash a conviction, after a finding of abuse of process in relation to the trial. The authors hope that given the exceptional nature of the abuse doctrine, and in the light of what an abuse of process actually stands for, that the circumstances in which the Court could nevertheless uphold a conviction (or order a re-trial) would be very rare indeed. For if the Court has determined either that the appellant should not have been tried, or that a fair trial did not occur, it is difficult to conceive of proper circumstances where it can still maintain the safety of the conviction itself.

What is the effect of pleading guilty on an appeal to the Court of Appeal?

8.91 In *Mullen* the Court of Appeal made plain that pursuant to its statutory jurisdiction to entertain appeals against conviction pursuant to the Criminal Appeal Act 1995, it was able to entertain such appeals based on the ground that the fairness of the trial was negated by an abuse of process. What however, is the position where before the Court a defendant alleges abuse and indeed did so at the trial, but having received an adverse ruling from the trial judge, then pleads guilty? In other words in order to allow a Court to have jurisdiction to appeal against conviction in this circumstance, is a defendant required to maintain a not guilty plea in order to preserve his subsequent appeal rights?

8.92 On the authorities there appeal to be two conflicting schools of thought. In *Chalkley*[1] the Court held that a conviction following a plea of guilty will not normally be deemed in any circumstances to be unsafe, even if the trial had been irregular in some significant way even if the trial amounted to an abuse of process. So far as the Court was concerned in *Chalkley*, the decisive factor overriding all others was if the defendant had entered a valid plea of guilty.[2] Following *Chalkley* in *Rajcoomar* which was a post-*Mullen* case, the Court ruled that *Mullen* did not effect the Court's ruling in *Chalkley*. As it pointed out in *Rajcoomar*, in *Mullen* the defendant had pleaded not guilty and had contested his trial.

1 At [1998] 2 Cr App Rep 79.
2 See for example, a plea which is not vitiated by mistake or duress.

8.93 The opposing school of thought based principally on a construction of the Court's judgment in *Mullen* is that the Court does have a jurisdiction to consider appeals against conviction even after valid guilty pleas. In his commentary on *Rajcoomar*, Professor Smith succinctly sets out the argument:

> '... But if, as the Court said in *Mullen*, ... for a conviction to be safe, it must be lawful; and, if it results from a trial which should never have taken place, it can hardly be regarded as safe', what does it matter whether the conviction results from a plea of guilty or a verdict of guilty by the jury? In both cases the defendant is in law guilty of the offence charged, but in neither case should the trial have taken place at all. According to the reasoning in *Mullen*, it is safe in both, or it is safe in neither'.[1]

1 Crim LR September at p 729.

8.94 The authors submit that Professor Smith's reasoning is to be preferred over the view of the Court in *Chalkley* and *Rajcoomar*. Moreover Rose LJ in Mullen appeared to cover the point when he summarised his judgment in the following terms:

'... by reason of this abuse of process, the prosecution and therefore the conviction of the appellant were unlawful' (page 157G).

8.95 The view of Rose LJ being that if the foundation for the prosecution was itself legally objectionable then it matters little how the defendant came to be convicted. One should also appreciate that both in *Chalkley* and *Rajcoomar*, the Court was not directly concerned with appeals based on abuse grounds. In contrast, *Mullen* was entirely focused on this point.

8.96 It is relevant to consider the position of the Court pre-implementation of the 1995 Act. For example, in *Schlesinger*[1] there was an unequivocal plea of guilty at the trial. Nonetheless, the Court unhesitatingly quashed the conviction holding that the entire prosecution of the defendant was an abuse.[2] It is submitted that the decision in *Mullen* is in conformity with the decision in *Schlesinger*. It is submitted that to deprive an appellant who has pleaded guilty from any avenue of appeal would be wrong in principle and inconsistent with the interests of justice. Moreover, on pragmatic grounds it would mean that a defendant, properly advised, would contest every prosecution no matter how hopeless his defence or how legally inescapable his conviction. A defendant pleading not guilty in such circumstances would result in his trial being almost a farce with defence counsel simply adopting a formalistic role. Nonetheless, bearing in mind the prevailing ambiguity in the authorities, it seems that for the purpose of preserving appeal rights, every defendant must be advised to plead not guilty for fear that other wise appeal rights may be precluded.

1 *R v Schlesinger* [1995] Crim LR 137 695.
2 Here the defendant had entered a guilty plea in ignorance of abusive behaviour committed by the prosecution. See Chapter 6 paras 6.69 to 6.71] for further consideration of this case.

Abuse of process as a novel ground of appeal

8.97 In the Court of Appeal can it be argued that the trial was unfair because of a specific abuse which was known to the defence at the trial but never complained about?

8.98 In *Mullen* the Court held that, where no ruling is sought by the defence on a matter within the trial judge's discretion, this will 'usually be fatal to any subsequent attempt to rely on that matter by way of appeal to this court'. In these circumstances practitioners would be well advised to make their abuse of process application at the appropriate time in the Crown Court, in order to avoid being precluded from arguing it on appeal. In *Mullen* itself the Court excused the defence's failure to argue abuse at trial for two reasons. First, the prosecution were responsible for non-disclosure of documents which were at the time of trial relevant to the abuse issue and second, the state of the law on this species of abuse was not so favourable to the defence at the time, the trial having occurred in 1990 pre-*Bennett.*[1]

1 At that time there were conflicting authorities on the issue of whether a court should ever inquire into circumstances concerning how a defendant had come into the jurisdiction.

RE-TRIALS

8.99 A less common area where abuse arguments arise is in relation to re-trials. They occur either after a first trial has had a 'hung' or discharged jury,[1] or by direction of the Court of Appeal. By the very nature of a re-trial, 'delay' will commonly be an issue, particularly where serious and complex proceedings are involved, but are there any additional abuse factors peculiar to re-trial situations?

1 See *R v Piggott and Litwin* [1999] 2 Cr App Rep 320 for an example of a retrial amounting to an abuse of process (where late prosecution amendments to the first trial's indictment significantly affected the fairness of proceeding to a second trial).

8.100 The Privy Council decision of *Charles v State of Trinidad and Tobago*[1] contains important statements of principle in this regard. In *Charles* the Privy Council found an abuse of process where a defendant had to endure a third trial for murder some nine years after the event, in circumstances where he had remained in custody under sentence of death. In the course of his judgment Lord Slynn made it clear that the Board ought to have regard both to the history to the protracted proceedings and, more significantly, to the personal concerns and anxieties that may be left by an accused. Lord Slynn emphasised the importance of the principles enunciated in the decision of *Barker v Wingo*[2] whereby:

> '... the United States Supreme Court considered that the right to speedy trial was designed to protect three interests of defendants, namely (i) to prevent oppressive pre-trial incarceration; (ii) to minimise anxiety and concern of the accused; and (iii) to limit the possibility that the defence will be impaired.'[3]

1 (1999) Times, 27 May.
2 407 US 514 (1972).
3 The Privy Council having previously acknowledged such principles in *Bell v DPP* [1985] AC 937.

8.101 While the facts of *Charles* are clearly in the extreme, nevertheless it is suggested that the general principle, namely that we should have regard to the personal distress of an accused, is of more general application.

Where the Court of Appeal orders a re-trial

8.102 Section 7 of the Criminal Appeal Act 1968 states that the power to order a re-trial is as follows: '(1) Where the Court of Appeal allows an appeal against conviction and it appears to the Court that the interests of justice so require, they may order the appellant to be re-tried.' The simple question thus arises: does this prevent one from arguing abuse of process on a re-trial?

8.103 In *Charles* Lord Slynn noted the potential for overlap between the two free standing decisions: the decision to order a stay and to order a re-trial:

> 'Whether a stay should be granted raised some questions analogous to those which arise when a decision has to be taken as to whether there should be a re-trial. In *Reid v The Queen* ([1980] AC 343, 350) the Board gave general guidance as to the factors which might be relevant in the exercise of the Court of Appeal's function in deciding whether to order a re-trial; 'The seriousness or otherwise of the offence must always be a relevant factor; so may its prevalence; and where the previous trial was prolonged and complex, the expense and the length of time for which the Court and jury would be involved in a fresh hearing may also be relevant considerations.'
>
> So too is the consideration that any criminal trial is to some extent an ordeal for the defendant, which the defendant ought not to be condemned to undergo for a second time through no fault of his own unless the interests of justice require that he should do so.'

8.104 The authors suggest that, where the Court of Appeal have fully and properly considered the abuse-type arguments, before making the order for re-trial, the defence will have considerable problems in even persuading the trial judge to entertain the abuse argument. Where the Court of Appeal have, for example, rejected a defence delay argument on the order of a re-trial, one would not expect a Crown Court judge (where the timetable for the re-trial has been followed) to allow the defence to resurrect the self-same argument as to abuse of process. This was the approach adopted by Turner J in the recent case of *R v Doran*[1] in relation to defence submissions which had previously been argued and ruled on:

> 'Not only has a court of competent jurisdiction ruled on those matters which were at present before it as issues, but that decision is one which is plainly binding this Court in respect of matters which were raised in the higher court.'

1 Bristol Crown Court (6 July 1999, unreported).

8.105 In *Doran* Turner J, however, naturally adopted a contrary position in relation to arguments which had not previously been advanced or ruled on. Indeed, it is further suggested that an abuse of process submission could still be made after an order for re-trial where there had been a material change of circumstances, such as a significant unexpected delay in the listing of the re-trial, which had not been within the contemplation of the Court of Appeal.

THE ABUSE OF PROCESS HEARING

Practice and procedure

No rules of procedure

8.106 There are no rules of court determining the correct way of conducting an abuse of process hearing. Bearing in mind the myriad of circumstances which abuse applications may be founded on, it would be unrealistic to impose a general set of procedural rules. Pragmatically, it is for the judge or magistrate to exercise their discretion on a sensible format for the proceedings. Ideally this would be in co-operation with the parties who seek to argue the matter.

Timing

8.107 Conventionally the abuse issue is determined at a pre-trial or pre-committal hearing specially fixed for the purpose. Otherwise the hearing occurs at the outset of a trial. Perhaps the only de facto rule in these applications is the requirement to give advance notice of the application on all parties. As this application can be classified as a question of law it is also becoming standard practice for skeleton arguments to be prepared and exchanged. In Crown Court proceedings Crown Court rules now require advance notice of any question of law to be given where the ruling may be binding; see s 40 CPIA 1996 and a similar requirement is found in a Pleas and Directions questionnaire. In the magistrates' court there are no similar rules. However, the practitioner in the magistrates' court would be well advised, as is commonly the practice, to give the court advance notice if only for listing purposes.

8.108 The application is normally instigated by the defence. However, it would appear there is some authority to suggest that where the court itself has some reason to suspect there is a ground for staying proceedings, it has a duty to raise it of its own motion, irrespective of the lack of any defence application.[1]

1 See *R v City ofLiverpool Stipendiary Magistrate, ex p Ellison* [1990] RTR 220n, 227 per Bingham LJ and *Gillick v West Norfolk and Wisbech Area Health Authority* [1986] AC 112.

Must the trial judge conduct an inquiry in to an abuse submission?

8.109 If, after hearing from the defence, the trial judge concludes that the submission has no justification or hope of success either because it is wrong in law or the facts appear very far from an abuse situation, it is submitted that the judge has no duty to conduct any inquiry.

8.110 In *R v Heston-Francois* the question arose as to whether there was a general duty on the trial judge to conduct such an inquiry when it was *justifiably* requested by the defence. The facts were that the defendant was on bail awaiting trial and the police, in the course of conducting another investigation, searched his home and seized legally privileged documents (documents prepared for use in his defence to the trial he was already facing). These documents were not only seized but they were then handed to the investigators who were involved in the prosecution of the defendant's imminent trial. At this trial the defence submitted abuse arguing that the conduct of the officers had been oppressive and justified a stay. The trial judge however, declined to conduct any inquiry into this, ruling that all relevant matters could be adequately explored during the course of the trial, and so a ruling could be made later in the proceedings. Post-conviction, the defendant appealed to the Court of Appeal.

8.111 The Court of Appeal emphasised that in circumstances such as an abuse application, a trial judge should be the master of his own procedure and therefore enjoy a wide discretion as to how to conduct an abuse inquiry. If the trial judge exercised his discretion wrongly or behaved unfairly, then of course this could be reviewed subsequently by the Court of Appeal and, in the view of the Court, it was well placed to conduct such a review.

8.112 A perusal of the judgment of Watkins LJ in this case reveals that the Court was vexed by several policy considerations which clearly led it to reach the conclusion that it did. Watkins LJ suggested that if a trial judge was to have a duty always to conduct a pre-trial inquiry in to allegations of abuse then this would tend to suggest that it was part of a court's duty to regulate the conduct of police officers. As no such duty existed then neither should there be a duty to always conduct a pre-trial inquiry. In relation to the trial process itself, Watkins LJ agreed with the trial judge's view that the trial was the best forum or procedure for eliciting facts relevant to an abuse application. Moreover, a trial judge having heard the relevant evidence had a variety of remedies available to him. Reprehensible conduct by the police could be dealt with within the context of the trial by judicial control over admissibility of evidence, the power to direct a verdict of not-guilty and the ability of a jury having heard all the evidence to return a verdict of not-guilty.

8.113 As a matter of practice Watkins LJ also pointed to several problems which would arise if a general duty on a trial judge was held to exist:

> '... for example, (i) of defining the issues claimed to exist, which may be very complex, (ii) of providing for representation of persons whose conduct is impugned, (iii) of ensuring that the persons affected are sufficiently aware of the case they have to meet. Whilst these problems may be overcome, the issues referred to are best left, we think, to be dealt with during the course of the trial and; if necessary, later by the Court of Appeal.'

8.114 In relation to such problems Watkins LJ also observed that: 'A pre-trial inquiry such as the appellant contends the judge in this case was under a duty to embark on would itself be open to abuse by unscrupulous and dishonest accused persons. The criminal trial system would be placed in jeopardy.'

8.115 In *Attorney General's Reference* Lord Lane CJ expressly approved the view of Watkins LJ expressed in *Heston-Francois*. He held that the trial process is equipped to deal with most complaints of abuse, for example the ability to ensure that all relevant evidence of this is presented during the trial and the ability of the judge to give directions to the jury.

8.116 On the basis of these two authorities therefore, it appears that there is no obligation on a trial judge to hold a pre-trial hearing even when it is justifiably requested by the defence. It is however, submitted that both of these authorities have now largely been overtaken by subsequent developments and perhaps by the growth of abuse applications generally. Certainly it is the experience of the authors that where, for example, an allegation of mala fides is made against police officers, it would be extremely unusual for a trial judge to hold that this matter need not be investigated until the relevant officers gave their evidence in the ordinary way in the course of the trial. Furthermore, an increased awareness on the part of the judiciary as to their responsibility to ensure that abuses do not go uncorrected, together with the growth generally in our criminal justice system of pre-trial or preparatory hearings, means that there has been an increased focus away from the belief that the trial process is the best and most efficient manner for determining matters. Especially those which if decided in a particular way would result in the entire trial being stayed.

Voir Dires

8.117 It is normal for applications concerned with the exclusion of prosecution evidence under s 78 of PACE or for a stay of the proceedings to be considered in a voir dire or a 'trial within a trial' held in the absence of the jury.[1] The usual procedure is for the prosecution to call witnesses to testify as to the circumstances about which the defence has made complaint, for the defence to cross-examine these witnesses and then for the defence to call any evidence it considers necessary. There is no obligation on the accused to give evidence although there is antiquated authority to the effect that he is not entitled to do so. However, it is submitted that if a fair determination of the issues makes it desirable for the accused to give evidence and he wished to do so, it would be wrong to refuse this. It should be borne in mind that if the accused does give evidence and the abuse application fails, the prosecution may lead evidence in the trial proper regarding this previous testimony. Prosecution cross-examination of the accused before the jury can be directed to expose any discrepancies and inconsistencies between the two testimonies in order to attack the credibility of the accused.

1 In *R v Barry Magistrates' Court, ex p Malpas* [1998] COD 90, DC, the Divisional Court acknowledged the Crown Court's use of abuse voir dires for dealing with disputed facts.

No power to order disclosure

8.118 The position of a trial judge conducting an abuse hearing was described by Watkins LJ in *R v Manchester Crown Court, ex p Cunningham.*[1] 'He is not in a trial situation nor is his role an inquisitorial one. He cannot compel any other evidential material to be provided.'

1 [1991] COD 23 This case is also known as *R v Manchester Crown Court, ex p Brokenbrow (1991) Times, 31 October.*

8.119 It was held in *ex p Cunningham* that a trial judge has no power to compel disclosure of documents from any party, including the prosecution, if such documents purely relate to the abuse application and do not fall under the prosecution's general duty of disclosure in relation to the trial. In relation to third parties, the trial judge has no power to issue a witness summons either for documents of for the giving of witness testimony pursuant to the Criminal Procedure (Attendance of Witnesses) Act 1965 (which has now been greatly amended by s 66 of the Criminal Procedure and Investigations Act 1996). In *R v Gokal*[1] the Court of Appeal upheld the refusal of the trial judge to make orders under the Criminal Justice (International Co-operation) Act 1990 in relation to the seeking of foreign evidence in order to support a forthcoming abuse application to be made by the defence.

1 (1997) 2 Cr App Rep 266, CA.

Argument and giving of reasons

8.120 In practice, a considerable number of abuse applications tend to be made in circumstances where, at the appropriate hearing, the defence and prosecution present the facts and argument without the necessity of calling any evidence. This is largely because the dispute between the parties will generally lie over the proper inference to be drawn from the facts, as opposed to the facts themselves. Alternatively, the prosecution may contend that, even if the defence's arguments or allegations are made out, they do not in law amount to an abuse. Where the defence do contemplate calling evidence in a voir dire, as part of the abuse application, they need to be ever mindful of the inherent dangers of exposing their witnesses to prosecution cross-examination. Indeed, practitioners are cautioned against the calling of defence evidence, unless they are confident first, that it is necessary and second, that it would be of positive assistance to the application.

8.121 The burden of proving assertions as to the alleged abuse and/or establishing the evidential foundations rests on the defence. In *ex p Cunningham* the court considered how a judge should rule on an abuse application. Watkins LJ said: 'In rejecting or granting an application the judge need only deliver a short judgment showing his command of the law and a summary of the reasons for his decision.' While it makes for good practice for magistrates to similarly provide reasons, there is no legal obligation on them to do so.

Divisible indictments

8.122 In *R v Munro*[1] the Court of Appeal held that the power to stay proceedings exists in order to enable a court to regulate the efficient and fair disposal of criminal cases. Lord Justice Steyn went on to acknowledge the good sense in a Court having an inherent jurisdiction to stay an indictment in part; whether that meant staying some counts and not others, or staying (in a multi-handed case) as against some defendants and not others. To that end, Steyn LJ held that it was 'an illusion to regard an indictment as an indivisible entity'.

1 (1992) Cr App Rep 183.

Defendant giving evidence in committal proceedings

8.123 In *R v Clerkenwell Stipendiary Magistrate, ex p Bell*[1] the applicant, B, was alleged to have committed an offence of theft at some time before May 1987. He was charged with the offence on 26 September 1989. On 22 January 1990 at committal proceedings, it was contended on his behalf that given the delay the magistrate should not commit him for trial because of abuse of process. The magistrate proceeded to hear evidence from a police officer explaining the delay, in relation to B moving address, but refused to hear evidence from B himself. He committed B for trial, which decision was then subject to a judicial review application. The Divisional Court granted the application and quashed the committal. It was held that the magistrate should have heard evidence from B, because any possible prejudice to B caused by the delay was a relevant matter and clearly B could give evidence as to this.[2] In short, the refusal to hear evidence from B amounted to a breach of natural justice.

1 [1991] CrimLR 468 QBD.
2 *R v Telford Justices, ex p Badham* was cited in support of this proposition.

Fairness to the prosecution

8.124 In *R v Derby Crown Court, ex p Brooks*[1] Sir Roger Ormrod in his famous dictum concerning the abuse of process said in relation to this subject as follows:

> 'the power to stop a prosecution arises when it is an abuse of the process of the Court ... the ultimate objective of this discretionary power is to ensure that there should be a fair trial according to law, which involves fairness to both the defendant and to the prosecution ...' (page 168).

1 (1984) 80 Cr App Rep 164.

8.125 Lord Lane CJ in *A-G's Reference (No 1 of 1990)*[1] emphasised that the Court's power to stay proceedings should never be used as a means of punishing the prosecution.

1 (1992) 95 Cr App Rep 296, CA.

8.126 The issue of whether the prosecution have been fairly heard in answer to a defendant's abuse application usually rises in the context of a magistrate's decision to stay proceedings about which the prosecution subsequently seek judicial review arguing that this was irrational. In *R v Crawley Justices, ex p DPP*[1] the Divisional Court heard a prosecution application for judicial review arising out of a justice's decision to dismiss the charges against the defendant on the grounds of prosecution delay. The justices held that the delay was so protracted and unjustifiable that it constituted an abuse. For its part the prosecution, while it did not deny the facts concerning delay, submitted that it had not received a fair hearing because the magistrates had not directed themselves to the essential issue of whether the delay had in fact prejudiced a fair trial. Furthermore, the magistrates had not considered who was responsible for the delay, the prosecution arguing that some of the responsibility lay with the accused. It transpired that at the particular hearing complained of, the justices had refused to hear any submissions from the prosecution and immediately proceeded to dismiss the charges. Unsurprisingly, the Divisional Court granted the application finding in effect that the tenets of natural justice have been broken and the prosecution had been treated unfairly.[2] Moreover, in the opinion of the Court, had the magistrates heard all the facts they probably would not have decided that there was an abuse.

1 [1991] COD 365, DC.
2 See also *King v Kucharz* [1989] COD 469, DC.

Fairness to third parties

8.127 Principles of even-handedness and fairness have also been held to apply, in the context of an abuse of process hearing where evidence is called, to the position of witnesses. In *A-G v Morgan, A-G v News Group Newspapers Ltd*[1] the Divisional Court held that where an application to stay had been founded on allegedly prejudicial publicity, it was irregular to have allowed the author of the criticised article (who was expecting to be a witness for the prosecution in the substantive trial) to be called as a witness on the application for a stay and then cross-examined at length as to his entire conduct vis-à-vis the article. The author should have first, been provided with an opportunity to take legal advice and second, having given evidence, should have been warned as to his privilege against self-incrimination.

1 [1998] EMLR 294, DC.

The burden of proof

8.128 The applicant making the abuse of process submission has the burden of proving it, and the standard of proof is the balance of probabilities.[1] As Mann LJ commented, in *Telford Justices,* the manner in which the applicant discharges such an onus will depend on all the circumstances of the particular case. The applicant must carefully decide whether to make the submission on the papers, and agreed facts, or whether some initial calling of evidence, perhaps in a voir dire, is required.

1 *R v Telford Justices, ex p Badham*; *A-G's Reference (No 1 of 1990)*; and *R v Cardiff Magistrate' Court, ex p Hole.*

8.129 It may well be essential for applicants to lay an evidential foundation for the intended submission. Indeed the Crown may take issue with the evidence presented, forcing the tribunal to make an initial determination as to the facts. The evidential burden would lie on the applicant. An example of such a situation might apply where a defence witness is called to testify to the effect that a number of important defence witnesses are unavailable by reason of the delay. The prosecution may challenge first, the assertion that they are important, second, the assertion that they are unavailable and third, that their alleged unavailability had anything to do with supposed prosecution led delay.

8.130 The *ex p Hole* decision provides clear guidance to applicants as to the manner in which the burden may be discharged. The Divisional Court there held that: 'If one is considering whether, on a balance of probabilities, the applicants are able to show that because of the delay they cannot fairly defend themselves against the charges, it is necessary to look at the charges and see exactly what defence it is that they are impeded from advancing.' In essence, the burden is to specify the alleged prejudice or unfairness and whether or not it applies to oral or documentary evidence, for example, to directly relate such matters to the particular charge(s) against a defendant. In the above non-availability of evidence type submission, the burden would clearly be on the applicant to identify the witnesses he would have wished to call.

8.131 While the actual burden on applicants may in practice be less onerous in delay cases where there has been an exceptionally long delay, the burden of proof always remains on the applicant. In the *Tan v Cameron* decision[1] the Privy Counsel considered the vexed question as to whether there should be shifting burdens of proof, reversals of the burden of proof and rebuttable presumptions. The Court held that the question as to whether proceedings ought to be stayed is a question to be considered 'in the round' and that nothing was to be gained by the introduction of shifting burdens of proof. The Court was clearly not prepared to accept that in a case of substantial delay, prejudice was presumed to exist to the extent that the prosecution took on a burden to rebut such a presumption of prejudice.[2]

1 [1992] 2 AC 205, PC.
2 See also *R v Bow Street Magistrates, ex p DPP* (1989) 91 Cr App Rep 283.

8.132 What was described as a 'heavy' burden in the *Tan* decision, which was a delay case, may well be an even greater burden on the applicant who seeks a stay on the basis of alleged mala fides. In the case of *ex p Thomas*[1] the added evidential difficulties of proving dishonesty were considered by the Divisional Court. The essence of the defence case was an allegation that the prosecutor, who had unsuccessfully sought to extend custody time limits for defendants charged with a drugs importation offence, had dishonestly contrived to manipulate the prosecution process. The prosecutor had the defendants re-arrested, before they could leave the court building, on new charges of possession with intent to supply the self same drugs. The Divisional Court, remitting the case back to the magistrates, stated that the justices must bear in mind that the burden of establishing dishonesty lay fairly and squarely on the defence, and that it was a 'heavy' burden. Where the defence take on the mantle of proving dishonesty, as opposed to an error of judgment for example, the evidential hurdle is an obviously high one given the seriousness of the allegation.

1 See *R v Great Yarmouth Magistrates, ex p Thomas, Davis and Darlington* [1992[CrimLR 116; and *R v Rotherham Justices, ex p Brough* [1991] CrimLR 522.

Presentation

8.133 Before presenting the abuse arguments at Court, the practitioner is well advised to have already taken specific client instructions on the matters raised. Certain species of abuse are clearly more directly connected than others to the clients' own particular recollection of a set of events: breach of promise or substantial delay cases being prime examples. Indeed the practitioner may also wish to question and take statements from defence witnesses in relation to abuse matters. Even if the client and his witnesses provide a long series of negative answers in relation to their ability to, for example, recall material events in the distant past, the same should be noted in their witness statements.

8.134 If an enquiry agent has, for example, also been used to investigate important aspects of a clients defence, the result of such investigation (if relevant to the abuse application) may also be reduced into an evidential format, possibly for use in a voir dire or in argument. Likewise, a compendious way of summarising the extensive efforts to prepare a client's case, which may have met with abject failure given the delay for example, could be for the solicitor in question to prepare a full, accurate and detailed affidavit.

8.135 In a sexual abuse delay case, for example, the solicitor could, in such an affidavit, succinctly set out matters such as:

(1) the names of defence witnesses who were to be traced; an outline of their relevance; the results of efforts to trace and proof the same;
(2) details of the disclosure sought from the prosecution (such as unused material); an outline of its relevance; the results of efforts to receive the same and/or the availability;
(3) details of efforts made to seek voluntary or other disclosure from third parties (such as social service files, medical records, educational records); an outline of the relevance of the same; the results of efforts to receive the same and/or the availability.

8.136 Such a solicitor could also annex the affidavit copy exhibits, such as letters or documents, which evidence the above-mentioned inquiries and their results. If the case has been thoroughly prepared and the solicitor's evidence is sufficiently relevant and material, such a document could be clearly be of assistance to the Court. Not only would it possibly save the courts valuable time, in terms of obviating the need for the calling of live evidence, it is presentationally more attractive, with more evidential weight than simple bland assertions in open Court. If it is intended to contain certain disclosure from the clients' instructions, or from his witness statements (for example, re their inability to remember), the solicitor is advised to ask for the clients' specific consent to such a course.

8.137 Practitioners are equally advised, wherever possible, to prepare a skeleton argument in anticipation of the actual abuse hearing. In so doing it is useful to summarise the chronology of events, the facts relied on, the relevant law and the basic arguments on fact and law. Indeed, it is sometimes helpful to annex to the skeleton copies of particularly pertinent abuse authorities. Having said that, practitioners are cautioned against the excessive citation of abuse authorities, which has been expressly disapproved of by the Divisional Court.[1] As with the service of any other skeleton argument, practitioners are urged to serve the same in good time on the appropriate parties.

1 See *R v Sheffield Stipendiary Magistrate, ex p Stephens* [1992] CrimLR 873.

Index